D. GARY YOUNG

The World Leader in Essential Oils

All rights reserved. No part of this book may be reproduced, stored in a retrieval system, or transmitted in any form or by any means, electronic or mechanical, including photocopying, recording, or scanning, without permission in writing from the publisher.

Young Living Essential Oils, LC
1538 West Sandalwood Drive
Lehi, UT 84043
USA
800.371.3515
YoungLiving.com

Copyright © 2019 by Mary Young

ISBN 978-1-7337015-2-5

Second Edition

Printed in the United States of America

The information contained in this book is for education and entertainment purposes only. Any reference to health, nutrition, diet, and food products should not be used to diagnose, prescribe, or treat any condition of the body and should not be used as a substitute for medical counseling. Neither the author nor the publisher accepts responsibility for such use.

D. GARY YOUNG

The World Leader in Essential Oils

Young Living
ESSENTIAL OILS

Gary teaching members on a Young Living trip to Egypt.

Table of Contents

Preface i
Acknowledgments iii
Foreword v
Dedication vii
Introduction ix
Seed to Seal x
Three Pillars—Seed to Seal Quality Commitment xii
A Path Unknown 1
    Destiny Speaks—A Terrible Accident 5
Recovery—Mexico and a New Path of Discovery 9
    Essential Oil Research in France 12
The Birth of Young Living 15
    Jean-Noël Landel—The French Connection 16
    Philippe Mailhebiau—New Spiritual Insight 19
    Marcel Espieu—Mentor and Friend 20
    Henri Viaud—The Father of Distillation 21
The Modern-Day Father of Distillation 25
    Distillation on the Kitchen Stove 25
    St. Maries—Farming Begins 28
    "Mechanizing"—The Planting Machine 34
    The First Harvest 36
    The Farming Learning Curve 36
    The First "Real" Distillery—1994 38
    The Art of Distillation 46
St. Maries Expands 49
    The Research Farm—So Many Questions 51
    Greenhouse Research 54
    Melissa 62
    Gas Chromatography (GC) Essential Oil Analysis . 64
Young Living Simiane-la-Rotonde Farm 67
    Trouble in France 68
The Move to Utah 75
    The Utah Farm and Distillery 81
    Marcel Espieu Comes to Utah 97
    Family Fun at the Mona Farm 100
    The First Annual Draft Horse Show 111
    Young Living Draft Horse Show and
        the 2018 World Percheron Congress 114
Photosynthesis—How Are Essential Oils Formed? .. 116
Quality and Purity 117
    The Proper Environment 117
    Composting 117

    Weed Control..............................118
    Organic Farming...........................118
    Distilling Clary Sage........................118

Einkorn 121

Ecuador–A New Opportunity 127
    Finca Botanica–Young Living Ecuador........127
    Research Nursery..........................158
    Brix Testing and Harvesting.................159
    Curing, Geographical Location, and
        Distilling Time........................160
    GC/FID/MS Combining Analytical Instruments
        in the Field...........................164
    Mera Ocotea Farm.........................167
    NovaVita Spa and Rejuvenation Center........168
    Essential Floral Water Spa....................169
    The Young Living Academy..................170

The Frankincense Trail 179
    Oman–Sacred Frankincense Distillery.........182
    Yemen–Going Into the "Forbidden Zone"......189
    Somalia–A Trip Into the Unknown...........199
    A Fascinating but Unnerving Adventure........200
    Three Different Species of Frankincense........205
    The Truth About Boswellia Frereana..........207

The Highland Flats Tree Farm and Distillery 211
    A New Logging Camp......................213
    The Unstoppable Mustang Man..............218
    Only 125 Miles to the Distillery...............222
    The Highland Flats Distillery.................229
    Automation–History in the Making...........238
    Steam Generators.........................240
    Highland Flats Reforestation.................244

Distilling Under the Northern Lights–
Fort Nelson, British Columbia, Canada 247
    Black Spruce Speaks.......................264

Croatia–Distilling in 19 Days 267
    Domesticating Helichrysum.................268
    The Battle to Find Helichrysum..............277

Skyrider Wilderness Ranch 279
    Tabiona, Utah–In Gary's Words.............279
    Skyrider River Ranch–Tabiona, Utah.........287
    Dogsledding–Gary's Last Great Adventure.....288
    The Ultimate Dogsled......................293

In Search of Ancient Knowledge 295
    The Ancient Secrets of Egypt................295
    Discovery in Pakistan......................298
    The Old World...........................298
    Masada, the West Bank of the Dead Sea.......299
    Israel–The Ancient Balm of Gilead–Liquid Gold...301
    Madagascar..............................309

Young Living Partner Farms
and Certified Growers......................311
    Global Farm Operations in 2019.............312
    Quebec Partner Farm......................313
    Australia–Outback Botanical
        Reserve and Distillery...................314
    Spain–Vida de Seville Distillery..............316
    Taiwan–Cooperative Farm and Distillery......320
    Hawaii–Sandalwood Reforestation Project.....322
    Australia–Ord River Sandalwood
        Farm & Distillery......................324
    Australia–Melaleuca Gihndagun Farm........325
    Washington–Labbeemint Partner Distillery....326
    South Africa–Amazi Amahle Farm and Distillery..327
    Wolfberry...............................329
    China–Ningxia Wolfberry Farms
        and Processing Plant...................332
    Philippines–Happy Pili Tree Farm & Distillery...334
    Mexico–Finca Victoria.....................336
    Italy–Bella Vista Farm & Distillery............337
    Turkey–Hediye Rose Farm & Distillery........338
    Brazil–Painted Stone Farm & Distillery........339
    Argentina–Esmeralda Farm.................340
    Philippines–Kalipay Coconut Farm...........341
    Wildcrafting.............................342

The Origin of Plants 345
    Carbon Dioxide (CO_2) Extraction............347
    Adulteration and Chemical Manipulation......348
    Scientific Analysis.........................349
    The Day of the Laboratory..................350
    Common Adulterating Agents...............350

Young Living Today.........................355
    Kevin Scholz, the Architect..................358
    Five Years, Five Key Goals, One Powerful Pledge...362

Warehouse and Manufacturing 365

Member Services Center 369

D. Gary Young, Young Living Foundation......371

International Offices........................379

International Grand Conventions 396

The Gifts of Conventions....................391

A Modern-Day Pioneer......................399

Gary's Quotes 404

A Love Story 406

Celebration of Life 411
    A Tribute to Gary.........................414

The Final Resting Place 437

Journey On 439

PREFACE

This is a book about the life of D. Gary Young and the path that led him to become the world leader in essential oils.

A lot is written about aromatherapy and the use and application of Mother Nature's essential oils. Many books have the word "aromatherapy" in the title, and people all over the world are buying them, looking for alternatives for emotional and physical well-being, skin care, household and environmental concerns, cooking, and other interests.

However, little is written about where these oils come from and why they are found in cosmetics, nutritional supplements, perfumes, soaps, used as food flavorings, and sold in little glass bottles that people purchase for their personal use.

Who knows where the plants, herbs, trees, etc., are grown; and who knows anything about distilleries and the extraction of the oils? Most importantly, who understands about their quality and the need for absolute purity? Even people who visit a distillery may see the plant material being loaded, hear the hissing of the steam as it begins spiraling upward through the chamber, and see the oil coming out of the separator. But the intricate details of making sure the distillation process is exactly right for the best extraction is unknown or elusive to most.

This book chronicles Gary's journey to deliver the purest essential oils to people everywhere. It's a book about one man, his gifts, and his gift to the world—Seed to Seal, which is the story of essential oils, from the planting of the seeds to cultivating, harvesting, distilling, testing, packaging, distributing, and educating.

This unexpected path began because of an accident that took away from him the only life he had ever known and led him down an unknown path that gave him purpose

Gary is thrilled to see the beautiful Juniper oil.

and a reason to live. That purpose led him into the annals of history and to the far corners of the earth, where he was continually learning more about essential oils and discovering fascinating lost knowledge, which he was driven to share with God's children.

His company, Young Living Essential Oils, is the vehicle through which his vision has been taken to the world, wherein millions of people have been blessed in numerous ways. This is the true-life story of one man's dream filled with adventure, heartache, pain, triumph, and success beyond measure. May his passion for life touch your heart and help ignite the fire within you.

Members attending Silver Club loved hearing Gary explain the "art of distillation" at the Young Living Lavender Farm and Distillery in Mona, Utah, 2015.

ACKNOWLEDGMENTS

When I started this book, I had no idea how complex it was going to be. Writing about someone's life is one thing, but showing that life of nearly 70 years in pictures became a huge challenge. Just finding pictures with good or acceptable resolution, especially from the earlier years, was like looking for a needle in a haystack. I could not have completed this book without the dedication and tenacity of those mentioned here.

John Whetten sat with me hour after hour, day after day, hunting for pictures, placing them, rearranging text and photos, and working Photoshop magic on many of the old pictures. With the use of his excellent language skills, John also helped with the editing and some of the rewriting. He traveled the world with Gary and was often there when "it" happened and took many of the pictures we used. For this second edition, he was again looking for pictures and giving me creative ideas and helping any way he could. He is extremely talented, dedicated, and willing; and I cannot thank him enough.

David Petty is a very talented graphic artist who has a wonderful eye for photography. David probably knows the archived pictures better than anyone and spent a lot of time finding "just the right one." His beautiful pictures are seen all through the book, and his clever photo editing enhanced so much of what you see. He has been with Young Living for many years and has been an invaluable part of creating this book.

Paul Springer used his beautiful graphic design talent to create the final layout and look of this book. He has been doing design work for us for many years and understands the nature of Young Living, our mission, and what we wish to convey to the reader. He has been a friend for a long time and has designed many of our publications, including Gary's historical novel *The One Gift*, as well as *Shutran's Apothecary*, the *Essential Oils Desk Reference*, *Ancient Einkorn*, and others.

Alene Frandsen head of Publications and Document Review, engaged the members of her staff, Erin Stewart, Jamie Moesser, and Shanna Davila, to help in the editing of the second edition. They meticulously read through the manuscript many times, catching all those "little mistakes" and inconsistencies. They rewrote awkward sentences and paragraphs and clarified what didn't make sense or could be expressed in a better way, saving us a lot of time and frustration. It was a very tedious task, but so rewarding, for which I am extremely grateful.

Karen Boren is a researcher and technical writer who documented dates, places, and explanations. She searched the internet and many history books to make sure that our information was written correctly and expressed in the proper scientific way. She found little errors that most people would not see and helped in many difficult areas with her writing skills.

Pei-Ling Cogswell a skilled graphic designer and a good friend, offered to help as we were beginning the work on this second edition. She spent many long hours laying in new pictures and text following Paul's original design and reorganizing some of the chapters.

Gary, Jacob, and Josef were often frustrated with me as I stayed up late writing the first edition. Gary really wondered if I would ever finish but helped so much with specific areas of writing in telling his story. He found pictures and edited for content, specific dates, and places, as only he could do, as everything had to be accurate going back so many years.

Gary was thrilled to see his story told and was deeply honored to sign books for members around the world. This magnificent historical journey has become a prized possession for millions of people as they come to value God's gift of essential oils to the world and marvel at Gary's accomplishments. The details of his legacy are unsurpassed, and it's wonderful for the boys to have this history of their father. I love my family and appreciate them very much.

Clint Walker starred in the TV series *Cheyenne* (left), 1955-1962, and in the movie *Yellowstone Kelly* (right), 1959.

Clint Walker at the Youngs' home, June 2013.

Clint and Susan Walker received the Spirit of Young Living Award at the 2013 Convention. Clint said, "Gary is like a modern-day Moses, leading the people from chemical bondage to the freedom of natural products and essential oils."

iv D. Gary Young | The World Leader in Essential Oils

FOREWORD

My life has been an exciting and colorful adventure but full of tremendous pressures and demands that have taken their toll physically and emotionally. I have spent almost 45 years of my life in the movie industry in grueling days of filming with long hours that demanded tremendous mental focus. It was always exciting to see the film or the series finish, but I often felt exhausted, so I was open to things that offered longevity and increased energy.

While in Hollywood I was told about a young man who had recovered from a terrible accident that was supposed to have left him in a wheelchair for life. However, this young man had a very strong will and had discovered many natural things and some of Mother Nature's secrets that he said helped him. It was amazing to many that he was able to get out of his wheelchair and, even though it took a long time, was able to walk again.

I, too, was interested in the gifts of Mother Nature, and so I decided to go and meet this young man to see what I could discover. I had grown up helping my father in his health food store, so I had some knowledge of herbs and different plants and was always interested in learning new things.

When I met Gary Young, I was impressed with his tremendous positive attitude. I had no idea that he was always in pain because he never let anyone know. He never talked about the life-threatening accident that destroyed his physical strength and powerful body.

Only when we became friends on a deeper level did he express some of his innermost feelings and how he was constantly looking for things that would help him on his road to recovery.

He shared his excitement about his discovery of essential oils and his feelings about their value to mankind. We talked about things that we both had experienced in the world of health and wellness and our mutual feelings of exploring Mother Nature's world. He was always so encouraging and supported my ideas and desires to try new things.

I watched Gary develop his farms and grow his business and was so honored when he invited me to speak at his convention and tell my story and just be a part of what he was building.

As I read through this book, which reflects over 40 years of our friendship, I am deeply impressed and touched with his dedication and unwavering commitment to his mission. Growing up in poverty with little education, getting out of a wheelchair and learning to walk again, and moving forward with his dream against what the world would say was impossible is surely a tribute to his unbreakable spirit and love of God, which has been his foundation.

We love the essential oils, the NingXia Red, and so many of the products he has developed. They all fit right in with our lifestyle.

Susan and I have enjoyed our association with his family and have delighted in watching Jacob and Josef grow up, ride horses, and be a great example of what their parents have taught them.

I am grateful that I have lived long enough to see Gary's vision become a reality and that Susan and I have had the blessed opportunity for many years to benefit from what he has created.

— Clint and Susan Walker

Clint Walker passed away on May 21, 2018, at the age of 90, nine days after Gary.
www.clintwalker.com

With his trusted horse, Sundance, that brought him years of enjoyment, riding in rugged mountain terrain, Gary reminisces in front of the old trapper's cabin, where he sometimes stayed with his father while hunting in the Idaho wilderness.

DEDICATION

Gary's great love was being with God in the mountains on his horse with his family beside him. Were it not for such a terrible, debilitating accident, he would have stayed in the mountains, the path that destiny took him down would never have come to be, and the gifts that he gave to the world would never have been given. His instinctive knowing about the essences hidden within the vast web of the life-giving flora that Mother Nature offers to the world and the quest to discover their secrets would never have entered his mind.

The curiosity of humankind has been ongoing since man first walked on the earth, and knowledge has been lost and found over and over as time has passed through centuries of discovery. Essential oils have been used since the beginning of time for perfume and cosmetics, for physical and emotional well-being, and for the most fascinating and deeply spiritual rituals that only the soul of each individual can understand. Only the Father of us all, the Almighty, has all the answers; and He has given us the challenge and the opportunity to figure them out. Throughout the ages there have been those who would delve into this universal knowledge, just scratching the surface, only to see it disappear into history or be squashed by those who would restrict this knowledge for profit and power.

In our modern world of the 21st century, there is more knowledge than ever before; and there are those of us who fight for our right to choose our desired way. The path that destiny chose for D. Gary Young was full of difficult challenges and opposition, but he never wavered in his determination to share with the world what he discovered—the gifts of Mother Nature.

This book is dedicated to all those who carry the torch of freedom, determined to live an abundant life of health and happiness and have a desire to share what they have discovered with those who are looking for the messenger who would bring them the same opportunity—the people of the world.

We enjoyed visiting with members at the Young Living International Grand Convention in Dallas, Texas, August 2015.

INTRODUCTION

A pioneer in his own right, D. Gary Young spent the last 30 years of his life researching the ancient ways and traditional methods of distilling from the last century. He sadly watched the true art of distillation slowly being lost to fast extraction with modern equipment and chemicals.

Plant care has gone to chemical fertilizers and pesticides that have weakened plant immunity and reduced the quality of the oil, causing lower levels of chemical constituents and even the loss of many valuable compounds. Nutrient-depleted soil is unattended, resulting in weaker plants and loss of quality.

Rural facilities without financial means remain crude and inefficient, often producing a lower yield and lesser quality. Some older distilleries in more remote areas of the world fuel fireboxes with old tires, wood, and often garbage to heat cookers made of carbon steel, which are most undesirable for plant extraction of essential oils.

High tech laboratories both manufacture chemical molecules to add volume and/or manipulate the chemical composition for a more "pleasant smell" and a greater marketing advantage.

A true, unadulterated, pure essential oil as God intended is difficult to obtain, as even many growers and distillery operators are lured into the practice of adulteration because of the desire for money and power.

From the time of his accident and his discovery of essential oils, Gary was committed to his research and the true art of distillation. Having used the oils to support his own personal journey and that of many others, he knew the difference between the pure and the adulterated, which made his path very precise. Purity and quality of the oils were most important to him, regardless of the time and money that it took to produce the desired results.

This book is a compilation of many things happening in many parts of the world, often at the same time. An exact chronology is impossible to write, as new activities continually transpire at the same time in different locations. The reader will jump back and forth from farm to farm with the development of the crops and the distilleries.

This historical journey also recounts the early years and life experiences of Gary that gave him the foundational experience and knowledge for the path that he took and how he acquired so many skills that enabled him to accomplish so much in the development of his farms, distillation, and becoming the world leader in essential oils.

The farms have been visited by tens of thousands of people, and many have participated in various aspects of harvesting, distilling, bottling, and seedling planting and reforestation.

Some of the pictures are not the best resolution because they are old and taken with old cameras, and because of the low resolution, they cannot be enlarged; but I thought a lower-quality picture was better than no picture.

May you enjoy your educational experience in learning about how aromatic plants are grown and distilled and come to a greater understanding about the decision you make when you choose to use an essential oil.

Mary Young

Mary Young
July 2019

25 years ago Gary Young established Seed to Seal®, the quality system that makes Young Living the most unique essential oil network marketing company in the world.

Seed to Seal uses specific protocols to monitor and control the production of every essential oil from our corporate farms, partner farms, and certified growers worldwide.

When Gary began visiting potential partner farms around the world, he saw tremendous differences in the way plants were grown, harvested, and distilled, so he began to put in place his criteria for the planting of the seed all the way to the distillation of that plant material.

Young Living has since developed its Three Pillars—Sourcing, Science, and Standards—by which our global corporate offices oversee production all the way to the labeled bottle.

SEED

It was critical to Gary that he produced and sourced the highest-quality essential oils to protect the commitment of his Seed to Seal process that ensured the very best essential oil production.

He worked with many botanists and agronomists to identify the plant genus and species to be certain that the seeds, cuttings, and seedlings would produce the highest essential oil benefits documented by historical use and scientific research.

A small amount of each crop is kept for harvesting seed for future planting. Today we have our own seed bank for many of the crops grown at the Mona and St. Maries farms, which provided the lavender seed that Gary took back to France for planting and restoring the lavender in Provence that was unhealthy and dying.

CULTIVATE

Gary knew that proper cultivation was critical, which demanded a lot of ingenuity as much of the equipment needed was not available. As he retrofitted farm implements, it took time to determine what worked best for both cultivating and harvesting.

He was also careful about harvesting wildcrafted plants to preserve the sustainability of their future growth.

The health of the soil–as determined by the use of compost, natural fertilizers, crop rotation–as well as proper irrigation, and monitoring of sun and temperature exposure, was critical to plant quality.

The country of origin and species for every essential oil are recorded, and partner farms and distilleries are periodically visited to offer assistance and document current practices for producing the highest-quality oil.

DISTILL

After seeing so many variations of distilling throughout the world, Gary decided that only stainless steel and glass materials could be used for distillation. Our grant program helps our partner farms and growers with new stainless steel for their distilleries.

Gary wanted the documentation of plant volume, curing time, steam temperature, time of distillation, and oil yield, so he could determine more specifics for the distilling process.

Only single species of plants could be distilled in the cooker; afterwards, it had to be steam cleaned before a different plant species could be distilled in the same cooker to prevent contamination. The ancient method of hydro-distillation for the extraction of the oil from tree resins is still used today, and cold pressing is usually the method of extraction for citrus oils.

TEST

Gary learned from leading experts in Europe to use his nose as his "instrument" for testing. He was remarkably accurate in determining the percentage of major constituents or detecting any imbalance in oil chemistry. He could tell if the oil had been scorched or if the distillation time was too long or too short. It was shocking the number of oils he rejected because they didn't meet the specifications of his nose. Surprisingly, many of those rejected oils were bought by other essential oil companies.

Eventually, pure oils would not meet the demand, and gradually adulterated oils began to enter the market. Gary wanted an in-house laboratory and bought the first gas chromatograph (GC) instrument in 1997. Today our chemists use millions of dollars of state-of-the-art equipment.

SEAL

Our Seed to Seal process ensures the highest quality of every essential oil poured into the bottle. Every oil container is assigned a batch number and then tested and approved by our Quality Control. Through batch number tracking, it is easy to trace the oil back to the distillation from which it came. If it does not meet our standard, it is returned to the distiller.

After the oils are released for production, they are sent for specific blend formulations or for various supplements or skin and body care products. They may also be bottled and labeled as single oils and then shipped to our members worldwide.

Visitors are welcome to see our magnificent process, from laboratory testing to bottle filling and packaging. This is truly Gary's vision that he generously shared with the world.

Seed to Seal Quality Commitment

Millions of people around the world have discovered the benefits of pure essential oils. Young Living is committed to establishing and maintaining the ultimate, industry-leading standard in essential oil products.

Our extensive Seed to Seal quality commitment helps ensure that our products meet strict specifications to achieve the highest quality of pure essential oils, so all people may enjoy the benefits of our global resources, industry leadership, and over two decades of innovation.

Our three pillars of Seed to Seal—Sourcing, Science, and Standards—are paving the way for all essential oil companies to improve processes that protect our planet and ensure the highest-quality standards.

THE THREE PILLARS

SOURCING—*Corporate-owned farms, partner farms, Seed to Seal-certified growers*

Young Living produces its own essential oils or sources them from carefully vetted partner farms and Seed to Seal-certified growers. Young Living and all of our partners must meet the highest standards of agricultural practices, harvesting, distillation methods, storage, and bottling. We select our growers according to our established relationships, Seed to Seal specifications, contractual agreements, testing, and ongoing audits.

We engage third-party experts to audit the process of each grower for certification, testing, and sustainability to ensure the Seed to Seal quality commitment is always maintained as a part of the Young Living Essential Oils Sourcing pillar.

Our distribution center in Spanish Fork, Utah, is a state-of-the-art production facility, where we use best manufacturing practices to test essential oils, supplement ingredients, and essential oil-infused products and to formulate and produce new and innovative offerings.

SCIENCE—*Testing and Research*

Science is a major component of our Seed to Seal process. As the worldwide demand has grown for essential oils, so has the sophistication of laboratories that produce synthetic compounds in an attempt to meet that demand.

Our D. Gary Young Research Institute (the R&D department) and our Quality Control departments employ many PhD chemists, scientists, technicians, and trained staff, who work with the most advanced scientific equipment available, directing cutting-edge methods of testing to not only ensure the quality of our oils but to also develop new products for our market.

The quality starts at the farm and is then proven in our laboratories, where many physical, chemical, and microbiological scientific tests are used to measure the exact components and properties of our essential oils. Testing begins at our farms and continues all the way through the final stages prior to bottle filling and shipping.

Our testing includes, but is not limited to refractometry, polarimetry, inductively coupled plasma mass spectrometry (ICP-MS), inductively coupled plasma-atomic optical emission spectrometry (ICP-OES), gas chromatography (GC), high-performance liquid chromatography (HPLC), Fourier-transform infrared spectroscopy, automated microbial enumeration, flash point, gas chromatography mass spectrometry (GCMS), Isotope Ratio Mass Spectrometry, and chiral chromatography.

We also work with more than a dozen of the world's leading, independent, and accredited laboratories with highly skilled scientists who specialize in advanced product testing. If our exhaustive tests show that an oil does not meet our standards, the shipment is rejected and sent back.

Our Research Institute employs cutting-edge science to develop unique products that lead the industry. This team also conducts ongoing research to support product claims and uses and develops new testing methods to help ensure the quality of our products.

STANDARDS—Sustainability and Compliance

Since the beginning of time, man has explored and exploited the natural resources of Mother Nature. The beauty of colorful, durable, and exotic wood has driven the entrepreneur to search out beauty for profit. Amazing, graceful, and ferocious animals have not only become prey for adventure and profit but also for the trophies that are hung on the walls to be admired and envied.

The danger of extinction of many species has caused concern around the world, with many organizations and conservation groups rising to fight against those who would exploit some of the beauty and grandeur that surrounds us. In the search for pure essential oils, many trees, such as rosewood, have been overharvested.

A United Nations agreement called CITES (the Convention on International Trade in Endangered Species of Wild Fauna and Flora) was signed by representatives from 80 countries on March 3, 1973, to ensure that international trade of wild animals and plants does not threaten their survival. The Lacey Act is a conservation law in the United States that prohibits trade in wildlife, fish, and plants that have been illegally taken, transported, and/or sold.

Young Living has joined with the United States Department of Justice to create a comprehensive essential oil compliance program specifically to help determine the viability of any plant, bush, tree, etc., to be harvested for commercial use and protect any species that falls within the jurisdiction of CITES and/or the Lacey Act, which protects more than 35,000 species of animals and plants, whether they are traded as live specimens, fur coats, or dried herbs.

Our comprehensive Lacey Act Compliance Program is the first in the essential oil industry to have been reviewed and accepted by the government. It is the gold standard for compliance programs, and we are proud to be the first to establish such a program. We work with top legal and environmental experts around the world who keep us advised of the most current laws and advise us on the protection and status of delicate and endangered plant species.

The Lacey Act Compliance Program includes five steps that demonstrate the world leadership of Young Living to protect our environment and the production of essential oil: 1. Education of the basic requirements, 2. Evaluation of product and supplier risk factors, 3. Certification of compliance, 4. Risk assessment of both suppliers and plant products, 5. Auditing and monitoring of all individuals and organizations in the supply chain.

Young Living is also committed to sustainable plant sourcing, reforestation of harvested trees, and educating local communities to comply with environmental laws. This includes recycling and zero-waste programs at the Young Living offices, as well as both LEED and Green Global (NC) certifications of our Global Headquarters in Lehi, Utah.

Life was harsh, but it made him strong, determined, and fearless.

A PATH UNKNOWN

"The time will come that if you don't grow it, you won't have it."

How could Gary have understood the significance of these words spoken by Mr. Henri Viaud? The Frenchman was speaking about his beloved lavender essential oil; but when he said this, lavender was plentiful.

That was in 1991 when Gary was studying distillation with Mr. Viaud, who at that time was considered the "father of distillation" in Provence, France, the lavender capital of the world. Tucked away on top of his mountain, Henri Viaud, a retired professor of mathematics and physics at a university in Toulouse, France, was joked about to have distilled everything, and jokingly, even rocks, in his life's work to explore all avenues of distillation for the advancement of understanding the process for the best extraction of essential oils known to man.

What did Mr. Viaud feel or sense about the future of what was so precious to him? Did he know that there would be a scarcity of oils with a demand that could not be met? Did he know that essential oils would become so popular that because the demand could not be met, they would be adulterated and made synthetically to eventually be used in everything from food flavorings to cosmetics and even soaps, a far cry from their amazing and intended benefits?

Sadly, families that have been distilling for centuries are closing down their distilleries. They are being dismantled, and the property is being sold as real estate for housing, restaurants, and other business ventures. Some of the land is also being sold for commercial use, while other crops are being taken out and replaced with quicker cash crops such as hemp, soy, canola, etc. The young people are heading to the cities for the "technical life," while pure oils are being endangered by growers and distillers willing to cut corners for profit.

But how did D. Gary Young, a farm boy from the mountains of Idaho, come to be in France studying distillation with the famous Henri Viaud? Why was he driven to learn everything he could about essential oils, how they were produced, and their benefits to mankind?

The story goes back to perhaps another lifetime in comparison—back to the mountains where Gary grew up, his emigration to Canada, and his dream to forge a life out of the wilderness. He could never have foreseen the change that would come into his life that would take him down a strange and unfamiliar path, a path that would change millions of lives for the better.

His destiny? For Gary, the world became his destiny—his teacher, his classroom, his encyclopedia, his destination—his life. Yes, his life revolved around discovering how to heal his broken body, riddled with pain, which would lead him into the annals of history and an ancient world shrouded in the mysteries of essential oils that had been lost to the modern world.

Gary is in front of his maternal grandfather. To the left is Nancy, Gary's older sister, who moved with him to Canada for a short time.

The Donald N. Young family in 1963.

At age 14 Gary tracked and shot this cougar, which had been killing their sheep for over two months.

D. Gary Young | The World Leader in Essential Oils

When Gary was born, his family lived in the 16x20-foot sod-roof cabin shown below. At age 4, his father built this 30x30-foot, four-room cabin, where he lived with his parents and five siblings until he was 17. When he was 16, his father ran a line for electricity and installed their first hand-crank phone that was routed through the forest service line that connected to the lookout and ranger stations for fire patrol.

The family raised cattle and sheep, milked cows, cleaned trails for the forest service, and logged year-round for a living. They also hunted and worked as game guides, 1955.

During the summer of 1967, Gary logged over 2,500 miles in the saddle in the Idaho wilderness, patrolling for fires, clearing trails, and packing supplies to the lookout posts.

Gary's father in front of the old 16x20-foot cabin on the ranch he bought in 1948 that was 12 miles from town.

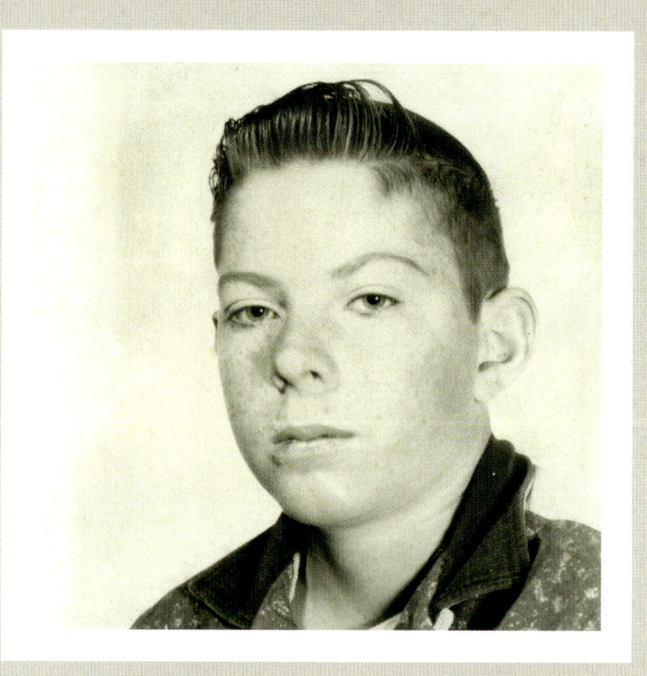

"As a young boy, I dreamed of going to Canada and homesteading a ranch on the Canadian frontier.

"In 1967, when I was 18, I loaded my personal belongings into the Mustang and began the long drive to Quesnel, British Columbia. In 1968 I got in on the last homestead act in the Caribou District and was given 320 acres 30 miles in the wilderness, where I could begin to live my dream and forge my new life out of the wilderness, building my horse ranch and logging business.

"Little did I know that here in the wilds of Canada, the destiny that awaited me would change my life forever."

In September 1967, at age 18, Gary packed his red Mustang and drove to Northern British Columbia, intent on living his dream.

Similar to his childhood cabin, Gary built a 16x20-foot cabin on the property he homesteaded 30 miles outside of Quesnel, B.C., 1968.

4   D. Gary Young | The World Leader in Essential Oils

At age 22 Gary was the youngest logger to have contracts with the two largest lumber mills in British Columbia. He worked hard meeting the daily logging quota, and the remaining time was spent building his dream, 1969.

Gary spent 27 months in a wheelchair before learning to walk again. This is a rare photo since Gary refused to have a picture taken of him in a wheelchair or using crutches or a walker, 1978.

Destiny Speaks—A Terrible Accident

At 24 years of age, on February 8, 1973, Gary suffered a very severe logging accident when a cut tree sheared off and hit him in the head, resulting in 3 open skull fractures, a ruptured spinal cord in 3 places that was classified as an incomplete break, 11 ruptured discs, 16 broken and/or crushed vertebrae, a broken pelvis, the right scapula broken in 9 pieces, a severed brachial plexus, and 19 broken bones, which included all of his ribs on the right side and several on the left side.

Suffering from intense pain and paralyzed except for his left arm, he was confined to a wheelchair with a medical prognosis that he would never walk again. His life was one of 13 drugs, including morphine and an antidepressant, and a world that seemed dark and hopeless with no light at the end of any tunnel.

After two failed attempts at suicide, he sunk into an even deeper state of depression. He had no insurance and slowly everything was sold to pay for his medical expenses—his logging equipment, his ranch, and his livestock—everything was gone.

In his third attempt, he decided to "fast" himself to death; it was the only way out. No one could rescue him or force him to eat; but after 253 days of only drinking water and lemon juice, the most unexpected happened—he felt movement in his right toe. The doctors said it was one of those unexplainable medical phenomena. They suspected that because of his fasting, his body did not get the needed nutrients necessary to manufacture scar tissue, enabling some nerve endings to reroute and reconnect, which was the beginning of many years of intense pain in his struggle to walk again.

He reconciled himself to living in the misery and hopelessness of his condition. He became determined to find a new path of life where he could survive. Because he couldn't go back to logging and farming, his mind began exploring different avenues of healing through the world of books.

He stopped all his medications to clear his mind, disregarded the diagnosis of paralysis, and began experimenting with new modalities. He attended a community college, went to massage school, opened his own health food store, and grew in his knowledge of herbs and healing. His amazing road to recovery brought attention from many people wanting help.

Gary's emotional recovery was dramatic. Told in his own words, his story gives us a slight glimpse into his life at that time and is a tremendous insight into his life; his tremendous anguish, deep pain, and determination:

"The lowest ebb in my life was when I tried to commit suicide and failed, not once, but three times. I had no place to retreat to when I realized I couldn't even die. Never before had I felt so disconnected from God, my family, and the world. I felt so rejected and was sure that God hated me because He wouldn't even let me die. I had nowhere to turn.

"Had it not been for my father, who came to my hospital room, and shaking his finger at me, told me to grow up, quit feeling sorry for myself, accept the hand I had been dealt, and figure out a way to get on with life, I might have continued to wallow in self-pity, depression, and eventually succeed in ending my life. But my father knew my temperament, and he pushed the right button, called 'tough love.'

"After speaking those words in a tone of disgust and anger, he turned and walked out and never came to visit me again. He made me so angry as he walked down the hall, never looking back, while I was bawling and crying out to him, 'That's easy for you to say. You don't know what it's like to be paralyzed and in constant pain with no drugs that help. If it's the last thing I do, I will get out of this bed, and I will walk and ride my horse again!'

"When I finally got out of the hospital to go home for a weekend, I discovered that my family was on welfare, which sent me deeper into depression, and I cried, 'No, I will not be on welfare; take it back!' My wife asked me what she should do. The ranch was gone, the horses and cows were gone, the logging equipment was gone, and there was no more money. Eventually, my wife took the children and left me, unable to cope with my current condition and the burden of the future.

"Alone, I cried for hours, and no one came to sympathize with or console me. When there were no more tears to run down my face, I started to think about what I could do. I asked my mother if my paint box and canvases were still in storage and if she could get them for me. Perhaps I could earn a living by painting; at least one arm worked. I started that night and by the end of the next day had painted a beautiful, scenic picture of the mountains.

"Everyone loved it and expressed their feelings of support. I continued to paint and on the weekends someone would drive me to a shopping area in town where I could sit and sell my paintings. Soon I was getting jobs to paint murals in lawyers' and doctors' offices and homes. But in a small town, there was not enough business to support me as an artist for very long, and so the jobs became fewer and fewer.

Unable to work, Gary sold his paintings on a street corner in town on the weekends to earn a living after the accident.

This was the second truck that Gary had retrofitted with a hand clutch and brakes, so he could begin working again.

Gary's Spine
May 29, 2013

An MRI of Gary's spine taken 40 years after the terrible accident, which left him with unending pain that he blocked from his mind to accomplish all that he did in his life.

Note the hole in the top vertebra and the hairline cracks in almost all the vertebrae that were either broken, chipped, crushed, or disfigured from the various accidents and activities throughout the last 40 years.

That he learned to walk again is a miracle that defied his medical prognosis.

Cervical

Lumbar
- Hole in vertebra
- 45% crushed
- 50% crushed
- Discs pressing into the spinal column.
- Small, faint, dark gray hair-like lines are fractures, cracks, and breaks in the vertebrae.
- Crack

Disc 11 was ruptured and driven through vertebra 12, forcing bone marrow out through the shell from the sandrail accident in 2013.

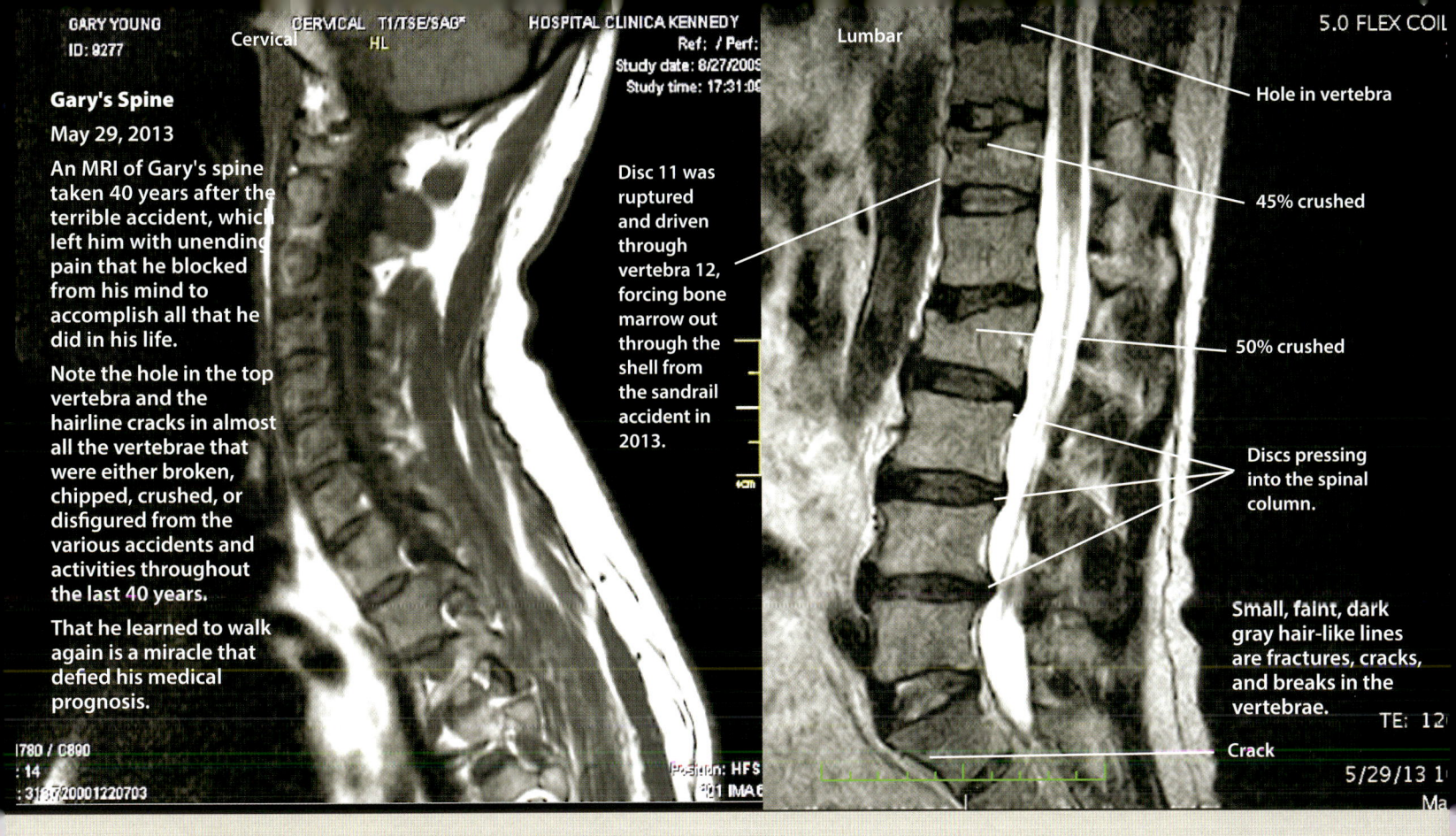

"One night while reading the paper, I saw a job listing for a truck driver to haul chips. A friend drove me to the mill office; but when I told the owner what I wanted, he laughed and asked me how I was going to drive a truck in a wheelchair. I told him that if he equipped the truck with hand controls, I could drive it. With a dubious look, he pointed to a Mack day cab tractor in the yard and told me that if I could drive it over to a semi chip trailer, hook up to it, and drive it back to the office, we would talk about a job.

"I wheeled my chair through the gravel yard to the truck, pulled myself up on the steps, pulled my chair up beside me, and shoved it behind the cab. I got in the seat and started the truck, and once the air pressure was up, I released the brakes, turned the truck off, put it in gear, and started it again.

"I pulled around in front of the trailer, turned the motor off, put it in reverse, and started it again, backing under the trailer. When it locked on the bull pin, I set the brakes and turned off the motor at the same time.

"I slid out onto the step, lowered my chair to the ground, and then slid along the frame so that I could hook up the air hose and power cord. Then I slid back to my chair and wheeled myself to the landing gear handle, cranked it up, wheeled back to the step, and got back in the truck.

"I started the engine, built the air for the trailer, released the trailer brakes, and turned the engine off. Putting it in the lowest gear, I started the engine again, coasted down to the office door, shut it off, set the brakes, and got out over the steps into my chair. It took me almost an hour with climbing up and down and pulling my chair up and down. As I started to wheel myself to the owner's office, he came out to meet me and, with tears in his eyes, told me I had a job.

"On my first trip, when I backed the trailer up the unloading ramp, I was concerned that the foreman would get upset with me for taking so much time to unhook, dump, and rehook my trailer, making the other trucks wait. I moved as fast as I could, sliding out, lowering my chair, and grabbing the rod that I had made so that I could reach under the trailer to hook the fifth wheel release lever and trip it.

"I noticed him watching me and thought that my job might not last. I wheeled back and started to crank the landing gear down when he came out of the control tower and down the steps. To my surprise, he told me to get back in my truck and said he would take care of hooking and unhooking me whenever I came.

"It was amazing how a feeling of wholeness started to come over me now that I was working again."

D. Gary Young | The World Leader in Essential Oils

Gary renovated this motel and leased it for $1,300 per month to use for his research center.

8   D. Gary Young | The World Leader in Essential Oils

RECOVERY
Mexico and a New Path of Discovery

Gary moved to Southern California, where he continued with his education by enrolling in a naturopathic college. At the same time, he opened a small office in Chula Vista, California, and built a research center for physical and emotional well-being in Rosarito Beach in Baja California, Mexico.

His single desire was to help people find answers and solutions to their own problems. Through 13 years of constant debilitating pain and frustration, Gary went from a wheelchair, to a walker, to crutches, to a cane, to very painful, slow walking. But walking again, as painful as it was, kept him determined to discover new possibilities of healing.

During this time in 1983, a lady by the name of Annemarie from Switzerland brought her sister, who was not doing well, to his research center to see if she could find some help. Annemarie had grown up working in the natural health products industry, had her own laboratory, and formulated various health products. She had been studying essential oils for many years and was very interested in their health benefits. She handed Gary an envelope with some research that she had translated from French about essential oils because she felt he would be interested. Gary stayed up all night reading and in the morning called her and said he wanted to know more. She then invited him to attend a conference that was taking place the following week in Geneva, Switzerland, where medical doctors were presenting their research on essential oils and their effects on respiratory illness.

That was the beginning of his path that led to thousands of discoveries about essential oils and the immense possibilities they offer for physical, emotional, and spiritual application.

1985

Some of Gary's first supplements infused with essential oils in 1986.

It was fun recording with Donna Riley, a singer from the Lawrence Welk TV show, and Clint Walker, from the movie series *Cheyenne*, along with Clint's wife Gigi, singing together while at the research center.

The clinic kitchen where Gary first began experimenting with infusing oils into food supplementation. VitaGreen (MultiGreens) and ComforTone were his first formulations on the market.

Gary was passionate about live- and dark-cell microscopy and used these techniques extensively in his research. He believed that the blood carries the history of the body and is a window into each individual's health.

The original apothecary was filled with many herbs that were ground from plants gathered on weekend excursions.

D. Gary Young | The World Leader in Essential Oils

Gary welcomed Dr. Bernard Jensen and his wife, Marie, 1986.

Essential Oil Research in France

Gary was invited by the French medical doctors to travel to France and join them as they made rounds in the hospital in which they were conducting their research. Gary was fascinated and driven to learn more. His questions were endless, as this new world continued to open his mind to greater understanding and new possibilities.

He returned home from France with 13 oils and began experimenting with them to discover and learn more about their usage and application. There were no books available written in English about essential oils, let alone anything on usage and application; and the French medical doctors were publishing in journals that were only in French.

This truly put Gary on the frontier of essential oil science as he began to discover what oils and oil combinations to use, what worked better, and how to apply them. With no written information in the U.S., no internet, and virtually no one with any conclusive experience, the frontier was his. So he boldly went forward, against tremendous criticism and warnings, determined to unlock the hidden mysteries of this ancient science that he instinctively understood.

He even began infusing his herbal formulas with essential oils and was impressed with the increased efficacy of the supplements. He felt so much excitement that he wanted to share his findings with the world.

But the world was not ready for his discoveries; and people laughed at him, slandered him, and told him it was impossible to do what he was doing. But the few who had been using Gary's new products infused with essential oils began to spread the word, and more and more people wanted what he had.

He decided to sell his research facility and start his own marketing company. The demands were increasing and he felt a new passion growing inside. He could teach many more people at the same time than he could by helping one person at a time, day after day. The experience he had gained was tremendous, and now he wanted to teach and share his new knowledge, to begin a new chapter.

Dr. Jensen, well-known for his research in the field of health and natural healing, presented Gary with one of his most-popular books.

In 2008 the marquee in Bonita, California, still showed Gary's Young Life Wellness Center.

He did a lot of experimenting with the first oils he brought home from Europe and made many exciting discoveries. His thirst for more knowledge heightened with a desire to study distillation. With his farming background, he had a natural interest in growing, harvesting, and extracting the oils from aromatic plants, adding a new path of research and discovery. It seemed that France was the place to go, but he didn't know anyone there and didn't have the slightest idea how to make a contact, besides the fact that the French were not open to sharing their "secrets." French lavender was their claim to fame, and they didn't want anyone else, especially an American, getting involved or interfering.

Gary flew to France a couple of times a year, determined to learn everything he could about distillation. He carried a backpack and a sleeping bag, prepared for anything. After all, he grew up in the mountains, and comfort was not a consideration. In a small rental car, he drove the countryside looking at the fields and distilleries from the roadside. He found a few people who spoke English, but there was little they would tell him, which created a lot of frustration.

Typical French portable distiller abandoned years ago.

D. Gary Young | The World Leader in Essential Oils 13

There was a lot of excitement as Young Living started to grow.

Young Living headquarters in Spokane, Washington, 1989.

Gary was a guest speaker at many expos and seminars.

14 D. Gary Young | The World Leader in Essential Oils

THE BIRTH OF YOUNG LIVING

When Gary started his new business in the spring of 1988, he was a "one-man band." From Monday through Thursday, he answered the phone and took orders and then packed them and had them ready for shipping. He filled the oil bottles by hand in his little lab and hand wrote the labels for them. He did everything he could; and that which he couldn't do, he contracted out piece by piece.

Thursday evenings he would put the answering machine on and fly out to a different city such as Phoenix, Los Angeles, or Dallas and then travel around with his members and friends like Eldon and Nancy, Loretta, and Anna-Maya, doing meetings to grow his new little business.

Sunday night he returned home to get ready for all the orders that he hoped would start coming in on Monday. Once a month he would spread all the orders out on the living room floor and calculate the commissions by hand. That continued for months until the business had grown enough that he felt he could start hiring a few employees.

It was truly a simple beginning with real intent to give something to the world that he loved and that he believed would benefit mankind.

In August 1992, even with a broken ankle, Gary took the first group of members to France to see the lavender fields and distilleries.

The Landel family with Gary in Provence, France: Jane, Jean-Noël, Véréna, and Nicolas, in the backpack, 1991.

Nicolas, now the manager of the Young Living farm in France, was tutored by his father and Gary. Here he is teaching visitors about distillation, 2014.

Jean-Noël Landel—The French Connection

In 1990 Gary was lecturing at a Whole Life Expo in Anaheim, California, and had a group of members running the booth. Jean-Noël Landel was visiting from France, hoping to find someone to whom he could sell his lavender oil. Since 1985 Gary had been experimenting with oils and infusing them into his supplement formulations and had some of them with a few single oils on the display table. As Jean-Noël walked by the booth, he saw them and stopped to talk. He was still talking when Gary came off the stage. They quickly discovered a mutual interest, and Jean-Noël invited Gary to come to France for a visit, not thinking he would really come.

One month later, Jean-Noël was absolutely shocked when Gary called him from Paris. Gary didn't know when he would travel, so he didn't contact Jean-Noël ahead of time to let him know he was coming. Jean-Noël and his wife, Jane, who is an American, welcomed Gary into their home, which was the beginning of a great and lasting friendship that opened so many doors for Gary in the world of the French lavender growers. Their daughter, Véréna, was four years old; and their son, Nicolas, was just six months old. Jean-Noël and Jane had never used the oils in their home for their personal needs; and so when Nicolas was crying and spitting up and would not go to sleep, they didn't know what to do. Gary held Nicolas in his lap and showed Jane how to massage his feet with lavender oil until he fell asleep. Gary also taught Jane how to do Vita Flex to enhance the use of the oils.

Today, in 2019, Nicolas Landel is a young man following in his father's footsteps, managing our French farm and the lavender harvest. He works on various Young Living projects that include helping with einkorn production, sourcing new aromatic plants, and visiting current and potential partner farms. Little did Jean-Noël and Jane know that their lifelong friendship with Gary would involve many exciting adventures of discovery.

The Young Living cooperative French distillery in Simiane-la-Rotonde has now been upgraded with stainless steel equipment and more efficient technology.

Gary, Dave Anderson from Sweden, and Jean-Noël load the cooker with lavender at the farm in France.

This distillery was in full operation when Gary started studying distillation in France in the summer of 1991.

Some of Gary's first distillation training was with this French portable distiller, which he purchased in 2006, now on display at the farm in Mona.

Philippe Mailhebiau—New Spiritual Insight

On one of Gary's trips to France in 1991, Jean-Noël introduced him to Philippe Mailhebiau, who was writing and teaching about essential oils.

Philippe had a laboratory and was conducting research on both the physical and emotional aspects of essential oils. Philippe opened Gary's mind to the emotional aspects of the oils, which Gary found fascinating, since he believed the oils carried a spiritual essence that greatly influenced how an individual responded to the oils. Studying the emotional and spiritual characteristics of the oils was soul-stirring to Gary, opening another world of learning.

However, Philippe was not a farmer and had no distilleries, so he could not teach Gary anything about growing and distilling, but Philippe and Gary shared a mutual interest in discovering the unknown benefits of the oils. They became good friends and Gary invited Philippe and his associates to come to Idaho to teach the members, which was a rewarding time for everyone.

Philippe visited the farm in St. Maries in 1993.

Philippe opened Gary's mind to explore the emotional aspects of the oils, 1991.

D. Gary Young | The World Leader in Essential Oils

Marcel Espieu—Mentor and Friend

Gary traveled back and forth many times learning about France and the essential oil industry from Jean-Noël. One year after Gary's first visit, Jean-Noël introduced him to Marcel Espieu, the president of the Lavender Growers Association, who was not too open or receptive to this curious American who kept asking questions. However, with time Marcel could see how serious Gary was and eventually invited him to see his distillery. Gary volunteered to work filling the firebox and doing anything that Marcel asked. Gary stayed late into the night keeping the firebox filled, and Marcel would then come to trade places with him until morning.

Marcel began to trust Gary more and more and developed a friendship that was destined to last a lifetime. Marcel taught Gary everything he could, and Gary would often drive with him to take the lavender oil to the perfumeries in Grasse, France. It was amazing that even though they did not speak each other's language, they were able to communicate through working together and accomplishing the desired goal.

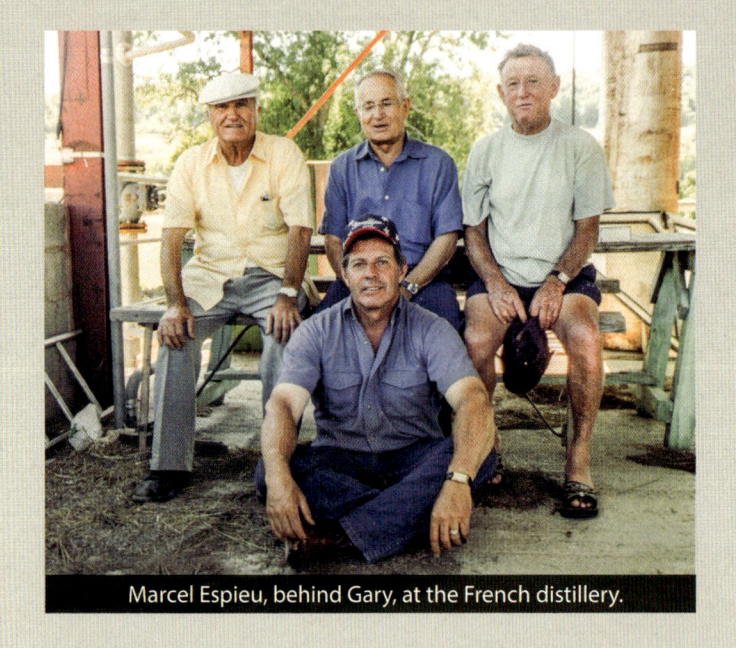

Marcel Espieu, behind Gary, at the French distillery.

As Gary learned more about distillation, he began to visualize building his own distillery. Everybody laughed and Marcel made jokes about the American who thought he could do what the French have done for hundreds of years. But the dream was there as though it had already begun.

Gary, Henri Viaud, and Jean-Noël and his family visit one of the nearby distilleries in Provence, France, 1991.

Henri Viaud working in his laboratory, 1991.

Henri Viaud—The Father of Distillation

There was yet another teacher of distillation who Gary wanted to meet. Henri Viaud, who at that time was considered the "father of distillation," lived in the mountains in Provence, not far from Jean-Noël; but he was not open to having visitors, especially "curious" Americans. However, Gary persisted; and one night, five years later, Mr. Viaud came to Jean-Noël's house for dinner when Gary was there.

In a very short but intense interview, Mr. Viaud asked Gary what essential oils meant to him. Feeling tremendous pressure and with much anxiety, Gary said, "I believe that essential oils are the closest physical and tangible substance that carries the spirit of God on earth." Pointing his finger at Gary and in a dramatic tone of voice with a heavy French accent, Mr. Viaud said, "You are right and anyone who messes with them should be treated like a criminal." Then he stood up, turned, and abruptly walked out the door.

Jean-Noël walked Mr. Viaud to his car; and when Jean-Noël returned, he said to Gary, who was feeling very defeated, "Mr. Viaud wants you on his mountain at 6 a.m." It was an exhilarating moment for Gary that left him sleepless and with great anticipation.

Gary spent many days with Mr. Viaud, cutting and harvesting wild lavender, thyme, and rosemary and then distilling them. He had only two 1,500-liter cookers, so the distilling was slow. The days added up to weeks and then months as Gary traveled back and forth from the U.S., going up the mountain to Mr. Viaud's distillery to work. Between Mr. Viaud and Marcel, Gary could not have had better teachers

Mr. Viaud's 600-year-old stone house on the mountain plateau, where Gary was taught and mentored in the art of distillation.

Jean-Noël and Gary exchange ideas with Henri about different oils and distillation.

Gary traveled all over France with Jean-Noël meeting growers and visiting distilleries. Jean-Noël and Gary leased their first farm in 1992. Then in 1993 they found an abandoned government farm that had a lease/purchase offering that seemed to be perfect for them. But after two years when the time came to buy, there was just too much paperwork, and the government was too difficult to work with; so Jean-Noël started looking elsewhere.

Over the length of four years, Gary traveled back and forth to France, spending as much time as he could studying and working in all aspects of the production, from planting, to harvesting, and to all facets of the extraction process.

Volunteering to help harvest, working in the distillery, and tending the firebox and boiler at night enabled him to study the cooking and distillation in detail. He made meticulous notes as he measured and drew plans. He learned everything he could with a "knowing" feeling inside that one day he would build his own distillery.

Jean-Noël and Gary had a lot of ideas about the second farm that was leased from the French government in 1994.

D. Gary Young | The World Leader in Essential Oils | 23

In 1989 Gary brought back the first lavender seeds from France and planted them three years later behind the Spokane office on a quarter acre of ground.

Second-year lavender (*Lavandula angustifolia*) that was harvested and then distilled in Gary's kitchen.

THE MODERN-DAY FATHER OF DISTILLATION

In 1988 Gary sold his research center in Baja California, Mexico, and moved to Reno, Nevada, to start his new business. A year later, at the end of 1989, Gary moved his headquarters to Spokane, Washington, where he devoted himself to his research and growing his Young Living business. On a quarter acre behind his building, Young Living's headquarters, he planted the small amount of lavender seed that he had brought home from France.

The seeds germinated and grew into beautiful, healthy plants, exuding the most intoxicating aroma. As the plants matured and grew bigger each year, Gary was anxious to see if he could produce oil from them.

As life took Gary down a different path and eventually into the essential oil world, he began to venture into many unknown areas, which became his world of discovery. He had taken many notes and made many drawings while helping Marcel in the distillery, and the memories from France were vivid in his head. As the ideas of distillation occupied his mind, he began drawing designs for distilleries on paper and mentally fabricating how he would build one.

In 1991 for his first distillation experiment, Gary welded two pressure cookers together, cutting holes in the bottom of the top container to allow water to be poured in and steam to rise up through the holes into the top cooker. He then harvested his beautiful plants that were only two years old and by French standard not quite mature enough to produce good oil. However, Gary felt he could not wait another year to determine if he could produce lavender oil.

Distillation on the Kitchen Stove

With the two pressure cookers welded together sitting on the stove top in the kitchen, Gary poured the water into the bottom through the holes that he had cut out and then packed the plants tightly into the top cooker. The gas stove was lit and as soon as the water began to boil, the steam started traveling up through the plant material. Shortly thereafter, a drop of lavender appeared, and Gary's first chapter of distillation was written.

These small cuttings produced 3 milliliters of the most exquisite lavender oil, which put more ideas into Gary's head. A good friend, Dr. Kurt Schnaubelt, analyzed this first lavender oil; and even Kurt was surprised at the quality of the oil from these two-year-old plants. It was Kurt's enthusiastic response that motivated Gary to keep going forward with his dream.

Gary's dream of distillation started with two pressure cookers welded together for his first distilling experiment in 1991.

Young Living members were willing and eager to help, 1991.

Gary built two more experimental distillers, each one a little bigger than the previous one. The second distiller built in Spokane in 1992 had a 25-liter cooking chamber, enabling him to distill a larger amount of lavender.

He experimented by distilling pineapple sage (*Salvia elegans*) and common sage (*Salvia officinalis*), which he had also grown in the garden plot behind the office. The pineapple sage smelled nothing like pineapple as he was hoping, but the fragrance of the sage was beautiful. As his curiosity increased, he decided to plant thyme.

All of the crops that were planted in the garden in Spokane and grown from seed, including the lavender seed from France, were the original starts that Gary eventually transplanted to the farm in St. Maries.

The second distiller was built in 1992 and was more advanced in design.

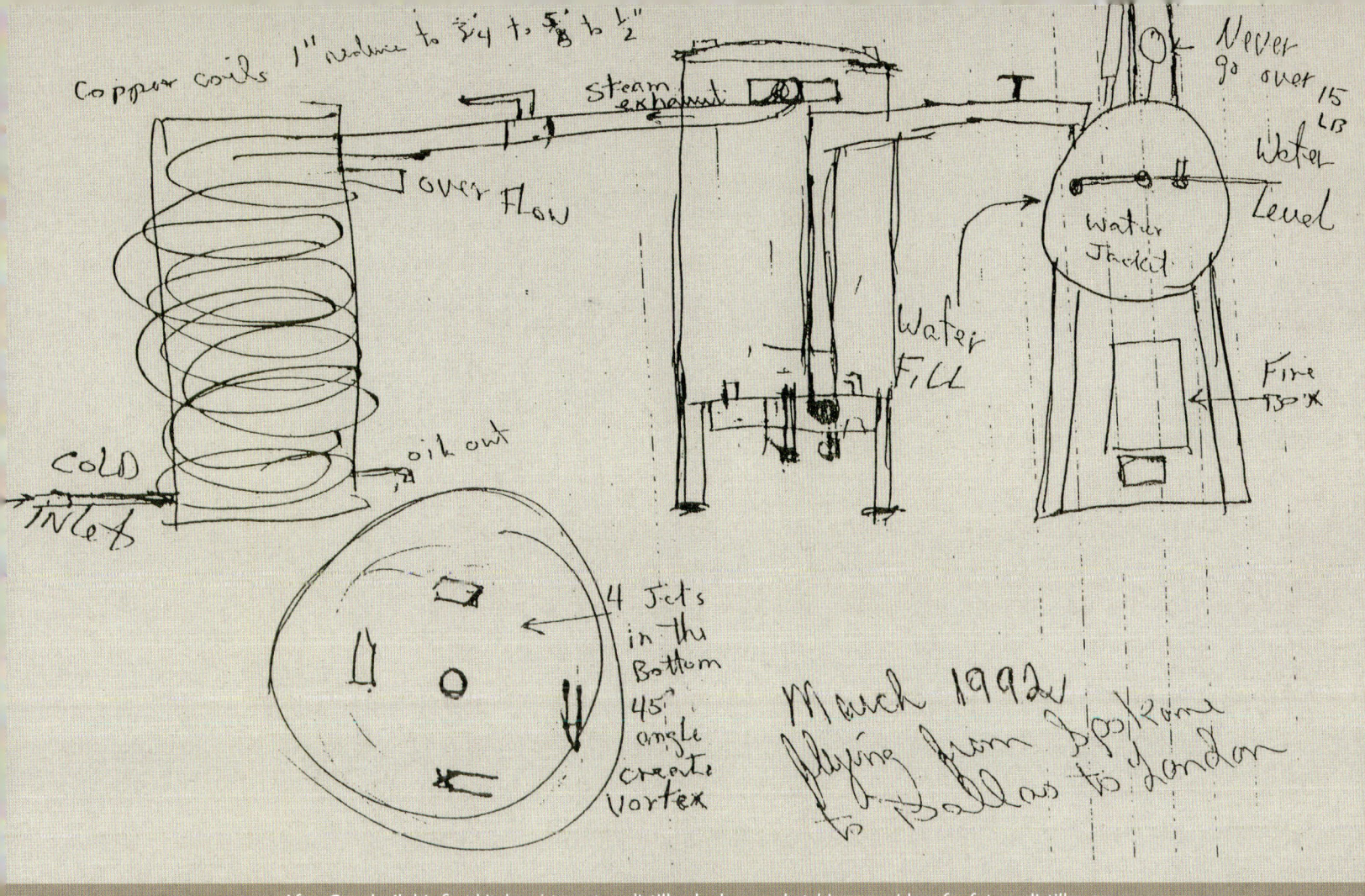

After Gary built his first kitchen/stove-top distiller, he began sketching new ideas for future distillers.

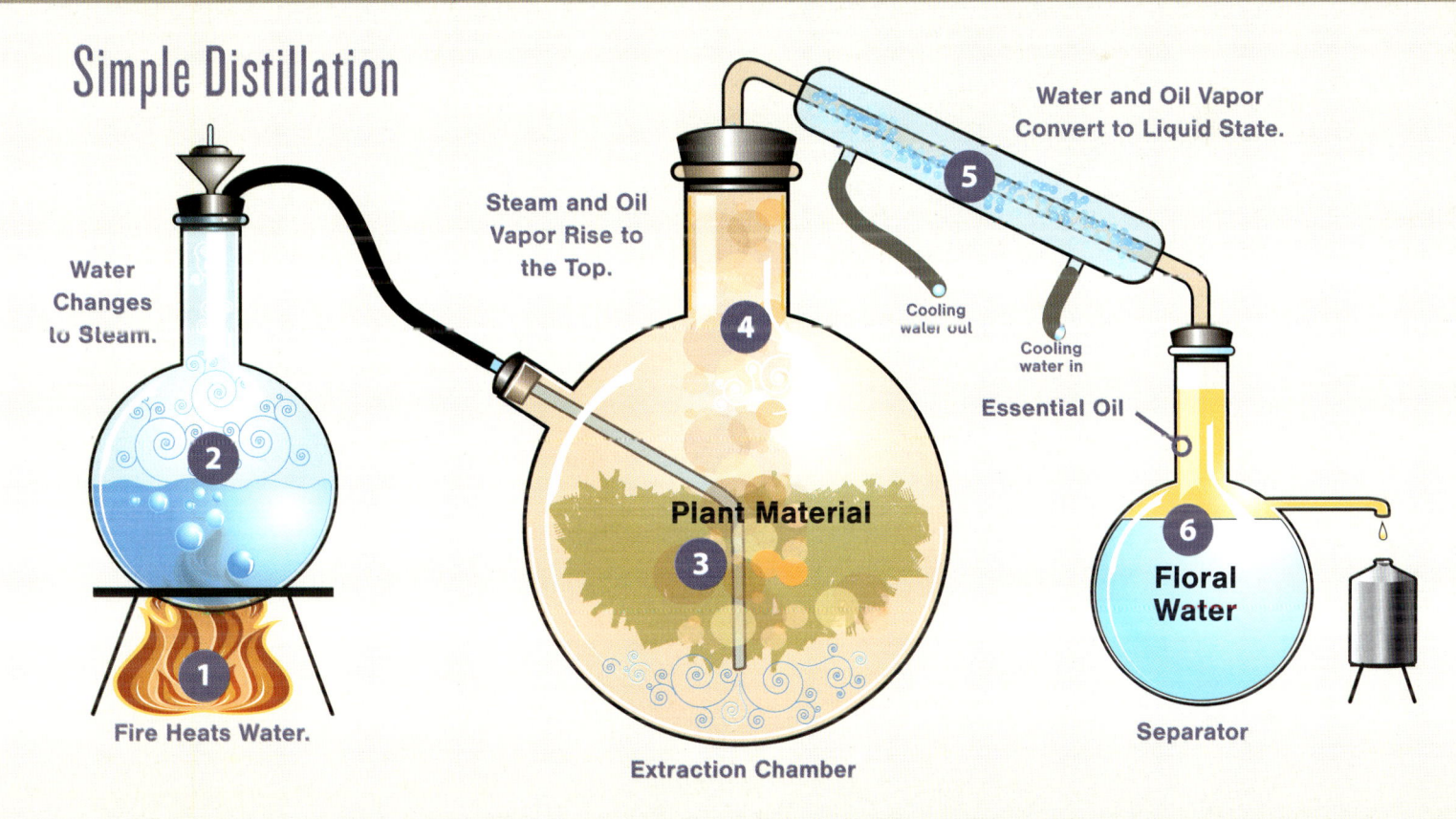

Simple Distillation

1. Fire Heats Water.
2. Water Changes to Steam.
3. Plant Material — Extraction Chamber
4. Steam and Oil Vapor Rise to the Top.
5. Water and Oil Vapor Convert to Liquid State.
6. Floral Water — Separator

Cooling water out
Cooling water in
Essential Oil

D. Gary Young | The World Leader in Essential Oils   27

In 1992 Gary began plowing the ground at the St. Maries farm, which had not been tilled in over 50 years and had never had chemicals on it. The soil was especially hard, with a pH of 4.5. It took 10 days to plow 40 acres with a 250-horsepower tractor and an 8-bottom plow. Burning the weeds, breaking the sod with the Dyna-Drive, discing, harrowing, and leveling the soil were done twice during the summer and spring of 1993 before planting.

St. Maries—Farming Begins

It was obvious to Gary that he needed more land in order to grow more plants for production to further his research, so in May 1992 he purchased his first farm of 160 acres nestled among the trees in Benewah County in the mountains of St. Maries, Idaho. The farm was remote and untouched by chemicals. It was perfect for his needs, and he aggressively began to till the land that had not been plowed in 50 years. The land had grown only grass for cattle pasture in the summer. However, the soil had an acid pH of 4.5, which was not conducive to growing lavender.

He had to till in several tons of manure, microbes, enzymes, and foliage feed to start bringing up the pH. Every year more calcium, nitrogen, and phosphate was plowed into the ground, gradually bringing the pH to 7.5, the desired level for lavender. He knew from experience that he had to build the soil, since aromatic plants did not grow well in conifer-type soil. He tilled 1 acre of ground in front of the barn and transplanted the lavender, thyme, and peppermint from his backyard in Spokane to this "gigantic" farm, as it seemed to Gary, beginning what would become his great farming legacy.

Gary injected liquid enzymes and microbes that are critical to building the soil for sustaining good crop growth. This was the first field of clary sage.

Gary spent 1993 preparing the farmland and increasing the soil pH, so he could plant small crops of peppermint and clary sage that he planned to harvest and distill. He designed a firebox boiler with a 250-liter distilling chamber and had it built in St. Maries in the machine shop at Fleet Parts and Service. Gary went several times to the shop to give direction and check on the fabrication. He was very exacting and wanted to make sure that it would work the way he wanted.

It was a 30-minute drive of great anticipation when Gary hauled it out to the farm. He quickly hooked up everything to prepare for distillation. Peppermint was the first plant distilled, and it was exquisite.

Bob Skinner, the owner of the machine shop, said: "It was fascinating to listen to them discuss how they were going to build this distiller, but I was more astounded when I knew how much peppermint was distilled and all the excitement that Gary felt when just a few drops of oil fell from the spout into the quart jar that was sitting on a tree stump. It was obviously a great triumph for him."

The distiller worked so well that Gary's vision began to grow bigger as he saw in his mind more crops planted, bigger extraction chambers, and more liters of oil. He was soon drawing the plans to make his vision a reality, and the farm expanded with that reality.

Members volunteered their time to help plant the clary sage and lavender starts that came from the garden plot in Spokane; Memorial Day weekend—38°F. Without the help of the members, it took 12 farm hands 12 hours to plant 1,800 starts.

The water was pumped with a small 5-horsepower fire pump running seven Rain Bird sprinkler heads that the irrigation company said wouldn't work, 1993.

Gary's third portable, wood-fired distiller, built in St. Maries, was a good prop for the ol' country doctor in the Steven Seagal movie *The Patriot*, 1998.

Gary dug out the pond on the farm for a reservoir to catch the runoff from the rain and snowmelt and pumped the water with a 5-horsepower Briggs and Stratton fire pump to the fields through 2-inch PVC pipe with risers and Rain Birds.

Chuck, the owner of Dickerson Pump and Irrigation Co. in Spokane, said it wasn't possible; but after Gary called him to tell him that it was working, he drove all the way to the farm to see what he thought was impossible.

Chuck became a lifetime friend and helped Gary many times over the years with the irrigation needs of the farm as it continued to grow.

For years that little pump served the farm very well, but as more crops were planted and the farm expanded, the pump finally had to be replaced with a much larger pump and several wheel lines in order to meet the increased irrigation demands.

The first clary sage field and Gary's PVC irrigation system that he built in 1993.

Cutting peppermint by hand, separating out weeds, and carrying it to the truck was "back-breaking" work. Clary sage is being irrigated in the background.

Members helped move PVC sprinkler lines, which was the beginning of Gary's dream to create opportunities for members to come and work on the farm.

When Jack and Carma Young managed the St. Maries farm in 1994, Aunt Carma was often out in the field working with everyone else.

In 1994 Gary and Uncle Jack built a three-row planter in the garage of the farm house. The planter worked perfectly and saved a great deal of time and is still in use today, 2019. Note: I am sitting on the right.

"Mechanizing"—The Planting Machine

In the beginning, many members came to help. In 1993-94 members planted 45,000 lavender plants in the unusual, freezing-cold spring month of May. However, this just wasn't fast enough and would never meet Gary's production goals, so he started designing again. Gary and his uncle, Jack Young, who died in 2001, built the first planting machine that was pulled by a tractor. There were three seats on the back with small platforms next to each seat for the trays so that three people could sit on the machine and plant three rows at the same time, greatly increasing the number of starts planted every day.

It was very rewarding for Gary to go from his crew of eight people, who had worked so hard to plant 1,500 starts by hand in 10 hours, to just three people planting 1,500 starts per hour and one more person operating the tractor.

Tansy

One summer afternoon in 1994, while walking from the house down to the distillery, Gary noticed tall, wiry plants with little, yellow, button-type flowers growing along the ditch bank. The aroma was strong and enticing, so Gary decided to distill it and see what it would produce. The yield was low, but it appeared that flying insects didn't like it, so it seemed like it would be good for experimenting.

Wild tansy was abundant in the fields and ditches, and farmers were very happy to have it cut and taken away, so it became a good wildcrafting crop. Strangely enough, each year when we went back to the fields where we had harvested, there was less and less tansy. Two of the biggest fields where the tansy was so thick and lush were completely gone within two years and what was left wasn't worth the time to cut.

We knew that tansy was considered a noxious weed by the farmers, and they were always looking for ways to get rid of it. The fact that there wasn't as much rain for two or three years while we were wildcrafting also didn't help.

Tansy was quite popular, especially for the horses when the bot flies attacked them, but the amount of oil we were able to produce was small compared to the demand. Eventually, Gary started looking for alternatives that had similar actions as tansy. He was very pleased with the results of Palo Santo in combination with other oils high in sesquiterpenes.

The thought was that perhaps in a couple of years, we would be able to go back to producing tansy, but with the new insect repellent that Young Living has currently formulated, which has proven to be quite effective, and due to the immense expense of wildcrafting, it doesn't seem necessary to go back to tansy. However, future possibilities always remain.

Interestingly enough, there was a lot learned with the tansy harvest and distillation. Even the idea to chop the plants in the field and blow them into the trucks began with tansy and has been a very efficient way of harvesting with many other crops.

Tansy was first cut by hand, 1995.

Upgrading to a tractor was an immense improvement.

I packed a lunch in the morning, and we would leave at 5 a.m. for the fields and come back at dark to help with the distilling. Gary chopped the tansy, blew it into the truck, and laughed as I enthusiastically swathed up and down the hills, even though my rows weren't as straight as he would have liked.

Gary discovered that chopping the tansy didn't hurt the oil and increased the production five times. Naturally, it was faster, more efficient, and definitely less taxing on the back muscles.

The First Harvest

The first harvest was very exciting as the lavender was packed into the 3,500-liter distiller. It was a tremendous accomplishment, and everyone was thrilled with the 4 liters of oil produced. The farm grew as Gary's vision expanded, and it became obvious that more cookers were needed. Different crops were being distilled, and fields were increasing. Soon three more cookers were added; and by 2006 a total of eight cookers were in operation at St. Maries.

The Farming Learning Curve

Clary Sage

Through trial and error, Gary learned a lot about aromatic crops. Clary sage grew extremely well, but the deer loved it and ate it down to the ground. One summer evening Gary and I flew to Spokane; and by the time we arrived in St. Maries, the sun was gone, and it was dark. As we drove up the hill and the car lights hit the field, illuminating the tops of the plants, more than 100 pairs of eyes stared into the headlights, obviously disturbed by these "intruders" who had interrupted their eating delight. Clary sage was like an aphrodisiac to them.

Gary used electric fences, air cannons, dogs on leashes, different scents, every means possible; but there was no way to keep the deer out of the fields. It was hopeless, so Gary decided to grow clary sage only in Utah. Interestingly, those well-fed does that next year had the highest rate of twin births ever recorded by a fish and game office.

Thyme

Most of the thyme plants looked alive but didn't seem to be growing. Further examination revealed a very disappointing discovery: the thyme plants were just sitting on top of the dirt. They had no roots because the gophers had been feasting. Perhaps they loved how it made them feel. Who knows, but that was also hopeless.

Peppermint

Peppermint grew well, but when it rained, the grass grew faster. Organic practices were becoming more challenging; and with the cool nights and early frost, the menthol in the peppermint did not reach the level Gary desired; so he decided that peppermint would be grown only in Utah.

Gary was thrilled with the first clary sage crop, 1993.

Collecting clary sage seeds by hand, 1993-1995.

Gophers enjoyed eating the roots of the first-year thyme, which made it impossible to have a reliable crop, 1997.

Gary cut the peppermint with a small sickle-bar mower—like a giant lawn mower. After the cutting, starts were dug up to replant in a larger field.

The beautiful first peppermint crop went moldy because of too much rain and too little sunshine—another learning experience. The crops grew extremely well; but fighting deer, rain, and mold made it impossible to grow some of the crops that Gary had hoped would be oil producing, 1994.

The hot climate in Mona was perfect for the peppermint, and it grew very well. The production was tremendous and the aroma was exhilarating. To our great relief, the clary sage also thrived, and the deer didn't have any interest in eating it. The plants grew with their vibrant fuchsia color, the aroma was exquisite, and the production was wonderful.

Gary designed a conveyor system for the peppermint and spearmint so that as the plants were harvested and cut with the swather, they dropped onto the conveyor that carried them up and into the truck that was driven alongside the harvester, and when full, driven to the distillery. It worked very well and greatly increased the efficiency of the harvest.

In 1994 Gary began to prepare the ground for the new distillery site.

The First "Real" Distillery—1994

In the summer of 1994, Gary began the construction of his fourth distiller, but this time it was to be a "real" distillery. He logged and peeled the white fir trees growing on the farm, prepared the ground, rented equipment, pounded the logs into the ground with the bucket on the excavator. With plans for a new design, he began construction of his first stationary stainless steel, vertical steam distiller.

He had only one 3,500-liter extraction chamber in which the first lavender, clary sage, peppermint, thyme, and tansy were distilled. Because it took so long to steam clean after each different crop, Gary could see the need for more cookers. The distillery grew as Gary had more cookers fabricated to meet the demand of the increasing amounts and different types of plant material that needed to be distilled.

Gary cut and sized the logs that he used for the support beams in the construction of the new distillery, which worked very well.

This old, rusty 25-horsepower boiler, which Gary bought for $500, was found in a farmer's hay field outside of St. Maries.

The garage was the perfect place for fabrication, because it was only two minutes away from the distillery site.

D. Gary Young | The World Leader in Essential Oils

The first extraction chamber, built in the garage, was moved to the distillery site at the bottom of the hill.

This is the first stationary distillery that Gary built with logs because concrete was too expensive.

Starting as a "one-man band" in 1992, 27 years later, hundreds of people are employed in Young Living's distilleries around the world.

The distilled plant material weighed about 1,200 pounds, but with larger cookers and more weight, that would not work in the future.

As Gary opened the valves and the first steam sizzled through the pipes, the cries of triumph from Gary and Uncle Jack were heard around the farm.

Seeing the first steam was a historical and joyous moment for Gary, June 1994.

Gary found an abandoned 25-horsepower boiler that was left to rust in a farmer's field outside of St. Maries, which he bought for $500. He had it cleaned and retubed and then had to begin assembling everything for the big moment of production. When the boiler fired and the steam sizzled through the pipes into the cooker, the cheering of triumph was heard all around the farm.

Gary was continually thinking about distilling and mentally making new designs for the extraction chambers, condensers, and separators. He had a different idea about the steam delivery into the chamber, so he drew out his plan and had the new design fabricated. He wanted the steam to travel through the plant material in a circular motion so that there would be a more even and better penetration of the steam that would carry the oil vapor with the steam up and into the condenser.

The water discharge pipes from the condenser were built with PVC pipe because PVC is lighter to move and cheaper than steel; but what a learning experience it was when the next morning, after the first distillation, Gary found that the hot PVC pipes had collapsed and stuck together because of the heat from the steam and condenser water. Naturally, the PVC pipe had to be replaced with steel.

Every aspect of the harvest and distillation was important to him because he knew that it all had to work in harmony to achieve the best results. Each crop was different so he made many adjustments and modified his system according to what he saw. The early years of harvesting and distilling brought about many changes from the traditional old ways to new, innovative, and more efficient production methods. The more discoveries he made, the more his head spun with ideas, and the more Gary's art of distillation evolved.

The aesthetic look was wanting, so on went the paint. Gary loved the beautification, although it didn't help produce any more oil.

Machinery for harvesting aromatic plants did not exist in the U.S., so Gary was constantly buying equipment that he had to modify. He imported an old lavender harvester from France for St. Maries that worked quite well, making the harvest a dream in comparison to cutting by hand the first year and then by modified sickle-bar mower the second year.

The harvester worked very well for the small acreage in St. Maries; but when lavender went into production in Utah, the need for another machine became apparent. Gary drew the blueprints, and the men in the fabrication shop in Mona went to work to build an even better harvester.

Gary was always designing equipment to make harvesting more efficient, and that kept the Utah fabrication shop very busy. He could look at a piece of equipment, see how it worked, and make changes that improved production, often fabricating out of necessity. After all, there was no money to buy farm equipment that cost tens of thousands of dollars; besides, there was little, if any, equipment even available in the U.S. for planting or harvesting aromatic plants.

The first lavender harvester that Gary designed and retrofitted was from a hay sickle-bar mower, which didn't work as he had hoped.

Gary thought that tying the lavender in bundles would make the harvest more efficient; but unfortunately, it proved to be just a waste of time and didn't make a difference. I am wearing the sun hat on the right.

This beautiful first-year lavender will grow into big, bushy plants.

When Gary imported the first lavender harvester from France in 2004, harvesting became an exciting time.

D. Gary Young | The World Leader in Essential Oils   45

The Art of Distillation

The mechanics of distillation vary little from one distillery to another. First, you have the boiler or heating source for the water to produce the steam that flows into the cooker, or distilling chamber, in which the plant material is packed. The steam travels up through the material, causing the plant membranes to open and release the oil vapor, which is carried up with the steam into the condenser, where the steam and oil begin to separate as they convert back from a gas state into a liquid. Oil droplets bubble up through the separator to the top of the water, so they can be poured off into a container.

The "art of distillation" is in knowing all the details. Finding an experienced teacher for this "dying art" is the first big challenge. Then, one must have good mechanical skills and an aptitude for distilling. A good operator knows how much to compact it, the appropriate size of an extraction chamber, the length of time the material needs to be steamed, how much pressure, and the time to ramp the temperature based on the sound of the steam in the chamber.

The steam "sings" with a different harmonic pitch as it moves up through the plant material and must be even and constant. If the pitch is not consistent and the temperature is not ramped soon enough or is ramped too fast, the chamber will flood, causing reflux and homogenization; and the oil will fall back into the plant material and usually cannot be recovered. Any oil that is recovered will most likely be scorched and will certainly be missing many important oil compounds.

Every aspect of distillation can make a difference in the oil quality: the design of the distillery, the temperature of the water going into the boiler, and the water purity. Then, of course, the seed quality, the soil pH and nutrients, planting and cultivating, time of harvest, Brix testing, curing time if needed, and so many more intricate details all affect the quantity and quality of the oil produced. Distillation is truly an art acquired through meticulous study, experimentation, and knowledge of plants and farming.

1. The water is preheated and the minerals are removed.
2. The boiler turns the water into steam.
3. Plant material is loaded into the cooker.
4. Steam travels up through the plant material, releasing the oil vapor.
5. The steam carries the oil vapor into the condenser, where they both return to a liquid state and separate.
6. In the separator the oil rises to the top, where it is drained off.

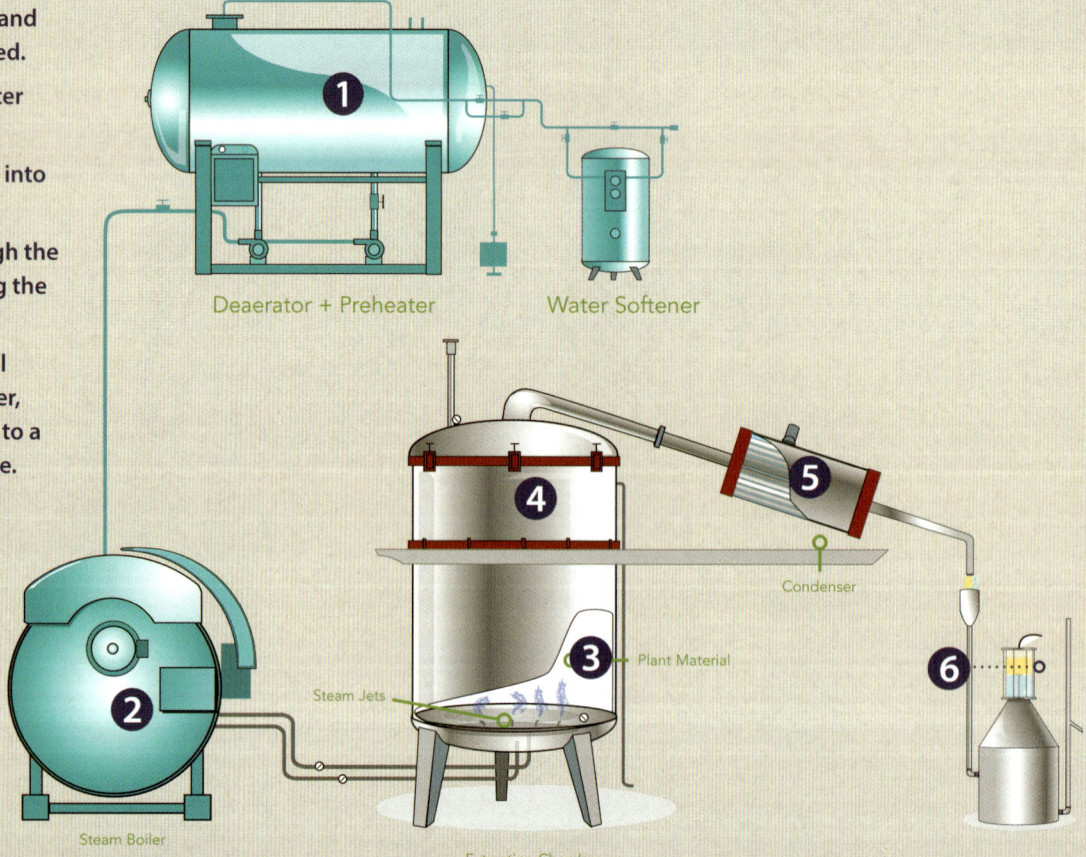

The first Young Living Essential Oil convention was held in 1995 in Spokane. On farm day Gary was very anxious to show everyone his new distillery in St. Maries and share all his visionary plans for farming and producing oils in the future.

Can an individual learn to do this from a book? Perhaps the very basics can be learned, and possibly a distillation could be started; but one will never learn the "art" from a book. Learning the art of distillation takes years of experience with logical thinking, trial and error, learning the many facets of farming, the exactness of mechanical functionality, and an analytical and creative mind.

It is a combination of skills that few people have. Gary learned many of the fundamental skills growing up farming, having to figure out how to fix old equipment and trucks, trying to figure out the best way to get the job done, what worked and didn't work, and what "just made plain, good sense." The fact that he had lived in the mountains and logged with horses was just an added benefit.

There weren't any calculators, adding machines, computers, or internet. Everything was done by hand or figured in the head with mental calculations, along with hours of hard physical work. All that he learned in his youth gave him a tremendous advantage, as those skills came together because of his passion to learn the art of distillation.

With every crop, every harvest, and every distillation, Gary learned more, and he incorporated this new knowledge into the many facets of his Seed to Seal standard. Originally in those areas where little was known, through the many years of farming and distillation, strict standards developed. Today there is less trial and error due to the vast knowledge that we have acquired, and when new challenges arise, we are able to quickly solve any difficulties. It takes years of experience dedicated to learning not only the art but the science as well. The entire process of distillation, although very complex, is also very fascinating.

Perhaps the challenge and opportunity to make new discoveries with a completely new list of questions to be asked and answered is part of what drove Gary's pioneering spirit. His quest to bring new and exciting additions to Young Living was a driving force in his life.

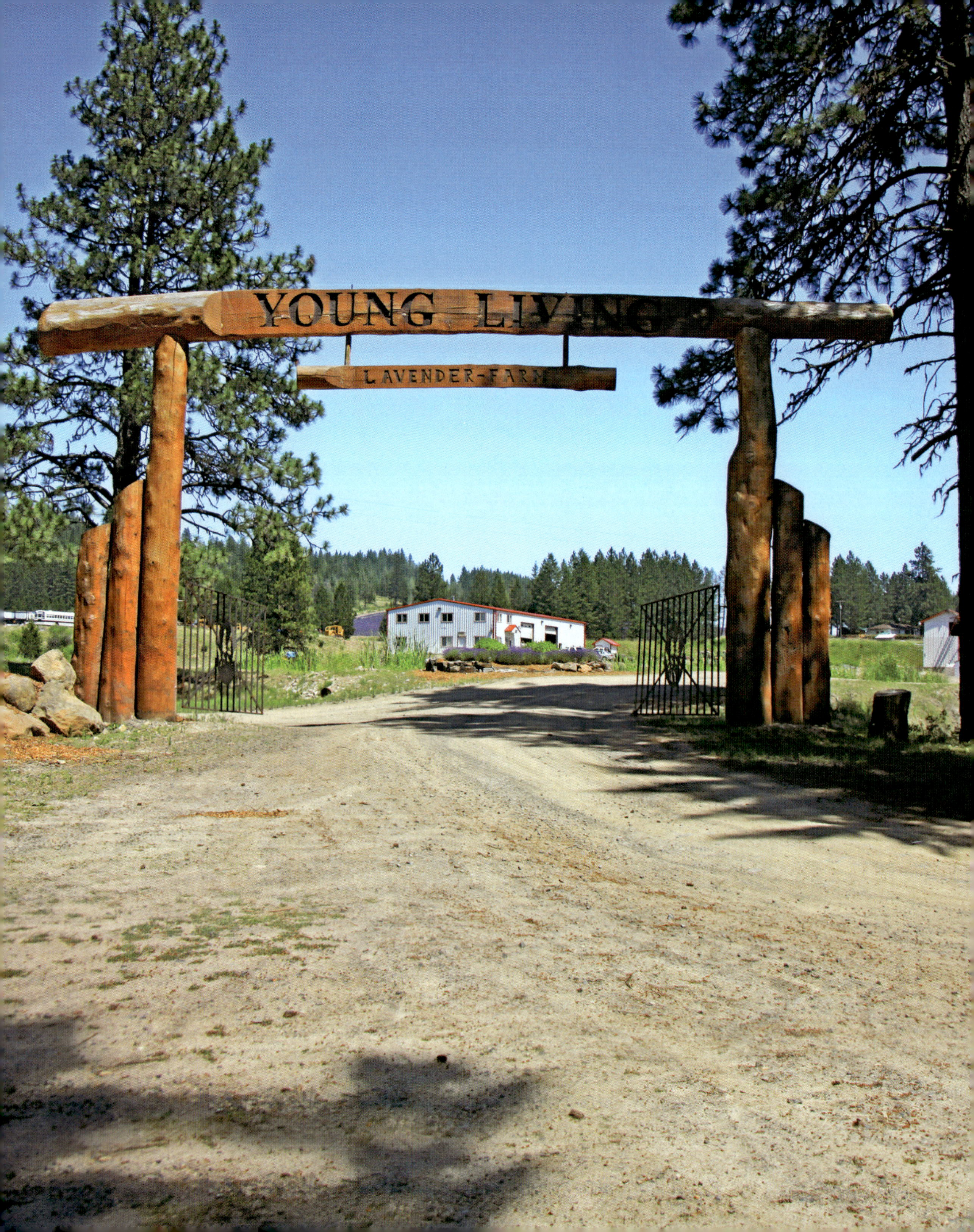
YOUNG LIVING
LAVENDER-FARM

ST. MARIES EXPANDS

All the hand-cut logs, the old boiler from the field, the hand-sawed boards, and all the nails Gary pounded made the distillery a special accomplishment.

In 1997 it became necessary to add more cookers and separators to expand the distilling capacity. Sadly, Gary had to cover the foundation logs with concrete and steel. As he became more experienced in distilling, he continued to make various changes and improvements to his design.

The Research Farm—So Many Questions

St. Maries was the great beginning of Gary's research and discovery. He used all that he had learned in France and his knowledge of the soil and farming while growing up with his father. He soon learned that the plants, soil, temperature, and climate affected each crop differently. The French always distilled lavender the same way, the way their families had distilled for years. They had it down to a science, and research and experimentation were not necessary—they thought.

But Gary was always looking and wondering, what if? How? Why? He was constantly asking himself questions. What about a different steam injection system? Would this make a difference? Yes, his vortex spiral steam injection system did make a difference. What size cooker was best for what amount of plant material? What were the different needs of different plant materials? Was the distillation yield better when the plant material was whole, coarsely chopped, or finely chopped? What was the yield with branches and leaves together or separated? How long should the plants be left on the deck after cutting to cure? Should all plants be cured and for how long or distilled immediately after cutting? What was the needed temperature for different plants? How long should the plants be steamed and at what temperature?

The questions were ongoing, and even today with the tremendous accomplishments at the farms and all that has been learned about the plants and the operation, questions continue to be asked.

How can we make the planting, the harvesting, and the distillation more efficient? Is there a better way? It was Gary Young's nature to ask those questions and is the legacy that Young Living carries on today, as we continue to make new discoveries and advances that benefit all those in the essential oil world.

The first condensers were vertical and the swan necks were rigid tubes connecting the cookers to the condensers at a 90-degree angle. Gary changed to flex tubes with camlocks, which made it faster to connect and disconnect rather than having to bolt and unbolt them.

In Gary's second generation of condensers, he changed the angle to 58 degrees, so there would be a smoother flow to capture all the oil droplets.

More cookers were built as more crops were planted. After the swan neck was changed to a flex tube, it increased the amount of oil captured. Oftentimes, droplets were caught in sharp corners and any uneven edge, so the objective was to make the flow as smooth as possible.

When the plant acreage increased, the need for more distillation capacity increased as well, as did the amount of time needed to clean the cookers after each distillation. The cookers were first steamed for an hour, and then soap was put into them and steamed for another four hours. Then they were rinsed and steamed again for another two hours. The water was then drained off, and the cookers were steamed again for another two hours. It made more sense to put in more cookers and designate different cookers for specific plants than to spend so much time cleaning the cookers.

In 2011 the first spa was installed near the separators so that it could be filled with the floral water containing micromolecules from the distillation. This water in the past was just drained off and wasted. Gary kept wondering what could be done to find value for this water. The idea came to him to install a hot tub and fill it with the floral water so that people could relax in it.

Since that time everyone who sits in this floral water is thrilled with what they experience. Some say it gives them an ethereal feeling, others say it is rejuvenating and energizing, and still others feel a total renewing of their well-being. Adults and children alike are thrilled to soak up those micromolecules.

It was a rewarding and inspiring moment every time drops of oil began to bubble up into the separator.

Every cooker had to be steam cleaned, which took several hours, before different plant material could be distilled.

The original St. Maries hot tub was inviting to Jeffrey Lewis, but usually people took off their shoes and hats before getting in the water.

D. Gary Young | The World Leader in Essential Oils | 53

Greenhouse Research

The St. Maries farm was Gary's hub of research and discovery, not only for the distillation process but also for the plants he was growing and intending to distill.

Gary began a research project in 1996 with enzymes and soil nourishment that provided valuable information about germination, foliage feed and nutrients, transplanting, and the needs of the new plants.

He learned to test the sugar concentration in the plants with a Brix refractometer, enabling him to determine the best time to harvest. Higher sugar levels indicate that the plants will produce a greater volume of oil.

When Gary began the development of the Mona farm in 1995, flying back and forth between both farms was very demanding because they were equally important, and Gary wanted to have the same positive results in Utah, even though the conditions there were different, such as soil, climate, and temperature, which required more research.

An additional small greenhouse was built in St. Maries to grow more starts to be trucked to Utah. It was an arduous task, but there was no other way to get crops in the ground before the arrival of winter in Utah.

Gary moved the two small greenhouses in Spokane to St. Maries in 1992 and then increased the size, so he could grow more starts and conduct research.

Untreated

Treated

Frequency-treated seed & Biogenesis-treated soil

Biogenesis-treated soil

Untreated

Frequency-treated seed

Treated vs. untreated clary sage. Plants were treated with enzymes and foliage feed, resulting in three times the growth.

A   B   C   D   E

Plant and root growth were measured and recorded.

D. Gary Young | The World Leader in Essential Oils   55

The first lodge, built in 1999, felt roomy; but with more members coming to the harvest, it began to feel cramped.

The lodge continued to expand and now has a large kitchen, dining and training room, showers, and laundry facilities.

The new addition, built in 2010, seats about 350 people comfortably and is a wonderful place to teach and learn.

The cabins at St. Maries are toasty warm during the winter.

More land had to be cleared to expand the crops in St. Maries.

The St. Maries shop and distillery are enveloped in a magical moment of peace and serenity at sunset.

Jacob was always out in the lavender field in St. Maries, 2002.

To the left is the office and mechanic shop, and to the right is the distillery. To the back, nestled among the trees, are the lodge, the cabins, the barn and old farm house, and the greenhouse with the white roof. The lavender and melissa fields are growing well, and newly plowed fields are ready for planting.

D. Gary Young | The World Leader in Essential Oils 59

Gary wondered if melissa would even grow in cold, wet St. Maries. The original seed came from France in 1991 but was first planted in 1997 and harvested in 1998. The St. Maries climate was perfect and similar to France; melissa grew beautifully and produced an exquisite oil.

Currently we have about 60 acres of organically grown melissa, which is harvested in early June or late July depending on the heat and sunshine that dictate growth and maturity. The weather in St. Maries is often unpredictable, so the time of the harvest is a little different every year.

Gary designed the conveyor to work with the harvester so that as melissa was cut, it would go directly into the truck, rather than being left on the ground. The harvest went from needing 18 people to 3 and reduced the harvest time from 14 days to 4.

Melissa

When melissa was first planted in 2000, the oil was not abundant in the world. However, in the last few years, more farmers have been planting melissa and making it more available, so it was not necessary to produce as much, so more acreage could be allocated for other crops that we needed.

During two years of harvesting and constantly testing the Brix levels, Gary was able to determine the right time for harvesting. He discovered that melissa did not produce well when cut and left on the ground, so he put tarps underneath the swather to catch the plants as they were cut. When the tarps were full, they were lifted onto a flatbed trailer and driven to the distillery.

Members loved operating the equipment.

This was very slow and labor-intensive, pushing past the best time for distilling. Gary designed equipment to mechanize the harvest and started the fabrication in the shop. He and several others worked on it during the summer but didn't finish it in time for the harvest, besides the fact that Gary broke his hand while working on the harvester and had to have surgery.

However, the following summer the new machine was ready and went into the field; and within a week's time, the harvest was finished, and the oil production increased greatly.

In addition to lavender and melissa, testing will be done to see what other crops will grow in this climate. In 2019 41 acres of goldenrod were planted, producing an oil that is difficult to find in the world. St. Maries is the perfect climate and elevation for this crop, so we will be able to have our own supply of this oil. Goldenrod is very supportive to the immune system and soothing to tired, aching muscles. It has become a favorite of our members.

Other crops will be planted and tested for their viability and sustainability. We will also distill conifers such as blue spruce, white pine, and western red cedar, which will keep the distillery in operation throughout the winter months. There are several logging operations relatively close to the farm that leave discarded limbs and bark in unsightly piles.

Getting melissa out of the tarp wasn't easy. Whether it was winter or summer harvest, members, like Cherié Ross (on the right), always brought many of the people in their organizations with them to be a part of Seed to Seal.

We can drive to the site and chip the slash into trucks and haul it to the farm. By distilling the slash, we are also helping to clean up the environment.

When St. Maries is in operation almost year-round, there will be more opportunity for members to come and be part of the Seed to Seal process both for winter and summer harvests, as well as spring planting and reforestation.

The hot tubs will be waiting for all who have time to enjoy the uplifting and soothing floral waters after a good day's work in the field. The St. Maries farm is 12 miles south of the town in a remote area surrounded by the dense mountain foliage. Everyone feels the amazing peacefulness there far from the noise and pollution of any city. It is like entering an enchanted forest with aromatic plants growing within—a beautiful experience.

The bees love goldenrod, as you can see in the picture. By the end of 2019, Mona will be growing 56 acres of goldenrod, and by the end of 2020, St. Maries will be growing 239 acres of goldenrod. Surely, thousands of bees will enjoy the new crops of goldenrod and will produce a unique flavor of honey.

Gas Chromatography (GC) Essential Oil Analysis

Early in 1996 it became evident to Gary that he would need to be able to do testing within Young Living. Third-party testing was important, but Gary wanted to know for himself; so he began to look for teachers and places he could go to learn about analytical instrumentation for testing essential oils. He wanted to be able to do the testing himself and interpret the results. That began a whole new path of education.

In 1992 Jean-Noël first introduced Gary to Dr. Hervé Casabianca, a highly trained analytical chemist of essential oils in France. Dr. Casabianca is well-known in the industry and helped write the French AFNOR standard for essential oils. He became a mentor for Gary and taught him about how to do the testing and how to interpret the analysis.

This opened Gary's eyes to yet another facet of essential oils. As his interest heightened, he began looking for opportunities to learn more about the chemical structure of oils that would give him the scientific foundation to determine their benefits and enhancements through blending different oils.

Gary completed 120 hours of GC/MS instruction with Dr. Baser.

In 1996 Gary went to the Anadolu University in Eskisehir, Turkey, to study with Prof. Dr. Hans Baser, who was teaching a course on gas chromatography (GC) analysis. Gary completed 120 hours of intense study and was excited about the world of essential oil analysis.

With this new knowledge, he could differentiate between different species of the same oil to understand why one species had greater benefits than the others or why different chemotypes of the same species each had their individual benefits. He found that combining oils could be very specific depending on their chemical compounds, and the response could be amplified.

Blending oils was an aromatic adventure; and with experience, he learned that depending on the compounds of different single oils, he could greatly change or enhance the aroma of the blend. Gary's instinctive understanding of the oils and his fabulous sense of smell gave him an amazing edge in the aromatic world of essential oils.

When Gary returned home, he bought his first GC instrument and hired a microbiologist for his new laboratory, which filled a very small room in the old Payson building. Dr. Casabianca came to set up and calibrate the new testing instrument to the exact column-wall thickness used in his CNRS laboratories in France. This tiny beginning has evolved into a very large laboratory today with millions of dollars of highly specialized instruments for scientific analysis and research of essential oils, as well as scientific equipment for testing other Young Living products.

Dr. Casabianca came to Utah to instruct Gary and Sue Chao, biochemist, on the new GC in the Payson office in 1996.

Dr. Casabianca provided continuing education for Gary and Chris Packer on GC/MS in France, 2010.

As Young Living grew and more distilleries were built, Gary wanted to have the testing capability to give him immediate information for making decisions about distilling.

There was a small room in the office/shop in St. Maries that Gary used for testing during the few weeks of distilling in the summer months. But when he started hauling chips from Highland Flats to distill during the winter, more testing was needed.

In 2012 a whole new addition was built onto the St. Maries distillery for a new laboratory in which a GC instrument was installed so that the oils could be tested for their chemical composition during and after distillation. This gave Gary instant information, enabling him to see if he was achieving the results he wanted. With this on-site testing, Gary was able to determine if he needed to modify the distillation time, temperature, or volume of plant material, as some plant materials yielded a higher quality oil when distilled in smaller batches.

Because Gary had immediate access to the analytical results from individual distillation batches, he was able to see how small changes affected production and was able to improve the process. Bottling and labeling machines were also installed, so members could participate in the process.

In the new addition, an entirely new spa was built with three hot tubs and five immense holding tanks that were installed in the basement underneath the tubs to hold the floral water so that it could be pumped into the spa tubs on demand. After working hard all day in the field, relaxing those aching muscles in the soothing floral water that calms and clears the mind is an amazing experience. Just spending time in the spa and visiting with other members is one of the highlights at the farm.

Today, in addition to the main laboratory in the Spanish Fork Warehouse, Young Living has laboratories at the farms in St. Maries, Idaho; Highland Flats, Idaho; Guayaquil, Ecuador; Northern Lights, Fort Nelson, British Columbia, Canada; and Split, Croatia.

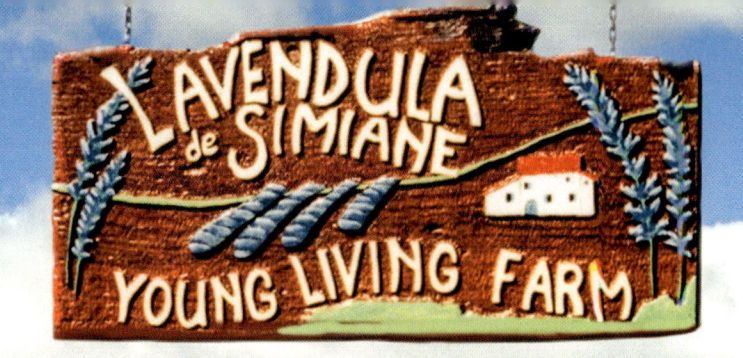

The third Young Living farm in France in the town of Simiane-la-Rotonde.

The castle overlooks the Young Living farm, outlined in white above.

Some of the first European members who came to help with the harvest.

YOUNG LIVING SIMIANE-LA-ROTONDE FARM

In 1996 Jean-Noël found a third farm in the Simiane Valley about an hour north of Marseille. It already had lavender growing on it that had not been treated with chemicals; so plans were made, papers signed, and the first foreign-owned lavender farm was bought by Young Living in Simiane-la-Rotonde, France. The farm has 55 hectares (136 acres) and sits in the Simiane Valley looking up at the amazing 12th-century castle Château des Agoult, which brings thousands of tourists every year to see its magnificence in the heart of the lavender capital of the world.

Sadly, the new farm had not been well-maintained and needed a lot of care, so Gary issued a call for help. Throughout that year Young Living members came from around the world to help with planting, harvesting, and distilling. Today hundreds of members travel great distances to participate in our Seed to Seal process.

At first the farmers were skeptical about this American who had moved into their valley. Foreigners were not very welcome, but Gary began getting acquainted; and as they saw his dedication working on the farm and the care he gave to the plants, they became curious, wanting to know about Gary and his company. As time went on, they wanted to know what Gary thought about farming and why he was adamant about not using chemicals. "Feeding and nourishing the soil will produce better quality oils," was always Gary's motto.

Gary made the statement that one day he would bring seed back to France from the lavender plants growing on the St. Maries, Idaho, farm that had grown from the original seed he had carried from France and planted in 1989 in Spokane, Washington, and in 1992-94 in St. Maries, Idaho. Everyone laughed at such a ridiculous idea. What could an Idaho alfalfa farmer offer a French lavender farmer? Only time would tell.

Members come from all over the world to participate in the Seed to Seal harvest and distillation.

Gary was saddened by the dying lavender fields in Provence in 1992.

Trouble in France

The farms continued to expand and produce more oil, and the number of Young Living members who came to the farm to participate in the Seed to Seal process firsthand continued to increase. All the farms were producing well except the farm in France. Gary saw trouble on the horizon in the heart of Provence, and now that trouble was staring the French lavender farmers in the face.

Gary's own words were alarming:

"Twenty years ago I saw things changing in the lavender fields in France with the true species *Lavandula angustifolia*. I watched it closely and it wasn't long afterwards that the lavender started dying off.

"When I went back to France in 1985, '87, '88, '89, and '91, when I started working with Jean-Noël, I kept taking seed back home and planting it. From 1992-94, I began expanding my fields at the St. Maries farm and had enough lavender seed to plant 45 acres.

"Every time I went to France, I saw the worry of the farmers watching their dying lavender. Part of it was an unknown virus that came through the region attacking some of the fields. Other fields developed a fungus, which I believe weakened the immunity of the plants after years of growing with fertilizers and being sprayed with pesticides. The lavender just wasn't resistant to some of the bugs and fungus any longer. Then a severe drought crippled the lavender for about seven years, followed by a one-year reprieve; and then another drought that was even longer took its final toll.

"I had a feeling that one day St. Maries lavender would reestablish the lavender in France and create a rebirthing of true lavender. As we talked about it, there were some laughs; but in 2010 I brought seed from the St. Maries farm back to France. First, we grew starts, and then two years later we transplanted them to the fields. It was amazing that this lavender, originally from France, and then brought back after 20 years in the U.S., was the only lavender on our farm in Provence that went into full bloom.

"Our St. Maries lavender was growing in the same field with original French lavender that hadn't died, and the comparison was dramatic. The lavender grown from our St. Maries seed had multiple stems with heavy, lush flowers of beautiful multiple colors from white to deep purple and seemed to dance in the sunlight as they reached farther and farther toward the blue sky. There is not a more beautiful true lavender than what is growing on our farm now.

"Benoît Cassan stated, 'The St. Maries lavender looks like the true French lavender we grew 50 years ago and is the only lavender that produced two crops this year.'

"The other part that thrills me is that this lavender produces seed that Jean-Noël and Jean-Marie Blanc, our production manager, gathered for propagating new starts for next year, starts with strong immunity that will produce the rich Lavender oil that the French farmers remember from years ago. I feel honored and humbled that I can give back to France for all that France has given to me all these years."

The contrast between the lavender grown from the St. Maries seed (left) that was germinated in a greenhouse in Simiane and the French lavender (right) is most remarkable. Planting healthy seeds in nutrient-balanced soil produces healthy plants. Unhealthy seeds and soil produce just the opposite.

The first Young Living harvester used on the Young Living farm in France.

Members watch the immense amount of distilled lavender lifted out of the 20,000-liter chamber after distillation.

In 2013 D. Gary Young, with the help of Jean-Noël Landel, his partner of 20 years; Benoît Cassan, the president of the French Lavender Growers Association; and Jean-Marie Blanc, the farm manager who oversees the farm production of planting, cultivating, harvesting, and distilling, merged their farms together as one Young Living farm. In doing so, they bridged two continents and three decades in the beginning of a bold undertaking: bringing a thriving, healthy *Lavandula angustifolia*—true lavender—from St. Maries, Idaho, back to its origin. Today the Young Living Lavender Farm in the Simiane Valley of southern France is the largest true lavender farm in the world!

The words of Jean-Noël tell the story so concisely: "What is really amazing is that this is the only time I've seen true lavender with such a life force in it. Nobody can believe it. The true lavender that has grown from the seed that Gary has brought with him from St. Maries hasn't grown here for over 15 years—it disappeared. But the way it looks now, there is a new future for the lavender farmers in France."

The pipe was laid for the first irrigation system in the Simiane Valley.

Jean-Marie, Benoît, Jean-Noël, and Gary merged their farms together to create the largest true lavender farm in the world, 2013.

In 2015 we irrigated our lavender for the first time in the history of Provence.

In August 2015 the equipment with the latest technology for harvesting arrived at the farm. When the lavender is cut, it lies for 24 hours in the field and is then loaded into the new stainless steel vat or distilling chamber and hauled by truck to the distillery.

72   D. Gary Young | The World Leader in Essential Oils

The lid is lowered and the steam pipe is connected at the bottom of the chamber to begin distillation.

The 12th-century Château des Agoult overlooks the Young Living distillery in Provence, France.

Gary arrived in Riverton, Utah, on Thanksgiving Day 1993. He was able to move everything he owned—including all the inventory and a small amount of office equipment—in one pickup truck and one small U-Haul truck and trailer. It was a very meager beginning for our new business that started in this dilapidated old building that we originally leased and then, a few months later, purchased. There was very little working capital and no outside investment, but Gary eagerly faced the new challenge, solving problems, making it work, and then making it work better.

In the laboratory that Gary built, he mixed the blends, and Rex Kidman and LaRue Billeter poured the oils by hand and wrapped labels around the bottles.

THE MOVE TO UTAH

In November of 1993, Gary moved to Riverton, Utah, where he and I started our new company, Young Living Essential Oils, in an old 8,000-square-foot building. Gary built his laboratory and production room, offices, shipping, and customer service area. It was a very tiny beginning with not a lot of promise from the onset, but there was great enthusiasm and determination—and so Young Living began to grow and was incorporated in April 1994. Naturally, Gary began to look for another farm; and in 1995 he bought 160 acres in Mona, Utah, where he built greenhouses and planted crops. Uncle Jack, a retired carpenter, who lived in Idaho, eagerly came to Utah to help Gary build the greenhouses when Gary called for his help.

Of the 8,000 square feet, only about 5,000 were usable. The building had been used as a mechanic and paint shop, movie house, church, and some "unidentifiable" businesses. The building was leased from a walk-through in the dark; and when the electricity was turned on the next morning, it was a shock to see the mess and deterioration. But that's what it was and so the work began.

My first "executive" responsibility.

Gary did construction and drywall and mixed the blends of Abundance and Purification into the paint. Mary and LaRue cleaned and organized the office.

The first day in business, the orders totaled about $950, but the orders kept coming; and by the end of the first month, the volume had increased to $1,800 a day, but that wasn't enough to pay the bills. So one night after the office was closed, the oil blend of Abundance was sprinkled throughout the office and over the keyboards. To everyone's amazement, the next morning the phones seemed to be ringing off the hook. The excitement mounted and the future looked a little brighter.

This is all there was. There were no big racks, warehouse, or cold storage.

76 D. Gary Young | The World Leader in Essential Oils

Alene Frandsen came in August of 1994 and took charge of the office and interviewed and hired new employees.

Alene and I put the first product catalog together and started looking at how we could create new literature for our members.

D. Gary Young | The World Leader in Essential Oils 77

A new "sophisticated" bottling machine increased production immensely, and the overhead bags with packing peanuts really helped get orders out the door faster. A small UPS truck stopped once a day to pick up between 30 and 40 orders.

Within a year's time, Riverton had become too small, and Gary began looking for a new home. Real estate in Salt Lake City was much too expensive, so the old Payson Elementary/Middle School became the next headquarters. It was a 45-minute drive south and seemed like a long way, but it was closer to the farm and a lot bigger, with 40,000 square feet, although probably only 30,000 feet were usable. So everything was packed up in September of 1996, and this little but growing business moved to the new Payson headquarters.

78 D. Gary Young | The World Leader in Essential Oils

The building was old and would have been torn down if Gary had not bought it. The wiring for the telephones and computers had to be run on the outside of the walls down the hallway in the middle of the building because the concrete walls were just too thick. Many windows were broken and a new roof had to be put on because there were so many leaks. The old kitchen became the laboratory, and in the first week, a main waterline broke, costing $10,000 in repairs, which was just astronomical at the time. The cafeteria was retrofitted for production, and the gym became the shipping department.

A loading dock had to be built for the UPS truck.

D. Gary Young | The World Leader in Essential Oils

Rex Kidman was excited about new blending equipment that came, and the walk-in cooler was perfect for the oils. LaRue Billeter loved the new lab with all the stainless steel. An automated Rota bottling machine arrived from Germany, which dramatically improved production, and one UPS truck was stationed all day at the dock for loading orders. Order Entry was growing, the business was flourishing, and the demand for more oils was increasing.

Order Entry/Customer Service took over the library, and air conditioners were installed in the breakroom for the computers and equipment in IT.

80   D. Gary Young | The World Leader in Essential Oils

The Utah Farm and Distillery

Lavender, clary sage, thyme, melissa, and many other plants were first grown in the small St. Maries greenhouse from where the first lavender starts were trucked to Mona. When the greenhouses were built in Mona in the spring of 1995, they produced thousands of starts that were not only planted in Utah but were also trucked to St. Maries for the expansion. In 1999 over 3 million lavender starts were grown in the Utah greenhouses and then transplanted to the fields.

In 1995 Gary purchased 160 acres in Mona and started preparing the land to plant lavender, and Uncle Jack came to help build the first greenhouses.

New starts were transplanted in the spring of 1996.

As more land became ready for planting, more greenhouses were built. The seeds germinated very well, and wheel lines and pipes were bought at auctions and private sales and trucked to the farm so that Gary could begin getting the irrigation system ready.

In 1996 Gary leased and then a year later bought a 1,600-acre farm close to the first farm, which was much more demanding, as it had more than 800 acres of undisturbed sagebrush. The Black Angus cattle farm had been in the owner's family for years and had been just that—a cattle farm. No chemicals had ever been put on the ground, so Gary was excited about this new "organic" farm. The manure was 4 to 5 feet deep in the pens, so Gary bought his first piece of new farm equipment, a manure spreader, and began to spread the manure and prepare the land.

The ground had to be tilled, seeded, and irrigated. He first planted lavender, clary sage, and peppermint; and they all did very well. Gary fabricated a new planting machine three times the size of the first one in St. Maries. He designed and built a new harvesting machine and several other pieces of equipment to make the harvest more efficient.

Gary and I went to many farm auctions and private sales, where they found tractors, cultivating equipment, trailers, and all kinds of farm implements. Gary bought his first semi-truck for $3,500, which was used for many years on the farms.

Gary designed and fabricated a six-row planter that was critical for getting all the plants into the ground when they were ready, to keep them from becoming root-bound from overgrowth in the cups.

The planter worked very well and hundreds of thousands of new starts went in the ground.

The starts were hauled with Gary's semi-truck from the St. Maries greenhouse for planting in Mona. When the Mona greenhouses started producing more starts, they were then trucked to St. Maries to meet the expansion there.

We went to many farm auctions, where we found tractors, cultivators, trailers, and all kinds of farm implements. Gary bought an ugly, green, 1973 Peterbilt semi-truck for $3,500, his first since 1978. The truck made many trips after being painted with the Young Living logo and was proudly driven by Gary, who was happy to be behind the wheel of a semi again, which brought back a lot of early memories.

The first automated air seeder for the farm put millions of seeds into small cups for germination in the greenhouses.

The distillery began to grow when the first cooker and boiler were installed for the first distillation in 1996.

Gary was disappointed that he had only one cooker for Farm Day at the 1995 convention. However, it was obvious that big plans were in the making.

The "straw" is lifted from the cooker and then transported to the compost pile to become fertilizer for the fields.

Solar-powered pivots were built in the Mona fabrication shop, saving thousands of dollars of electricity.

It took two weeks to harvest and distill all the peppermint because we had such a good crop that year, 1997.

The office and mechanic shop were completed in 1997.

The demand for oil required expansion everywhere, and the farm became a very busy place.

Gary built a small 4,500-liter extraction chamber to distill the first harvest. In 1997 he added larger chambers of 6,500 liters and every year continued to build more chambers to meet the needs of his expanding crops.

The last two 12,000-liter chambers were built in 1999, totaling 12, in which 10 to 15 crops were distilled each year, depending on what was planted, as well as wildcrafted.

Spearmint, German chamomile, hyssop, goldenrod, and thyme were subsequently planted. Each year different crops are planted, and others are taken out, depending on how well they grow and produce oil. Thousands of acres of juniper trees grow in abundance on the neighboring foothills and have been wildcrafted, producing a lot of oil since 1999.

Gary continued to develop both farms as he commuted back and forth between St. Maries and Mona; but when this third farm was finally purchased in 1997 (the second in Utah), the farming of aromatic crops took on a new dimension: more acreage to prepare, more seedlings to plant, more equipment to buy, more inventions and fabrications, more extraction chambers, more employees—just more of everything.

One summer evening, while standing on the porch of the old farmhouse that was being renovated as the Visitors Center, Gary looked out over hundreds of acres yet to be cultivated and, with that visionary look in his eye, said to me, "One day this farm will be a worldwide destination for people all over the world, welcoming thousands of visitors wanting to learn about essential oils and the amazing Young Living Seed to Seal story."

It was a huge undertaking and money wasn't readily available, but Gary knew it was all possible and went forward with that knowing for what the future would bring.

The chickens, pigs, and mice that lived in the old farmhouse had to be relocated, so renovation could take place for the beautiful Visitors Center that emerged and now welcomes thousands of people every year.

Gary continued to experiment with the distillation process and to modify his equipment. He even climbed into one of the extraction chambers with a flashlight and had them turn the steam on so that he could see how it moved against the dome lid of the distiller. He got the information he wanted; but needless to say, he didn't stay long in the chamber.

From what he saw, he immediately designed a new lid and again climbed back inside the cooker to see how it worked, but this time he poured water over his head to reduce the chance for burns. As he watched what happened with the steam, he was able to modify the lid for even better oil recovery. The GC analysis showed that nearly 15 percent more of the finer molecules were now being recovered than were being lost with the old design. "It's all about discovery so you do what you have to do to get the information you want," Gary said, laughing.

Dr. Hervé Casabianca flew from France to see the new distillery and was impressed with the oil quality.

One of 12 greenhouses, where at one time over 3 million starts were propagated that supplied both the Mona and St. Maries farms.

The second imported lavender harvester worked better, but it was still too slow, as the plants had to be forked or dumped onto the trailer.

The third harvester, imported from France the following year, was more efficient. However, the plants were so big and bushy that the motor on the conveyor wasn't strong enough to carry them all the way to the top, so the men had to be there constantly to keep them moving. Eldon Knittle usually flew up from Texas to help, and he and Gary would take turns on the harvester to keep everything going.

The lavender is magnificent when in bloom during June and July and can be smelled for miles around.

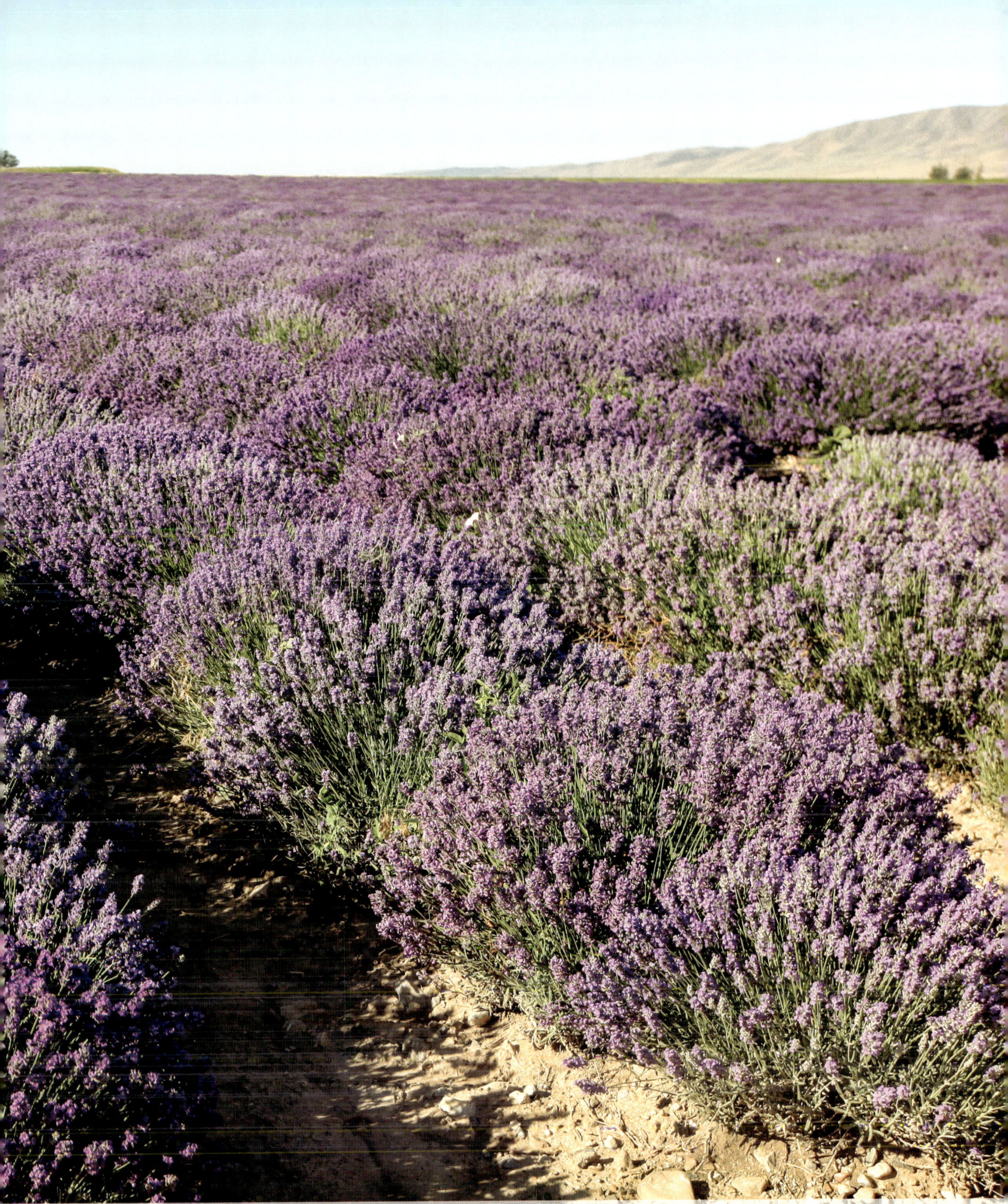

Gary redesigned the French harvester and built a better one in the fabrication shop in Mona.

The first crop of clary sage harvested in 1997 was spectacular and produced a very beautiful oil.

Dense and lush peppermint ready for harvest, August 1999.

I loved operating the swather. Hmm, stuck again? At least the aroma of the spearmint was refreshing.

Gary designed another conveyor system for harvesting peppermint and spearmint.

In 2003, as the peppermint harvest increased, more cookers were needed to meet the demand.

Gary, Marta and Marcel Espieu, and Jean-Noël holding Jacob stand between the rows of baby lavender in St. Maries in 2002.

Marcel Espieu Comes to Utah

Finally, the time came to invite Marcel Espieu and his wife Marta to the convention to see what Gary had built. Marcel had often laughed at this American with big ideas, until the moment he arrived and saw what Gary had accomplished. Gary flew with them and Jean-Noël first to Idaho to see St. Maries. Marcel was amazed at the beautiful lavender and melissa and was thrilled to see the new baby lavender growing so well.

They flew back to Utah and drove down to the farm in Mona. Before the car had completely stopped, Marcel opened the door, jumped out with great excitement, and briskly walked through the lavender field, touching and smelling the plants as he hurried toward the distillery.

At the 2002 Young Living Convention Farm Day, with tears in his eyes as he spoke to the group surrounding the distillery, Marcel said, "The student has now become the teacher." It was the greatest compliment that Gary could have imagined.

Every day during convention, thousands of members visit the farm to explore the many facets of Seed to Seal by walking through the beautiful flowering fields, watching the crops being harvested, or seeing them be transported to the distillery.

The fields are stunning when in bloom, with an aroma that wafts through the air for miles away. Hundreds of people come to participate in the harvest and/or the 5K or 1K run through the lavender fields. Children and adults alike enjoy the happy, calming effects of lavender. Lavender essential oil is said to be the "mother of all oils."

A tour of the distillery is a must and is what the farm is all about. It is an awesome sight and a breathtaking moment when the oil drops bubble up from the condenser into the separator, and the "essence" of Seed to Seal is right before your eyes.

After the distillation has finished, the oil is taken to the decanting or filtering room. Usually, a little plant debris escapes into the separator that has to be filtered out. The oil is also weighed and entered into the log book with other details specific to the distillation batch. When this is finished, the oil goes into large stainless steel containers that are taken to the warehouse. Samples are sent to the laboratory for analysis to make sure the compound structure is within the proper range, and when all the specifications are met, the oil is released for bottling and production.

> "The student has now become the teacher."
> — Marcel Espieu, 2002

Members listened intently to Gary, Marcel, and Jean-Noël, Convention, 2002.

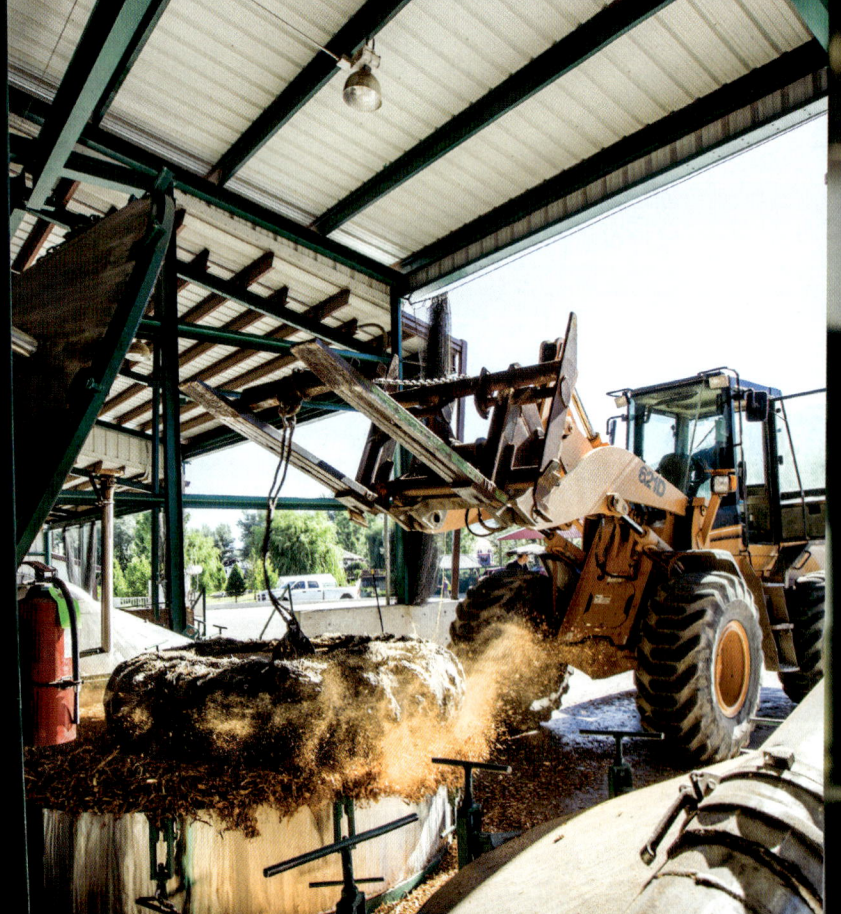

Juniper is wildcrafted in the mountains south of Mona, Utah. The landowner is giving Young Living the trees in exchange for clearing the land.

An old tractor tire filled with concrete works very well for packing the cooker.

The beautiful red color appears when sunlight hits the juniper oil.

Beautiful, fluffy, snow-like German chamomile ready for harvest.

Tons of German chamomile being forked into the cooker for distillation.

D. Gary Young | The World Leader in Essential Oils | 99

Family Fun at the Mona Farm

Everyone loves an old-fashioned wagon ride. Just as Gary envisioned in 1995, the Mona farm has become a worldwide destination for the entire family. You can't help but leave the farm with a tremendous appreciation for the drop of oil you are glad you have when you need it. The immense amount of time, effort, money, and dedication that is all part of our Seed to Seal commitment is easy to visualize and indelibly imprinted in the mind forever.

Members and staff have fun together playing in the Western show. Everyone laughed when the town clown wanted to share his NingXia Red.

Gary, Josef, Mary, and Jacob at the Provo Parade in 2015. Gary loved everything about the Old West, especially when his family joined him.

The boys following in Dad's footsteps, 2007.

Grandma LaRue still yodeling at age 92, 2016.

D. Gary Young | The World Leader in Essential Oils 101

All the children love running through the lavender fields.

102　D. Gary Young　|　The World Leader in Essential Oils

Josef and Dad are ready for those bad guys.

Josef was intensely focused during the chess tournament at the farm, 2015.

The 5K Run Through the Lavender has become a very popular event each year with people from all over the world.

D. Gary Young | The World Leader in Essential Oils 103

The joust begins with Mary singing the National Anthem as a tribute to those who have gone before us.

The procession was enacted by farm employees and many local residents.

The medieval village hosts many events at the farm.

The barrel swing is fun and takes the kids back in history.

Pony rides are very popular with the children.

When Gary brought jousting to the farm, it became a very special and exciting event.

Jacob and Josef kept the crowd entertained as they threw the javelin while riding their miniature horses, 2014.

D. Gary Young | The World Leader in Essential Oils 107

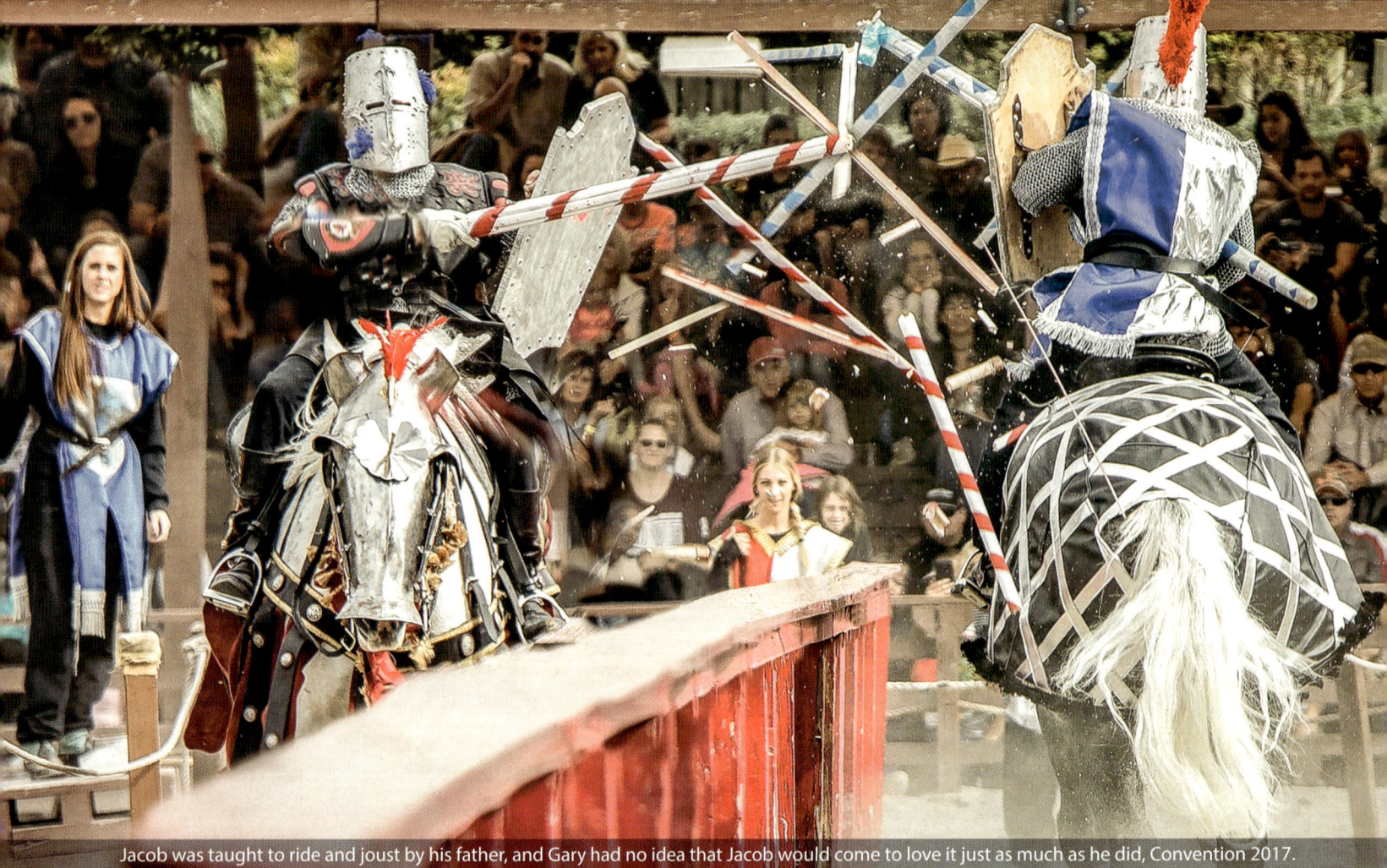

Gary said that jousting combines, skill, strength, and expert horsemanship, a challenge he loved. The protective armors and chain mail weigh 90 to 100 pounds, and the lance weighs about 40 pounds. On a hot day, the temperature inside the armor is 5-10 degrees hotter than the outside temperature.

Jacob was taught to ride and joust by his father, and Gary had no idea that Jacob would come to love it just as much as he did, Convention 2017.

Count the rings. Just like Dad—the skill is in Josef's blood.

Gary led the procession for the opening ceremony with Felix and Jacob, while Mary sang the national anthem.

The First Annual Draft Horse Show—Young Living Utah Farm, September 2015

The newest event took place at the Young Living Lavender Farm in September 2015 with the first Fall Festival and Draft Horse Show, including a rodeo and concert. The new arena was beautiful and spacious for the six-up and eight-up horse teams as they showed their precision and beauty to the spectators. Draft horse teams came from all over the United States to compete and enjoy the peace and beauty at the farm.

The Lane Frost Challenge Bull Riding competition entertained everyone as the bulls snorted, the riders rode hard, and the clown kept everyone laughing, except the riders. An array of wagons, stagecoaches, "school bus" wagon, and penitentiary wagon took everyone back in time. The miniature horses pulling a miniature stagecoach were fun to watch as they bucked and kicked up their heels while trying to feel their independence.

The event was magnificent and as many new people learned about aromatic crops and distillation, the excitement spread everywhere. It was a marvelous event that promised to bring fun and excitement every year.

The dancing Friesians were exquisite in their performance and will certainly give the powerful jousting Percherons a challenge for taking center stage. Different equine events have been a great addition to the farm, and there will certainly be plenty of manure to add to the composting for the natural fertilizer that feeds the crops.

It was a thrill for Gary to drive his magnificent team of Percherons—a lifelong dream come true.

Bandido de Amores, the dancing Friesian, loves to entertain, making his trainer, Felix Santana, very proud.

Reliving the Old West filled Gary with great happiness and satisfaction.

Spectators love a good rodeo with a lot of action.

Bull riding? Not for everyone—just for the brave cowboys.

D. Gary Young | The World Leader in Essential Oils 113

Young Living Draft Horse Show and the 2018 World Percheron Congress

Young Living's equine ambassadors fulfilled a 20-year dream, as Gary's team of prized Percheron horses swept in three elite categories at the 17th World Percheron Congress in Des Moines, Iowa, on October 13, 2018.

Horses were always an important part of Gary's life. He rode with his father as a baby and by the age of five was saddling his own horse and riding by himself. As Gary grew to manhood and began living his dreams, he came to a strong conviction that a life could not be balanced unless animals were part of that life. Horses were Gary's balance; although he loved all animals, it was his love of horses that led to the beautiful show horses that find their home at the Young Living farm in Mona, Utah.

In 1996, after Gary bought the farm in Mona, he felt that he needed to have horses there for everyone to enjoy, especially the children. He knew how the gentle spirit of a horse could evoke a feeling of peace and security with young people looking for understanding in our busy world.

Gary went to many farm auctions, buying trucks, trailers, tractors, heavy earthmoving equipment, horse-drawn wagons, and even his first semi-truck after giving up trucking many years earlier. He bought many fun antiques for the Mona Visitor Center and farm implements for cultivation and harvesting. He also bought a vintage steam engine from the 1900s to power the old thresher and binder to bring history to life at the farm. As he watched the horse-drawn wagons and buggies go up for auction, he saw an opportunity to bring the "Old West" to the farm and soon started to frequent horse auctions, as he needed horses for all of his carriages.

At the Waverly auction in March of 2003, L.D.'s Prince Heidi, a champion show horse, came into the arena. As Gary watched her beautiful movement, his head started spinning with new ideas for the farm. Winning the bid was a thrill for him, and he started making plans. He built a show barn and over the next few years, he bought more show horses and hired trainers and drivers as his vision evolved to the professional circuit.

Draft horses are powerful, gentle, and very smart, which motivated Gary to enter the world of draft horse competition. He went to many draft horse shows and enjoyed seeing the Young Living hitches take winning ribbons home. One day, while sitting in the bleachers at the Denver Stock Show, Gary leaned over to me and said, "I'm going to have a draft horse show in Mona." I felt overwhelmed again at the idea, but I knew that once he spoke it, the energy of creation was in motion, and it would soon come to fruition.

Young Living's world champion eight-horse hitch has become famous in the draft horse industry.

An arena was built with 2,500 seats, filling one fourth of the seating area for the first Young Living Draft Horse Show that took place in September 2015, with 12 hitches competing. Gary was so excited as participants came from all over the U.S. and Canada; the wheels were in motion for a world-class event.

In 2016, as the enthusiasm grew, another 2,500 seats were added to accommodate the 15,000 to 20,000 who attended over the three-day event. Numbers grew and the news spread about the beautiful arena and facility in Mona, Utah.

In 2019, 18 hitches registered to participate, and between 25,000 to 30,000 attendees came to watch the competition, enjoy the concert at sunset, and cheer for the rodeo cowboys in the evening, all while basking in the breathtaking beauty of the farm and learning about our world of essential oils.

Every time Gary saw his horses hitched to a wagon, he thought about competing in The World Percheron Congress, held every four years, known as the Olympics of the Percheron world. What started as a love for these gentle yet powerful horses turned into a commitment to compete with the best.

In 2018 The World Percheron Congress awarded Young Living's Percherons the Premier Exhibitor title, the best team overall. Young Living also claimed the titles of World Champion in the eight-horse hitch and six-horse hitch, which are the most competitive classes in the industry, as well as the three-horse Unicorn hitch.

Jason Goodman, Young Living's draft horse manager, said, "These horses tie into Gary's passion for quality—quality for products and quality for horses. Everything Gary did had to be the best."

Tim Sparrow, Percheron show team manager and driver, was thrilled to take our hitches to the top. His feelings were that "The immense love with which the horses are trained and the trust between us, with a lot of hard work, are the keys to this fabulous accomplishment."

The Young Living Percheron teams show the dedication that Gary had for every one of his passions and mirrors how hard work and unwavering pursuit made Young Living into a global leader of health and abundance.

Jason and Rose Goodman, Mary Young, Brittany and Tim Sparrow, and Madison Trott display all the ribbons and trophies when Young Living won the title of World Champion in the eight-horse hitch, the six-horse hitch, and the Unicorn three-horse hitch.

Photosynthesis
HOW ARE ESSENTIAL OILS FORMED?

1. ELECTROMAGNETIC ENERGY (SUNLIGHT)

2. CHLOROPHYLL — Molecules inside the plant cells convert sunlight into energy.

3. WATER

4. CARBON DIOXIDE

5. C_3 SUGARS

6. $3C_3$ SUGARS

7. C_6 SUGARS = FRUCTOSE

8. ENZYMES SECRETED BY CELLS

9. C_5 ISOPRENE

10. PLANT ESSENCES

The photosynthesis process is an example of the elegance and wonderful complexity of nature. Plants are efficient molecular factories that use carbon dioxide, sunlight, water, and enzymes to create aromatic compounds. These aromatic compounds (essential oils) are important for plant survival, as they assist with communication, protection, and attraction.

QUALITY AND PURITY

Gary's commitment to quality and purity began with his Seed to Seal commitment. So what determines a genuine, pure, therapeutic-grade essential oil?

Every plant created by God contains DNA and messenger RNA (mRNA) (or what Gary liked to call "memory RNA"), which contains decoding instructions or the blueprint for the enzymes and sugars that produce essential oils.

So how are essential oils formed? In the process of photosynthesis, plants not only produce food but in addition, some also convert nutrients into volatile aromatic compounds in order to protect themselves from sickness and insect damage. In the event of a forest fire, these compounds will cause the dry leaves on the ground to burn more quickly, so the fire has less to burn and does not penetrate into the ground and damage the roots. The aromatic compounds, or oils, are stored in glands on plant stems and/or leaves. The essential oil is released under low temperature and low pressure after varying lengths of distilling time.

The Proper Environment

With the proper environment, soil nutrients, water, timely cultivation with the right equipment, and careful management, the highest-quality essential oils can be produced that support the body's natural chemistry for health, heightened spiritual awareness, and emotional balance.

The proper seed species is critical to produce the highest quality. But how do you know if you have the proper plant species unless you are the grower, or work with the grower, and have the laboratory to test and validate the right chemical consistency? What is the origin of your seed? How do you know that the seed is not genetically modified?

Most seeds are commercially grown in a nursery not subject to the challenges of nature: sun, water, wind, and temperature changes. The harshness of nature develops strength in the plant's immune system that is expressed in the essential oil. Seeds grown in a controlled environment generally produce genetically weak plants, which usually produce a low-quality oil.

Growing healthy plants begins with understanding the physical and chemical properties of the soil, along with the nutritional needs of the plants. Insufficient soil nutrients and poor soil conditions will result in poor essential oil quality.

Geographical location, soil type, climate, elevation, humidity, temperature, sunlight, frost-free days, rainfall, and many other variables determine the growth and health of the plants and thus the quality of the essential oil.

Aromatic plants grow best in well-drained soil rich in nitrogen, potash, and phosphorous with a pH of 7-8. Clay soil needs an abundance of compost, humus, enzymes, and microbes to break down its naturally rigid structure and change it to the ideal composition.

Composting

Nitrogen is released from the plants through composting, which is critical for organic farming and is practiced on all Young Living farms. Fruits that fall from the trees to the ground and overly ripened vegetables, along with discarded food scraps from our restaurant on the Ecuador farm—such as banana peels, coconut husks, and the skins from mangoes, papayas, apples, and other exotic fruits—are added to clover and alfalfa to begin fermentation. This is later mixed with manure from the goat dairy and the liquid worm castings from the six worm houses to make an excellent fertilizer that is nitrogen-rich, providing a unique source of food for the plants.

Weed Control

Weed and pest control are always major challenges in organic farming. Gary developed a natural herbicide made with essential oils, neem oil, and castile oil. His pest control spray is a combination of Cinnamon, Palo Santo, Basil, Idaho Tansy, Pine, and Citronella, with neem oil as a carrier oil. Their efficacy is quite remarkable. It has been very interesting to watch how the different plants respond in a positive way to the essential oil spray.

Weed and pest control sprays made with essential oils can dramatically improve the organic environment of the plants. Soil sprayed with certain essential oils has been shown to digest unwanted chemicals in the soil as well. Naturally, it is much more expensive, but the results are well worth it.

Weeds can be a farmer's worst enemy and one of the biggest challenges when growing organically. For that reason it is important to control the weeds through early cultivation.

1. Summer fallowing cuts the weed growth and prepares the ground for planting.
2. Planting cover crops such as beans, corn, triticale, clover, etc., helps choke out the weeds and adds more nutrients when they are plowed into the soil.
3. Rotating the crops is always beneficial and adds different nutrients to the soil.
4. Some aromatic crops like chamomile and clary sage grow so close together that they choke out weeds.

Organic Farming

Gary never permitted the use of any chemicals on the plants growing on his farms. Young Living continues to follow his direction using organic farming methods and requires the same from all partner farms and certified growers. The Young Living farm in Ecuador is very rural and far from any industrial and city pollution. The air is fresh and uncontaminated, which lends well to organic practices and certification.

In 2013 the Ecuador farm received organic certification for the plants, raw farmland not yet planted, and CERES, which is a German organization accredited by the U.S. Department of Agriculture, comparable to USDA Organic certification.

A worker applies an essential oil-based spray to the plants.

Distilling Clary Sage

Gary had been distilling clary sage at the Mona farm for over an hour one day when the water-supply pipe to the boiler broke, shutting down the distilling. The oil yield was good and the distillation was almost finished, so the workers wanted to unload the cooker and prepare for the next one. But Gary had a thought: "Let the material sit in the cooker until we are ready to start again, and then let's distill for another hour and see what happens."

He was amazed when he discovered that during the second distillation period, there was greater extraction of the very desired compound sclareol. Allowing the clary sage to sit in the cooker until the pipe was repaired softened the fiber channels, which released even more sclareol. The oil from the two cooks was combined, achieving a greater balance of all of the constituents. The Young Living farm in France is now using this same distillation technique.

The environment greatly affects plant growth and quality of the oil that's produced. Latitude is a complex factor that determines the compounds produced in the plants.

Many questions can be asked about distilling each plant; but for each plant, there will be many different answers. Only someone like Gary Young, who grew, harvested, and distilled plants in different countries with different climates and soil conditions, could give complete and in-depth answers.

Sometimes it takes years of working in the same area on the same farm with different plants to answer some of these questions. Many people can visit a farm, watch the workers in the field, observe the entire distillation process, and think they know all about distilling; yet they couldn't duplicate what they saw or answer detailed questions about the operation.

Preparing the soil, planting, cultivating, distilling, and testing are all part of the process, as well as understanding how to deal with the problems that come with climate change and the solutions for those problems.

Extensive research will always be an ongoing part of Seed to Seal, including soil composition, climate and environmental statistics, planting, cultivating, harvesting, distilling, and analytical testing. Planting a new crop is very expensive and can be very costly if a wrong decision is made.

Helichrysum grew beautifully in Utah, but due to the high elevation and the cold winter temperatures, the neryl acetate compound was too low for Gary's approval. Even though it had a nice aroma, it was dug up and replaced by a different crop.

A truckload of clary sage arrives at the distillery.

The first einkorn grain was planted on the farm in France in 2006.

EINKORN

Today, on the Young Living farm in France, non-hybridized einkorn seed is harvested the old-fashioned way by letting the cut stalks stand in the field for 7 to 10 days to allow the germination process to start before threshing.

When Gary began searching for this ancient grain back in 1990, he found it to be very elusive. He discovered small patches growing in Hunzaland, in remote areas of Turkey, and eventually on the east bank of the Jordan River Valley.

A few years later, Jean-Noël became interested in einkorn and talked to Gary about it. Neither of them knew a lot, but they wanted to know more, so Jean-Noël planted some for testing in 2006. Then one of our co-op farmers was engaged to plant some seed, which increased our productivity and produced enough seed so that Gary was able to bring a small amount home to test plant to see if it would grow in Utah. The einkorn crop grew very well and produced good seed, which increased every subsequent year and prompted Gary to clear enough acreage at the farm in 2012 to plant 150 acres. Several farmers in the United States and Canada have been sent seed from the farm and are growing and experimenting to see how well the seed produces in their areas.

The history of wheat is very interesting, and much can be learned from the evolution of what some historians call the "ancient, original grain of man" to the hybridized "dwarf" wheat of today. As the population of the world increased, so did the need for more food. Wheat seemed to be a good choice that could feed millions of people. Scientists began looking for ways to increase the yield, which led to the hybridization not only of wheat but of other grains as well.

The "new" wheat made the harvest easier and faster and reduced the cost to the farmers. However, the consequences of altering Mother Nature's wheat were not taken into consideration. Now that there wasn't time to germinate or activate the enzymes, the wheat was difficult to digest and rendered many nutrients unusable, causing more and different digestive problems to appear. Sadly, the results didn't seem to bother anyone; or people simply didn't put two and two together.

As Gary continued to learn more about nutrition for strengthening his own body, his analytical mind kept asking questions, which took him down this path of discovery. Going back to nature—to the original grain—seemed to be the thing to do, which started him on his quest for einkorn. The more he studied, the more certain he became that this was an ancient food that needed to come back to the modern world. It was amazing as he realized the similarities of wanting to produce this non-hybridized grain and the ancient knowledge of the essential oils he wanted to research and restore to mankind. For more information on Gary's book, visit DiscoverLSP.com.

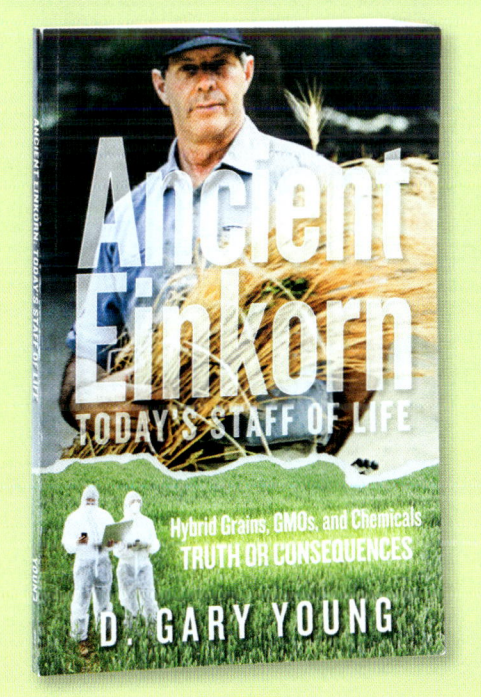

The first test crop of the ancient grain einkorn was planted in Mona in 2011.

An early 1900 steam engine powers this vintage thresher. Going back in history and seeing the old equipment in operation is a rare, intriguing opportunity. The einkorn, in the foreground, is left in the field for a week, so the kernels can begin germinating before being threshed.

Gary became driven in his quest to bring back the ancient grain, which first made its way into the Young Living market as the flour was made into pancake mix and spaghetti. Due to the demand, the flour was subsequently packaged for sale.

Members began experimenting with all kinds of recipes using the flour as well as the pancake mix. Several more products were developed, including Einkorn Granola, Einkorn Flakes Cereal, Einkorn Rotini Pasta, and Einkorn Crackers, many which have become favorites and some used in all kinds of recipes.

All of this comes to us because Gary had the vision and knew this would benefit so many and give an alternative to a vast number of products made with hybridized grains. It would seem that if this rediscovered einkorn grain produced the high nutritional value as it did anciently, then it would make sense that we could eat it and benefit from it in the same way the early people of our world did; and it certainly is a lot easier because we don't have to travel to the Middle East to get some.

Scientists who have been studying einkorn for years say that eating non-hybridized einkorn grain means that we are eating non-hybridized gluten. Therefore, einkorn is easier to digest; contains vitamins, minerals, and proteins that are important to our health; and is probably the most preferred grain to eat. It also has a delicious taste.

Gluten-free fad diets, which have become popular today, will eventually cause challenges down the road. Our bodies need and want what comes naturally in our food that has not been altered genetically. The body knows what to do with what God has given us to sustain life and should respond in a normal and positive way.

Due to the increased volume of kernels on the stalk as a result of hybridization, scientists thought that more food could be produced and more people could be fed. This seemed like a great solution for feeding the people of world. However, when the genes of a plant are altered, the God-given life force is changed within the plant.

Jacob received early instructions from Dad on the vintage cultivator pulled by the horses.

Einkorn on the left and modern hybridized wheat on the right.

Harvesting einkorn in Utah, 2013.

Dwarf wheat and other modern grains contain 42 chromosomes, with more and different varieties of genes for gluten proteins, causing possible body malfunctions. Other grains such as spelt (often called kamut) and emmer have 28 chromosomes, which is less than the more modern grains but is still more than einkorn.

Hybridized wheat—with 42 chromosomes—creates different genetic codes for new proteins that man was never meant to consume. With 3 genomes (A, B, and D), it is the hybridized wheat D genome that is the source of gluten-triggered responses. The perceived benefits of changing the genetic structure of a plant for whatever reason does not compensate for the negative effects.

The differences in the kernels of grain are easy to see. The einkorn stalks are long and slender, and the kernels are oblong and flat-looking, protected by a strong husk or chaff that clings to the kernels and is more difficult to husk. Because the einkorn hull is difficult to remove, it protects the kernels against negative environmental factors and destructive pests. Because einkorn has the simplest genetic code of all varieties of wheat, with just 1 genome and 14 chromosomes, it is easy for the body to utilize.

Nonirrigated or wild einkorn grows about 2 feet tall. In wetter climates and/or with irrigation, the cultivated einkorn grows 4½ to 5 feet tall with hair-like tassels that wave when the wind blows.

Hybrid wheat has been engineered to grow between 14 and 16 inches high, with shorter, thicker stalks to support the heavier grain heads. The common hybridized "dwarf wheat" of today has double the number of kernels that are thicker and heavier with less hair and a soft husk that is easy to remove, making it more susceptible to pests and various fungal diseases.

The kernels of the fully matured hybridized wheat fall to the ground as soon as the harvesting equipment begins to shake the stalks. For years farmers have been harvesting the wheat green in the soft dough stage to capture the kernels before this happened.

Hybridized wheat enables modern harvesting to bypass the different stages of development. Today the grain is cut and threshed immediately, so it has no time to go through the maturing stage to germinate and develop the enzymatic activity needed later for digestion.

The modern way wheat is harvested is for convenience, not for maximizing health benefits. In ancient times farmers would not have understood the science of harvesting wheat, but they must have known that the wheat was more health-sustaining when it went through all the stages of maturing.

This antique harvester was presented to Gary as a surprise when he visited the Young Living farm in France, 2014.

D. Gary Young | The World Leader in Essential Oils

Distillery site

This is what I saw as Gary and I looked at the dense jungle, November 2006.

This is what Gary saw it would become as he looked out over the immense jungle, July 2012.

ECUADOR—A NEW OPPORTUNITY

In 2005 Gary's path took another unexpected turn when he was invited to Ecuador by Dr. Edgar Rodas, the dean of the medical school at the Azuay University in the city of Cuenca, who had an interest in essential oils. He wanted Gary to develop an essential oils program with various research projects for his students. However, it didn't take long to discover that the university administration didn't have a lot of knowledge about the prerequisites and curriculum that would be necessary for this type of study in essential oils, and they were not prepared to offer such a course.

Gary did have the opportunity, though, to travel into the jungle with the volunteer Cinterandes medical team, headed by Dr. Rodas, to conduct research with essential oils.

Gary really enjoyed the Cinterandes mobile medical team when he was invited to travel with them into the jungle to conduct a research project using essential oils.

Gary invited his cousin, Tamera Packer, to join him to help administer the oils while he conducted blood analysis with his microscope in the jungle. He loved teaching about essential oils and becoming acquainted with Ecuador and the vast possibilities of new oils from its diverse ecosystem.

Was Gary disappointed with the university? Perhaps, but then maybe he was relieved. He was in Ecuador, a country with diverse climates and terrain and thousands of yet-to-be-identified plants and trees and so much still to be explored. He quickly realized that the warm tropical climate in Guayaquil would enable him to farm year-round. This untapped world of essential oils was very exciting to Gary, and he was anxious to start his new farming adventure.

Finca Botanica—Young Living Ecuador

The challenge of finding land was arduous and costly, and as inexperienced Americans, Gary and his family were often the targets of unscrupulous individuals. But Gary's vision was expansive, and he could see all the possibilities of a farm that could operate for 12 months of the year with so many new plants to be discovered and rare exotic essential oils for Young Living. He was determined and no matter what happened, he was going to continue on the path he had chosen.

In September of 2006, he found the perfect place—raw, dense, unwanted jungle on the edge of the remote town of Chongon about 40 minutes from the Guayaquil airport.

The task—conquering the jungle—seemed overwhelming; but with indescribable perseverance against the odds of unrelenting mosquitoes, stinging insects, no-see-ums, scorpions, boa constrictors, poisonous snakes, and monsoon rains that turned the ground into glue-like mud, almost impossible to traverse, 2,300 acres became the home of the next Young Living farm.

In September 2006 Gary found the perfect place, and in November, on Thanksgiving Day, the papers were signed for the land, and the transformation of the jungle began. The soil was dark and rich with nutrients but had high clay density, which took a lot of time with heavy equipment to move.

Operating the D8 bulldozer, Gary cut the first road, built the dam, and carved the beginning out of harsh, thorny bushes, shrubs, and trees. When the monsoon rains came, the valley quickly filled with water, ready for thirsty crops that would soon be growing in this tropical heat. The farm evolved into a working "metropolis," hidden from the world, surrounded by the dense jungle.

Gary built 2½ miles of road into the farm. During the monsoon season, it was especially difficult because of the sticky clay. When the rain stopped, tons of gravel had to be hauled and dumped the entire length of the road to build a stable roadbase.

It was a remarkable time and probably no other man in the world would have undertaken such a project; but Gary's dream was vivid, his determination unstoppable, and the challenge and constant discovery of new plants filled his head with endless ideas.

With a strait face, Gary told everyone that this was Mary's first house. Really?

The first greenhouses were built next to the dam.

Basil seed was the first to be germinated at the farm in Ecuador.

130 D. Gary Young | The World Leader in Essential Oils

Beginning of the distillery construction in January 2007.

Walls were formed with bamboo poles, and the concrete was poured by hand.

The 350-horsepower boiler built in Guayaquil in 2007. Parts and equipment for the boiler that could not be found in Ecuador were shipped from Utah.

The 14,500-liter cooker was ready to go to the farm.

Containers arrived from Utah with needed building materials and distillery parts.

As the steel beams were lifted in two places, the dream of distilling was soon to become a reality.

The battle with the monsoon rains was often frightening; but with Gary, it was about how to solve the problem and not let the problem stop him.

The torrential monsoon rains came down like sheets of water that were difficult to penetrate or see through. The culverts weren't big enough and the road was washed out. The clay soil turned to glue-like sticky mud and was as slick as an icy winter road.

Putting in bigger culverts and rebuilding the road after the monsoons washed it out.

During the monsoons, the water could rise 1 to 2 feet per hour. This small break in the dam could have been a disaster, but Gary made it there in time with the excavator, and everyone moved quickly to plug the opening and stop the rushing water.

Tamara, Marianne, Sabina, Jacob pushing Vallorie, Gary, Geoffrey, and Mary behind the wheel, with Josef next to her watching.

The pictures were never ending, but Gary and John Whetten loved it.

The road leaving the farm between the second dam and the field of dorado azul is the only road through the farm. Over 6 miles of electrical wiring were strung from the main road to the farm.

136   D. Gary Young | The World Leader in Essential Oils

Palo Santo is a very unique oil that is extracted only from dead wood that has fallen and has been lying on the ground. Gary learned about this wood in 2006 while traveling through Ecuador and had heard about Palo Santo oil from various people. He eventually found an elderly gentleman who had been distilling small amounts of wood and selling the oil locally.

Gary was intrigued with the oil and took enough wood back to Cuenca to distill in his small testing distiller. He sent the oil to Utah to be analyzed; and when the report came back, he decided this would be a wonderful addition to Young Living's growing line of products.

When he moved to Guayaquil and set up the small distilling operation before the farm was established, he began looking for villagers who could gather the dead wood for him. He learned that the longer the tree had been dead, the more oil was found within the channels of the wood fiber, a phenomenon known only to Mother Nature. The people in the remote jungle villages began to gather the wood and truck it to the farm.

Prior to this, the villagers had no opportunity to work, so this wildcrafting for Young Living has greatly improved their lives. With the money earned, they have been able to build two schools. The supply of wildcrafted plants will always be limited and without guaranteed availability, but those who have this oil know of the deep feeling it gives of being grounded and close to nature.

When Gary was clearing the land to prepare the new fields for planting, he discovered thousands of palo santo trees growing in the brush on the property. He sent the farm crew to walk ahead of the bulldozer to safeguard the trees until they could be moved.

Earlier, Gary found an area deep within the farm that had an abundance of palo santo trees. It seemed like a natural sanctuary and was designated as a special place. Over 3,000 trees were transplanted to this new location, now known as the Palo Santo Forest, which covers more than 100 acres of high rolling hills. The Palo Santo Forest is a quiet place for contemplation, meditation, and spiritual renewal and is enjoyed by everyone who comes to the farm and takes time to go there.

Palo santo was very intriguing and was one of the first that Gary chipped and distilled.

Dead palo santo wood is gathered and trucked to the farm to be distilled.

A small patio next to the house that Gary leased for the family was enclosed for experimental distilling of ruta (rue) and palo santo.

The Palo Santo Forest is a special place for meditation and quiet introspection and is uplifting and rejuvenating for all who visit.

In the highlands near Pelieo and Ambato, about 500 people grow ruta for Young Living. Local farmers who wildcraft in unfarmable regions are earning an income for the first time. New plants are constantly being distilled and analyzed for possible new oils for Young Living.

Gary built employee housing on the farm with electricity, hot and cold running water, and a complete kitchen, as well as a washer and dryer next to their housing, which was a new experience for most of the workers. There was a little bit of frustration with a lot of laughter as they were trying to figure out how to use the washing machine, but they never cease to express their gratitude.

Young Living provides jobs for hundreds of people for the first time, as well as income for over 2,000 families, including locals in the jungle and surrounding villagers who gather palo santo, ocotea, ruta, and blue eucalyptus that they bring to the farm for distillation. The farm blesses the lives of thousands of people in Ecuador, as well as people around the world who are blessed because of the oils produced at this farm.

Employee housing built on the farm has eight individual apartments, each with three bedrooms and two bathrooms.

Gary made eight expeditions into the Amazon jungle in Ecuador and Peru on foot, by canoe, speedboat, and whatever means was available. Even at the risk of his life, he continued to explore looking for new plants, which he brought out of the jungle to distill and analyze. When they met his specifications, he engaged the local people to harvest the plants or flowers and bring them to the farm, providing work and income for natives who had never had an income before this time.

Sometimes, the plants were so deep in the jungle and far from modern transportation that it would take two or three days to take the plant material by boat downstream where it could be loaded on a truck to be driven to the farm, which could take as long as 18 to 24 hours of driving. After several years local harvesters still bring the plants to the farm to be distilled, enabling Young Living to offer unusual, exotic, and beneficial oils that are part of the Young Living essential oil line.

Lush vegetation grows in nutrient-rich soil fed by the many volcanoes of Ecuador.

The shaman shared amazing secrets of the jungle with Gary, which gave him even more ideas

Exploring the Amazon by canoe sometimes took two days for Gary to reach the final destination.

The children in the Amazon rainforest were fascinated with this American who seemed so interested in talking to them.

New plants, flowers, and jungle vegetation were always of great interest to Gary.

Turkey hot dogs were a first for this young guide, and he ate them with gusto.

We could almost disappear in the field of dorado azul when it was ready to be harvested, 2008.

Shortly after establishing the farm in Chongon, Gary found a "worthless" jungle weed growing wild in the foothills northeast of Guayaquil, but to him this worthless weed had a beautiful aroma. He collected enough plant material to distill a test batch, and after analyzing the oil, he immediately knew this was going to be a staple crop of the new farm in Ecuador. Gary went back to the brushy jungle, gathered seeds from the wild, and started the first field domestication of this plant that he called dorado azul.

A local botanist could not identify it and suggested that Gary name the plant. Laughingly he said, "Let's call it *Guayfolius officinalis* found here in Guayaquil." However, the plant is well-known in the scientific world as *Hyptis suaveolens*.

Another interesting fact about dorado azul is that it thrives during the monsoon season, a time of the year when most other crops are drowned out by rain. This was also one of the first plants distilled at the new farm in 2007. Dorado Azul has since become a favorite oil in Young Living.

Gary joked that he built Mary's "first house" on the far side of the reservoir, but she declined to live there because of the snakes, spiders, scorpions, and other creepy crawlers. The second farmhouse was much more appealing.

Ruta was the first plant to be distilled in 2007.

It was a remarkable feat when the first distillation took place in August 2007. Those who visit today still stand in awe of that accomplishment. Gary carved this beautiful, productive farm with all of its attractions out of unusable, wasted jungle land.

Three 14,500-liter extraction chambers distill large quantities of plant material six days a week, 11½ months of the year; and during some harvests, the distillery operation runs 24/7 to extract the oils at exactly the right time. The glucose content (Brix measurement) of the plant is monitored closely to ensure that harvesting and distillation happen at the right time. Distilling even one day too soon or one day too late can reduce the amount and quality of the oil produced.

350-horsepower wetback boiler built in Guayaquil.

The shop is large enough to work on heavy equipment inside during the monsoon season. The office is on the second floor.

144   D. Gary Young | The World Leader in Essential Oils

A 6-ton block of distilled plant material is lifted from the cooker with a 10-ton hoist.

Everybody helps: early training.

D. Gary Young | The World Leader in Essential Oils

Because of the warm climate in Ecuador, supplying cool water to the distillery condensers was a challenge. Gary creatively reconfigured ordinary deep freezers with copper tubing and antifreeze to cool the water on its way to the condenser, which surprisingly worked well for years, but only as long as the flow rate of water was slow. However, with the increasing volume of plant material, the freezers could not keep up with the amount of water needed to supply the condensers, and coupled with the maintenance and cleaning, the cooling efficiency decreased, and they could no longer meet the need.

After analyzing the massive flow rate of the water going into the condenser, it became apparent that the condenser efficiency remained close to where it was when the freezers were working. Small modifications were made by increasing the size of the condenser discharge lines to facilitate the higher flow rates. Every oil distilled at the farm was tested to ensure that the chemistry and physical results were not altered and no negative changes in yield were found. Everyone was thrilled when the production rate increased and the quality of the oil remained the same.

Eugenio and Gary built a wonderful friendship over the years working together as Gary taught Eugenio the art of distillation.

There are 16 small cookers that are used to distill ylang ylang and palo santo as well as new-crop plant material for testing.

Two 14,500-liter cookers were added to meet the growing demand, and flex tubing was imported from the U.S. for Gary's modified design.

Members attending Platinum Retreat gather around Gary to learn about the distillation of dorado azul.

In June 2011 land was cleared for 24,000 ylang ylang trees. Members planted thousands of seedlings; and by June 2013 the trees had grown into very big, bushy trees that produce flowers year round.

Nicolas Chong, the farm general manager on the right in the white shirt, checks to see how the ylang ylang harvest is progressing. Field manager, Jose Solorzano (nicknamed Panchito), on the left in the green shirt, was the first local person from Chongon to be hired.

Happy ylang ylang pickers. Primo Chaves (in front) transferred from St. Maries to Ecuador because of his farming and distillation expertise, which he acquired after working for many years on the St. Maries farm.

The original 24,000 ylang ylang trees continue to expand and by the end of 2019 will total 70,000 trees.

The smell of ylang ylang is intoxicating.

150 D. Gary Young | The World Leader in Essential Oils

Ylang ylang flowers are sorted and distilled in the small distillers on the lower level of the distillery.

The restaurant serves over 180 nutritious meals every day to farm workers, spa staff, many members who come to help with the harvest, and many guests who come to visit the farm.

Employees in the kitchen prepare the meals according to Gary's direction: fresh and organic, no sugar, nothing fried, and no synthetic flavorings or additives.

During the monsoon season, the water level comes up so high that it creates the appearance that the restaurant is floating.

The entire restaurant is built with bamboo and sits on bamboo stilts over the reservoir, which creates a fabulous atmosphere for everyone who comes to enjoy a delicious meal. All kinds of garden-grown vegetables and delicious fruits are used in the preparation of the many meals that are served. Gary planted banana and mango plantations shortly after moving to the farm that are within a two-minute walk from the kitchen. They now produce the fruit that is eaten and is part of the exotic tropical fruit juices made daily.

Acres of rice are grown on the farm for the restaurant and the school, and goat cheese and yogurt are made from the organic goat milk that comes from the goat dairy on the farm. The meals are made without sugar, white flour, or other unhealthy ingredients. It is a delight for all those who come to visit.

Vallorie, Tamara, and I love the sweet bananas grown on the farm.

Nothing compares to the delicious taste of the thousands of organic tree-ripened mangoes that are enjoyed at the farm restaurant and the Young Living Academy.

Yacon is a sweet potato-like vegetable that has a dark, thick, mineral-rich liquid when pressed.

One entire hillside at the farm is covered with the favorite Ecuadorean Sasha cacao trees, which produce large amounts of beans that have a delicious flavor and from which organic chocolate is produced. One hectare (2.47 acres) with 1,000 trees can produce 2-3 tons of cacao beans per year.

Eucalyptus blue is gathered in the eastern Amazon region of Ecuador and trucked to the farm for distillation.

EUCALYPTUS BLUE

Components	Accepted Lot 26808	Rejected Lot 24921
Alpha-Pinene	19.9	28.9
Beta-Pinene	0.7	0.4
Myrcene	0.7	0.7
Alpha-Phellandrene	0.4	0.9
Limonene	5.4	5.4
Eucalyptol	66.2	4.1
Gamma-Terpinene	0.6	1.2
Alpha-Terpineol	0.6	1.8
Alpha Terpinyl Acetate	0.8	3.8
Aromadendrene	1.6	16.7

These are the major components that make up the action of the oil. Minor components have been left out.

Workers harvest lemongrass, which produces four crops every year.

Gary found the oregano species *Plectranthus amboinicus* growing wild on the farm in 2008 and distilled it in 2009. After analyzing the oil, he liked the constituent profile and decided it would be beneficial to cultivate it on the farm.

Plectranthus oregano in the greenhouse ready to be planted in the fields.

Constituent	Plectranthus oregano Lot 012706 (Area %)	Origanum vulgare median ISO values (Area %)
Alpha Thujene	0.70	0.85
Alpha Pinene	0.40	1.35
Myrcene	1.90	1.75
Alpha Terpinene	12.20	1.25
Para Cymene	3.80	7.0
Eucalyptol	0.40	—
Gamma Terpinene	17.90	6.0
Linalool	—	1.5
Terpinen-4-ol	1.20	1.25
Alpha Terpineol	0.60	—
Pulegone	0.50	—
Geraniol	0.30	—
Geranial	0.60	—
Carvacrol	32.90	70.0
Trans Beta Caryophyllene	10.20	2.25
Trans Alpha Bergamotene	6.70	0
Trans Beta Farnesene	0.30	0
Alpha Humulene	2.80	0
Beta Bisabolene	0.40	0
Delta Cadinene	0.30	0
Caryophyllene Oxide	1.70	0

D. Gary Young | The World Leader in Essential Oils

Worm Houses/Worm Castings
Millions of California red worms multiply in six worm houses on the Ecuador farm, creating liquid fertilizer and castings (manure), which are applied every week on the fields on a rotation basis and are also mixed into the potting soil for the greenhouses. The liquid produced from the composting is mixed with the liquid from the worm castings and goes through the sprinkler system for irrigating the crops. It is the best way to use the plant material after distillation and is a unique way for controlling automated fertilization and has proven to work very well. Over 5 million tons of our specialized fertilizer is spread on the fields annually.

California red worms

Holding tank for liquid worm castings, which are mixed with compost and goat manure from the goat dairy on the farm.

Manure is also trucked in from nearby dairies and used for soil enhancement and composting.

The goats produce organic milk and cream for the restaurant and the Young Living Academy. The manure is mixed with the compost for the fertilizer that goes back on the fields. Ramon Salazar has cared for the goats from the beginning, and they come when he calls them by name.

While traveling in Ethiopia in 2010 looking for different species of frankincense, Gary visited the University in Addis Ababa and learned of a trade school that he went to see where the students were making blocks from dirt mixed with a little cement and using them to construct different buildings and student housing on the school campus. It was a very simple and inexpensive way to build; and they even made different colors of bricks, depending on the color of the soil used, which enabled them to create very interesting and colorful design patterns.

Gary was so fascinated that in his investigation, he learned that the brick-making machine was made in South Africa. He decided that would be a fabulous way to do the construction of future buildings at both the school and the farm and possibly create a different source of revenue for the farm by selling the bricks to the public.

Two machines were ordered and when they arrived at the farm in Ecuador, instructors came from South Africa to teach Gary and some of the farm workers how to operate them. It was quite successful and now thousands of bricks are made daily. It was very rewarding to be able to build the new additions to the school with these blocks for a fraction of the cost of cinder block and cement.

Making bricks with soil and a small amount of cement was developed in South Africa, an educational and financial addition to the farm.

D. Gary Young | The World Leader in Essential Oils

Research Nursery

In the nursery we test and record plant and root growth in different soil conditions for adaptability, pest resistance, and weed control with oils. We also study new plants found in the jungle to determine their nutritional and therapeutic value and their water needs. When ready, seedlings are transplanted into the fields and studied for their growth and potential oil production. Chris Packer and Gary check to see if the plants are ready to be transplanted.

Juan Cardenas, who has managed the greenhouses for several years, takes pride in the plants that are grown from seeds that are germinated year-round and are continually being transplanted to the fields. New plants are grown and test-distilled to determine production viability.

This sophisticated weather station constantly monitors weather patterns, UV hours per day, temperature, humidity, barometric pressure, rainfall, and daylight hours. This data is used with the Brix testing to determine the best harvesting and distilling times to maximize production.

Examples of Brix testing:			
Lavender	St. Maries	Shade-dried for 62 hours	Brix 24
Lavender	Mona	Shade-dried for 48 hours	Brix 28
Lavender	France	Cut before the flower goes to seed, dried 76 hours	Brix 21
Melissa	St. Maries	Cut mid-bloom, shade-dried for 12 hours	Brix 14
Oregano	Ecuador	Cut before going to seed, shade-dried 120 hours	Brix 24
Dorado Azul	Ecuador	Distilled immediately	Brix 16
Peppermint	Mona	Cut in full-bloom, sun-dried for 3 days	Brix 28

Brix Testing and Harvesting

When is the perfect time for harvesting? Many variables determine when the plants are ready to be harvested, beginning with the weather.

1. A growing season that has had daily low temperatures or high temperatures, heavy rain, or little rain will greatly affect the maturing time of the plants.
2. As harvest time approaches, multiple daily Brix testing of the plants, which is the measurement of the plants' total dissolved solids (mostly glucose or sugar), helps determine the time of day to harvest. The higher the degree of Brix, the greater the oil production and the higher the percentage of chemical compounds.
3. When the plants are ready to be harvested, a small amount should be cut for a sample distillation.
4. The distilled oil is then scientifically tested with a GC/MS instrument to determine its chemical profile, which indicates constituents and their percentages for that particular oil. If the chemical profile does not meet Young Living's standard, then either more maturing time is needed, or the crop will not be distilled. This is one reason why new plants are test distilled to see if that particular plant has enough benefits to merit cultivating or further wildcrafting.

Panchito squeezes out just one drop of plant liquid, which is all that is needed to measure Brix with the refractometer.

Curing, Geographical Location, and Distilling Time

Curing is a very interesting and critical factor of distillation. Gary discovered in his early years of distilling that there is a difference in the volume produced and compounds found in the oil of each batch of plant material, depending on how soon it is distilled after being harvested. Some plants are very stressed when they are cut and will manufacture more oil within the plant fiber as a way of trying to protect themselves.

Gary did not realize this until he started distilling in different states and then in different countries. It was very revealing to see how the distillation process was different in Washington, Idaho, and Utah, and then in France, Ecuador, Oman, Egypt, Taiwan, Israel, northern Canada, and Croatia, as well as in our farms and partner farms located around the world.

It was interesting to discover that geographical location made a significant difference in the distillation. North and south of the equator and the 45th parallel, elevation affects the maturing time of the crops, which may require a modification of the distillation process in order to obtain the highest quality oil with the best constituent profile.

North of the 45th parallel, we have Washington and Idaho, but Utah is south of the 45th parallel. Then the elevation adds another factor to consider. Washington, north of the 45th parallel, is at an elevation of 1,500 to 2,500 feet; and the time for distilling peppermint is early August.

Below the 45th parallel and above 4,500 feet, in order to have higher levels of menthol and lower levels of menthone, the best time for distilling peppermint is late August to early September.

In the hot, humid climate of Ecuador, because we can farm year-round, there is more time to test and conduct research to determine the best distilling time.

Shade drying and maturing the plants before distilling varies greatly with different plants, even in the same geographical area, as you can see from the chart. Because shade drying is so important for so many crops, Gary extended the concrete pad and roof to protect the crops from the direct sunlight to ensure the proper curing time.

Only someone who grows, harvests, distills, conducts analytical tests, and keeps records would know these details.

Plant Material	Distilling Time
Dorado Azul	Immediately after cutting
Ruta	5 days after cutting
Oregano	5 days after cutting
Lemongrass	3 days after cutting
Vetiver	7 to 10 days after digging
Eucalyptus Blue	3 to 5 days after picking
Ylang Ylang	Immediately after picking
Ocotea	10 days after picking
Palo Santo	5 years after death of the tree

Too little sunshine, too much rain, or a dramatic change in temperature can change the distillation time, causing it to vary from year to year. A lot of experience is needed to understand the distillation of so many different plants with so many complex possibilities. Different plants may grow in many different types of soil, but will these plants produce oil?

Many questions need to be asked:
1. What is the condition of the soil, and what is its nutritional profile?
2. Can lavender grow in a 5.5 pH sandy or clay loam soil?
3. Can frereana frankincense grow in Oman?
4. Will ylang ylang grow in Idaho?
5. Will lavender grow on the tropical coast of Ecuador?

Many of these questions are constantly asked; but will these aromatic crops, planted outside of their normal growing environment, produce oil? Then even if the plants produce oil, will the oil have the right chemical profile with the right percentages of the compounds?

The answer is: No, they won't, or not usually. Essential oil compounds are produced from the plant's genetic profile and fed by the nutrients in the soil. If the right combinations of nutrients are not in the soil as well as the proper amounts of sunshine and rain, the oil compounds will not be the same.

Eugenio Caruajulca, who has been the distillery manager for 13 years, checks the Brix levels of the plants every two hours as they cure before being distilled.

Ocotea leaves start to cure from the time they are picked to when they reach the farm four days later. When the truck arrives with 8 tons of raw material, the leaves are spread out and turned twice a day until dry, which could take up to a week, depending on how wet they are. It is critical that the material is dry before distilling because when the steam enters, any moisture remaining on the plant material will cause the steam to prematurely condense, homogenizing the finer molecules of the oil, compromising their extraction. As Gary experimented with the ocotea, he discovered that to recover the highest volume of oil, ocotea needs to be distilled for 6 hours the first day and for 4 hours the second day.

Isaias Saldivar spreads lemongrass for shade drying and curing before distillation.

In Gary's own words: "For 60 years I have been working in the farming industry. I saw a lot growing up on a ranch where we raised oats, barley, wheat, and alfalfa at an elevation of 6,500 feet in central Idaho. My father tried to grow different species of alfalfa such as Ranger alfalfa, but it did not grow well in our environment or at our elevation. Besides that, it was quite common for the winter temperatures to drop to -20ºF to -35ºF for two to three weeks at a time. However, Ladak alfalfa grew very well and was very hardy.

"It seems logical that plants would grow well in similar climates; but when they don't, it is usually because the soil nutrient profile is different. When the aquifer is different, the subsoil water may be too much or too little for aromatic plants; and if that cannot be controlled, there will be problems.

"France has never in history irrigated lavender until 2015, but the climate has changed with less rain and higher temperatures. Many farmers have given up, and now only 30 percent of the lavender growers in France are growing lavender today. The rest have switched to other crops.

"When I consider planting a crop, I first evaluate the growing conditions. If the soil profile is right, then longitude and latitude elevations have to be considered because this will change the planting and harvesting time, which can change the quality of the plants. The number of warm days, cool nights, and UV hours of daylight are all variables that can change the oil components. Too little water will kill melissa, and too much water will kill lavender or helichrysum, etc."

We may think that the origin of the plant is the best place to grow the crop. However, that isn't always true. The same plants may not grow the same, depending on nutrient depletion of the soil, insufficient water and/or sunshine, dramatic temperature changes, and the use of chemicals.

The molecular structure of lavender in Utah is almost identical to France, but the harvested volume per acre is greater in Utah, which means greater oil volume per acre. In Utah our seeds are strong, because the soil has never had chemicals on it, and it is also treated with needed nutrients. Since we started to irrigate in France, other farmers are following, and lavender is growing where water is available.

It is a remarkable feat to see this beautiful, productive farm in the surroundings of a dense and almost impenetrable jungle.

There was no water on the farm in the beginning. After Gary built the dam, the monsoon rains filled the reservoir quickly.

This laboratory was built above the distillery in 2010, making it possible to rapid run analyses during and after distilling.

Gary combined three columns and multiple detectors into one instrument. When he told the manufacturer, they canceled the warranty, but it worked.

GC/FID/MS Combining Analytical Instruments in the Field

On the upper level of the distillery building, the laboratory was built, where each distilled batch of oil is tested for chemical composition. This was critical in the ongoing research to determine the length of time needed for curing and the best time and specifics for distillation. New plants were continually being test-distilled to determine their viability as new essential oils for Young Living. Verifying the chemical profile of any essential oil is critical to determining its potency and purity.

The gas chromatograph in the laboratory at the farm is combined with a mass spectrometer (GC/MS), giving the technicians a vital tool for separating and identifying chemical compounds. The GC/MS combined with other analytical instruments provide our scientists in Ecuador with detailed information about each oil.

After the laboratory's first year of operation, Gary modified the existing two-detector, two-column (polar and non-polar) GC/FID (flame ionization detector) to accommodate a third detector: a mass spectrometer. Two capillary columns were connected to a splitter at the inlet of the GC so that the injection of one essential oil sample is divided between both columns. A 60m-long, non-polar capillary column was connected to the GC/MS portion of the instrument.

With this GC/FID/MS system, many components in the essential oils could be separated and tentatively identified using Young Living's exclusive retention index and mass-spectrum libraries.

The mass spectrometer (MS) is an instrument that makes it possible to characterize new essential oil components from previously unknown aromatic plants. The MS helps to confirm the identification provided by the retention index library by matching the mass spectra to Young Living's extensive compound reference library.

Using sophisticated computer algorithms, the computer searches for the best match in the reference library. These mass-spectra data are then cross-referenced with the retention index data to identify key essential oil components.

This combination instrument uses one 50m and one 60m column for the FID and one 60m column for the MS. With the three columns, we are able to identify more oil compounds for a more detailed analysis. Gary wanted to combine the GC and MS instruments into one instrument to accelerate his field research, against the manufacturer's recommendation, which voided the warranty. Now, nine years later (2019), the instrument still produces valuable data.

Dr. Herve Casabianca (between Gary and Chris) loved the farm in Ecuador and was very impressed with the analytical laboratory.

Dorado Azul Chromatograms(s)

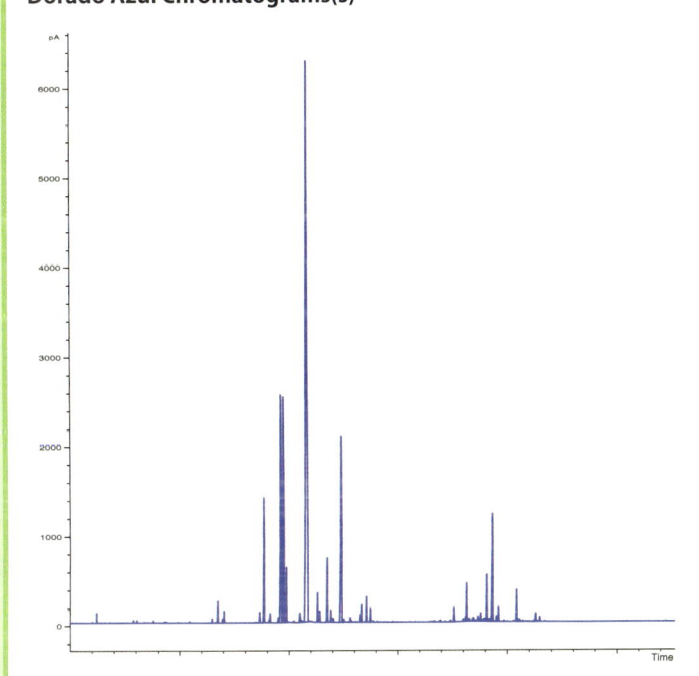

Many new plants are grown in the greenhouses for research to be test distilled and analyzed to determine their value in becoming new crops for producing exotic oils for Young Living.

Dorado Azul

Components	Dorado Azul Dry June 5, 2014 DA#001	Dorado Azul Green June 6, 2013 DA#001	YL Specification Min	YL Specification Max
Sabinene	8.6	9.1	0.6	17.4
Beta-Pinene	5.9	6.1	3.2	10.8
Eucalyptol	33.8	36.8	28.4	54.0
Limonene			0.2	7.0
Alpha-Fenchol	14.1	13.4	2.6	19.1
Bicyclogermacrene	7.7	7.1	Trace	9.4

Other Major Peaks				
Cis-3-Hexene-1-ol	0.5	0.6		
Alpha Pinene	2.9	3.1		
3-Octanol	0.1	0.5		
Myrcene	1.2	0.8		
Fenchone	2.9	2.9		
Terpinen-4-ol	1.2	0.8		
Alpha-Terpineol	0.6	0.5		
Beta-Caryophyllene	2.5	2.1		
Germacrene-D	2.4	2.2		
Spathulenol	2.1	1.9		
Tau-Cadinol	0.8	0.7		
Tau-Muurolol	0.4	0.4		

The main difference between the green and dry samples is that there is a slightly increased amount of monoterpenes in the green sample over the dry sample.

The farm crew is off to work on the new ocotea farm in Mera, Ecuador.

Hundreds of ocotea seedlings are ready to be planted.

Mera Ocotea Farm

Ocotea is a very important oil that Young Living produces in Ecuador. As the demand has grown, the need for greater supply has also become paramount. In the beginning, ocotea was wildcrafted and then trucked by the local harvesters to the farm for distillation. The soil and coastal climate of the farm was not suitable for growing ocotea. Land about three hours north of the farm, closer to where ocotea grows wild, would certainly be more suitable.

Gary decided it was time for Young Living to have its own ocotea farm where sustainable plants could be cultivated and harvested, so in 2016 Gary instructed Nicolas Chong, the farm general manager, to start looking for land.

On September 8, 2017, Young Living purchased 115.80 acres of land in Mera, which is part of the Pastaza province, located between Baños and Puyo, for the purpose of planting ocotea trees. In 2018 permits were issued from the EPA to clear 14 hectares (34.60 acres).

A sustainable ecological plan was developed to protect the waterways and prevent erosion in the ravines, maintain a sustainable percentage of larger trees, balance production with biodiversity of native trees and plants, and preserve an orchids sanctuary in the protected 14 hectares.

Corridors throughout the property are created for the wildlife, and GPS coordinates and drone images are used to plot the terrain for the mapping.

Orlando Pschecho, the farm agronomist and field and production manager, oversees the progress of the ocotea farm. He dug test pits between 80 centimeters to 1 meter deep to study the soil quality and take samples for specialized laboratory analysis to record the micro and macro nutrients in order to develop the best fertilization plan.

After the first 10,000 ocotea plants were planted, fertilizing and weeding became the focus in cultivation. Early care is very important so that the trees have a healthy start, as it takes five to six years before they will be ready for harvest. The farm is doing very well with the anticipation of growing strong trees that will produce the highest quality oil possible.

Orlando, Nicolas, and Eugenio enjoy the uplifting aroma of ocotea.

Lots of post holes.

Gigi, wife of Nicolas Chong, loved planting.

Natural corridors are preserved for the wild animals.

NovaVita Spa and Rejuvenation Center

In 2006 Gary opened a research center in Guayaquil to test the efficacy of the oils. New discoveries were almost a daily experience, and a great many people returned home with renewed health and vitality. However, the noise and pollution of the big city were not conducive to the well-being of everyone there. Gary wanted to move his center to the farm, so in 2011 the construction started and when finished, the new environment was beautiful.

NovaVita sits just a stone's throw from the distillery. Members love having an essential oil spa where they can enjoy the infrared sauna, massage, Raindrop, or even a chocolate masque with essential oils, besides the many other applications for rejuvenation.

In 2017 Gary decided to change his direction by creating a farm educational experience for members just as we do with our other farms. Members can work in the greenhouse and in the fields as well as pick ylang ylang flowers and then help in the distillery. They can also visit the Young Living Academy or spend a day in Guayaquil sightseeing and visiting the Young Living Experience Center and the new offices.

Members can enjoy a simple "tune-up" at NovaVita or spend a rejuvenating time in one of the spa tubs soaking up the micro oil molecules from the hydrosol that is piped underground from the distillery. Imagine soaking in the floral water of palo santo, dorado azul, eucalyptus blue, and the exotic ylang ylang—an indescribable, heavenly experience—a major spa attraction.

Delicious, organic meals are served in the restaurant, and the juice bar is open all day long for those wanting to drink exotic organic juices made from tree- or vine-ripened fruit while relaxing in the peaceful atmosphere of the farm.

For more information, visit novavita.com.ec.

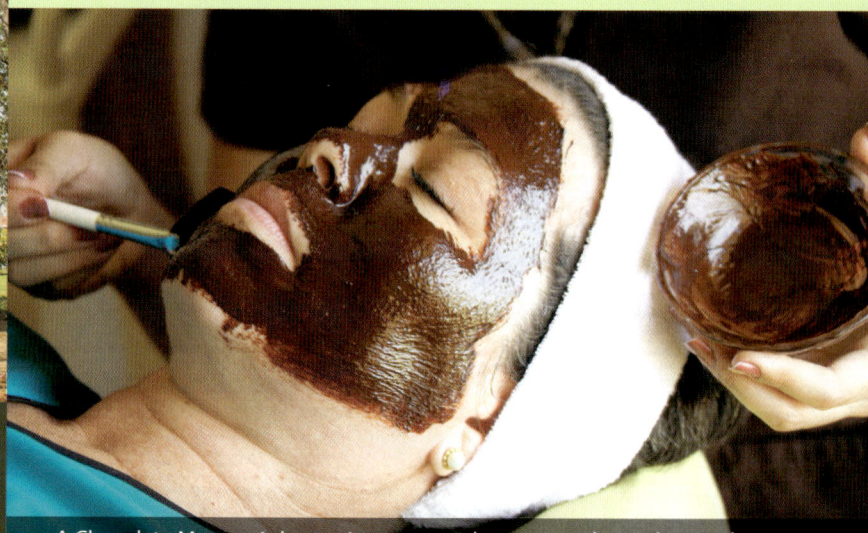

Lupita helps Osias, head chef, prepare exotic dishes for the spa.

The juice bar serves meals for those with spa appointments, and makes fresh tropical fruit drinks all day long for everyone.

The tree house originally started as a small family project with Gary and the boys. However, with Gary's imagination, it grew into a real functioning house with two bedrooms, bathroom, kitchen, living room, electricity, hot and cold water, an elevator, and even wi-fi. Many who come to the spa enjoy the comforts of their adventure high in the jungle treetops.

A Chocolate Masque is becoming more and more popular as the word gets out.

The NovaVita Center, first established in Guayaquil in 2006, was moved in 2011 to the farm, where the spa and rejuvenation activities were added.

Soaking up those micro molecules from the floral water is a rejuvenating spa experience.

Essential Floral Water Spa

Only five farms in the world have essential floral water spas, and all five are on Young Living farms growing these crops:

- Chongon (suburb of Guayaquil), Ecuador: Palo Santo, Dorado Azul, Eucalyptus Blue, Ylang Ylang, Mastrante, Lemongrass, and Vetiver
- St. Maries, Idaho: Lavender, Melissa, and Goldenrod
- Highland Flats, Naples, Idaho: Blue Spruce, Balsam Fir, Western Red Cedar, and Ponderosa Pine
- Fort Nelson, British Columbia, Canada: Black Spruce, White Spruce, Canadian Balsam, Yarrow, and Ledum
- Split, Croatia: Helichrysum, Sage, Juniper, and Bay Laurel

Floral waters vary depending on the plants that are being distilled at the time. Certainly, there will be other distilleries to come in the future, and many more beautiful oils will caress the skin of thousands of excited visitors.

This was the only school close to the farm, which had 42 children attending for all grades with one teacher, who came two or three times a week. There was no electricity, running water, or bathroom facilities, except for a covered hole in the ground outside.

The Young Living Academy

After passing through Chongon and driving toward the jungle down a windy dirt road, Gary saw on the corner of a turn in the road, close to the farm, the local schoolhouse that had been built with cinder blocks in 1959. It had no water, no electricity, and only holes in the walls to let the light in, along with all the road dust and flying insects; and the bathroom was a hole in the ground enclosed with broken and chipped cinder blocks. It was a deplorable sight for the 42 children who attended with one teacher for all grades, who showed up about three times a week; so Gary decided he had to change what looked to be a hopeless future for all of them.

He was told of an elderly couple that might be willing to sell their property located between the old school and the farm only five minutes away. The old gentleman was a bit reluctant; but when Gary questioned him further, he expressed his desire to have a motorcycle. When Gary offered to buy him a motorcycle (that cost $900) and build a small home for him and his wife in Chongon as part of the deal, a big grin came across his face. He happily agreed on the price, and a swampy, mosquito-infested piece of land became the beginning of Gary's vision for these poor village children.

Gary drew the plans, met with the Chongon town council, and construction began. A director was found, teachers were hired, and the doors opened on April 14, 2009. The school was built only for the children attending the dilapidated old school on the corner of the turn in the road just a short distance from the new school. However, more than double that number showed up the first day, and as the word spread, more and more children came. Classrooms were divided and soon plans were made to expand and build onto the existing building. A year later a preschool was built, and then more additions were added for the high school.

Many students spend school time at the farm in an apprentice-type environment. Classrooms were built next to the greenhouse, where they learn about soil amendment, planting, cultivating, and harvesting. They also help in the worm houses to learn how worm casting is used to make liquid fertilizer. Other students go to the mechanic and fabrication shops, the distillery, and the laboratory, as well as visit NovaVita to learn more about essential oil usage.

A very sad environment for children who are so eager to learn.

Gary loved playing Santa Claus for many children who had never received a Christmas present; a special moment for Gary.

D. Gary Young | The World Leader in Essential Oils

Gary designed and drew the architectural plans for the school.

Interestingly enough, the most popular areas of education are the distillery and the analytical research laboratory.

Some students work in the goat dairy or even in the restaurant, where goat cheese and other goat milk products are made. Extra milk goes to the school, and tons of rice are harvested at the farm for the restaurant and the school.

A large number of Young Living members have donated to the school, and the Sponsor a Child Program has been extremely successful. More and more children want to attend the academy that is already "bulging at the seams." Thanks to our generous members, in 2015 we were able to build a high school and a covered outdoor amphitheater/gym, enabling the children to play outside underneath the gym roof while the monsoon rains are soaking the ground.

It is hard to imagine such a modern school in the rural community of Chongon, but now more than 350 children each year have a previously unimaginable opportunity for their future. In March 2016 many Young Living members, parents, teachers, and students celebrated the first graduating class. In April 2019 students, faculty, the community, and many Young Living members were thrilled to celebrate the 10th anniversary of their school and Gary's amazing vision for them.

Music is important at the Academy.

When the Academy opened on April 14, 2009, people were astounded at such a beautiful school in rural Chongon, and now students come from all over Guayaquil to attend. Night classes for literacy are offered for the parents who can neither read nor write, as well as beginning English.

The students learn weights and measures as they pick rosa morta flowers, which gives them greater understanding when they go to the farm for special classes.

D. Gary Young | The World Leader in Essential Oils 173

Academy students were eager to learn about distillation from Gary.

174 D. Gary Young | The World Leader in Essential Oils

Really, cowboy boots?

All the students loved it when Gary played baseball at school, especially Jacob and Josef.

In 2009 the second building was constructed for preschool, kindergarten, and a large music room.

D. Gary Young | The World Leader in Essential Oils

A rewarding moment.

In 2014 construction for a covered amphitheater began and was completed in 2015. The addition for the high school was completed in March 2016, and the Academy celebrated its first high school graduation of 12 students.

The Young Living Academy graduating class of 2017.

The graduating class of 2018 is excited for the future.

The Young Living Academy graduating class of 2019.

High in the Al-Hasik Mountains of Oman, Gary made many exciting discoveries.

THE FRANKINCENSE TRAIL

Because of Gary's desire to study frankincense, he began traveling the world in 1995 to see if the stories of the famous frankincense were true. His first stop was in Oman. He was surprised to learn that *Boswellia sacra*, the resin of the sacred frankincense of Oman, had not been exported for distillation, nor was it being distilled for export at that time. Frankincense resin was a local commodity used by the local people, and only a very small amount had been shipped to the royal courts of Arabia.

Gary traveled to many different countries where it was reported that frankincense trees were growing. He wanted to see and document as many different species as possible, as well as to be able to test and analyze their different compound structures. He flew to Ethiopia and for several days journeyed by air and land from village to village to the farthest northwestern region bordering Sudan, and then to Kenya, crisscrossing the country from border to border in search of different frankincense species.

He traveled to many unpopulated regions, where he found *Boswellia papyrifera*, which is the most commonly sold frankincense resin in the world market and makes up over 75 percent of the frankincense resin sold to brokers worldwide. *B. papyrifera* is extensively used in the perfume industry and for incense. But while *Boswellia serrata*, *B. carterii*, *B. sacra*, and *B. frereana* have 574 scientific studies listed on PubMed, as of 2019 just 29 studies are found on *B. papyrifera*.

Many companies substitute inexpensive *B. papyrifera* oil for *B. carterii* oil and then mix in *B. frereana* and synthetic compounds to make the oil mimic the more expensive oils, enabling them to undercut the market. This is especially true of *B. frereana*, which in its pure state is triple the price of carterii.

Boswellia sacra tree flower.

The prized hojari resin of the *Boswellia sacra* frankincense tree.

D. Gary Young | The World Leader in Essential Oils | 179

In 1995 Gary and I first went to Oman to see the new excavation and archaeological findings of the ancient city of Ubar, about two hours north of Salalah. This rich, opulent city was the last enjoyment and connection to civilization that the camel caravaners had before entering the Rub' al Khali, or Empty Quarter. With great fear of the unknown, they began their treacherous, life-threatening journey through the vast and constantly changing desert of desolation, heat, and wind, from which many never returned.

It was exhilarating for Gary because he knew that thousands of sacks of frankincense and myrrh resins had been carried and deposited, exchanged, and distilled here. Many of those camels had continued on, carrying their precious cargo to such places as Damascus, Gaza, Alexandria, Ein Gedi, China, India, and even to King Solomon in Israel.

While walking through the marketplace and seeing tons of sacks of frankincense resin, especially the beautiful and prized hojari, the highest grade of *Boswellia sacra* (Young Living's Sacred Frankincense), Gary made the statement that one day he would build a distillery in Oman and produce this "holy anointing oil" for Young Living. It seemed impossible, but the dream was there and the vision was intense.

During the next 20 years, Gary made at least 16 trips to Oman because he desired to learn as much as he could and to verify the frankincense species of *Boswellia sacra*. He met Dr. Mahmoud Suhail, a medical doctor who also had a deep interest in frankincense. They developed a friendship in their desire to help people with this ancient oil.

As Dr. Suhail said, "It was not frankincense that made me and Gary friends. It was the man he was—the inspiration and positive energy that surrounded him."

After exploring so many of the Arabian countries, Gary decided to build the distillery in Salalah, Oman, the center of frankincense history. Dr. Suhail and Gary became partners in building a distillery and started with one single distilling chamber in January 2010. Five months later 25 liters of Sacred Frankincense had been distilled and a second extraction chamber added.

Just as Gary said in 1995, he built a distillery in Oman, which became the first large commercial distillery for the extraction of Sacred Frankincense in modern times, perhaps since the time of Christ—a dream come true. The farm was located on the edge of the city and had a deep-water well that provided cooling water for distillation.

Gary and I traveled to Oman in 1995 to see the archaeological excavation of the ancient city of Ubar at the edge of the Empty Quarter, north of Salalah.

Ubar was a very rich city and the last touch with civilization before the caravaners ventured into the Empty Quarter.

Young Living's first distillery and extraction chamber with Gary and Dr. Mahmoud Suhail in Salalah, Oman, 2010.

In 2008 Gary and Dr. Suhail met the Sheik of the Dhofar, who is responsible for the frankincense of the original Hadhramaut region in Oman.

Frances Fuller planted a new frankincense start with other Diamonds on the farm during the Diamond Retreat in Oman.

His Royal Majesty the Sultan of Oman sent his favorite plant, the Desert Rose, to be planted near the entrance. During our Diamond Retreat in April 2013, our members planted frankincense saplings that are strong and growing very well.

The Omani government is actively working to return Oman back to its rightful place as the frankincense capital of the world. The groves of frankincense trees are abundant in the Dhofar region, which is part of the Hadhramaut, spanning Yemen and Oman, once the ancient realm of Queen Sheba.

Dr. Suhail was interested in researching other biblical oils and decided to distill the resin of the biblical sweet myrrh, which is found only in Yemen and Oman. Sweet myrrh has been revered from the beginning of time; is known for its woody, sweet aroma; and has traditionally been used to support the spirit, mind, and body. Sweet myrrh, *Commiphora erythraea*, is commonly known as opopanax. This beautiful oil, little known to the modern world, was made available in Young Living's Exotic Oils Collection in 2014.

D. Gary Young | The World Leader in Essential Oils

Due to continuous growth, new extraction chambers were added for sacred frankincense (*B. sacra*), myrrh (*C. myrrha*), and sweet myrrh (*C. erythraea*).

Oman—Sacred Frankincense Distillery

Essential oils extracted from resins go through a process called hydrodistillation. The extraction chamber has an agitator that rotates back and forth, slowly grinding and stirring the resin in a continuous motion. Approximately one fourth of the chamber is filled with the resin and then filled halfway with water. The agitating action continues while the water is slightly heated to help melt down the resin and release the oil vapor into the water. The vapor is then carried upward with the steam, passes through the condenser, and goes into the separator.

This part of the process is very similar to normal steam distillation. Today the farm has 17 hydrodistillers, and Dr. Suhail is currently designing a new hydrodistiller that will again increase the distillation capacity.

Beautiful Sacred Frankincense.

Establishing a distillery in Oman was a huge accomplishment and started Gary thinking about other possibilities in the world. This led him to explore the opportunity of partnering with others interested in distilling and being part of our production.

As the demand for Sacred Frankincense (*Boswellia sacra*) grew, the need for expansion also grew. Currently, an estimated 15,000 collectors, divided into groups of 10 to 30, gather the resin from the local Shahri people in the Dhofar region for our distillery. Each tree can be harvested only once every 12 months, so that must be carefully monitored as well.

With so much growth and demand, Dr. Suhail soon found that he did not have enough time to work with local resin collectors, run an expanding distilling operation with its many details, and take care of growing trees.

Besides that, as a medical doctor, he wanted to continue his research to document the efficacy and medical protocols using the essential oils of both Frankincense and Myrrh.

He found a larger and newer facility in Muscat, where expansion would be easier, and Muscat, as the capital of Oman, offers more in the areas of testing and collaborative scientific research, as well as greater business support for import, export, and being apprised of the latest government regulations and attitudes.

The original Salalah farm went back to the original owners, who wanted to work with the government to develop more reforestation plantations to strengthen the frankincense industry of their country. Local farmers work several hours daily taking care of the trees, which are doing very well.

The new facility is in a protected area, has nine employees, and can run for 24 hours if necessary. There are 17 extraction chambers that can be in operation at the same time six days a week if needed.

Dr. Suhail utilizes a Grace Preparative Flash Chromatography for separation and also conducts specific gravity tests. All oils are tested using GC/MS and HPLC for boswellic acids through Young Living in Utah.

Bags of resin are stored until distillation.

The frankincense distillery in Muscat, Oman, since December 2016.

This building houses 12 of the 17 total extraction chambers.

①

Distilling Procedure   March 11th/10
        Salalaha Oman

① Clean and prep extraction Chamber
Never use solvents, Hot water only
IF needed a detergent only
Then Steam chamber for 6 hours before
preping to load

② Place water in extraction chamber
40 Liters or until water level is 20 cm
above the resin.

③ ADD Frankincense resin 20 kilos
Clean wood pieces best as possible
before loading.

④ Use agitator for 30 minutes with
heat on Medium to start to liquify

⑤ Close Lid make sure gasket is
secure before placing clamp

⑥ Check pop-off Red Plug in Lid
Make sure it is cleaned after each
cook and then replaced with
snug pressure not hard.

⑦ Attach seperater carefully then
attach water lines

②

⑧ Check Water Freezer Make sure it
is filled the night before cooking.
~~The next day if it is not.~~

⑨ Once hoe's are in place start col
water until condensor and retur
tube are full, Then Turn off
water pump, until condens
water starts to flow. You will
see the water starting to drip
first. Then Turn water pump
on.
    Make sure return tube is in
cold water Tank.

⑩ Very important to watch flame
if it is to low you will lose
the oil.
    If it is to high it will burn th
oil.
    Must listen to flame it will
make a hissing noise

⑪ Make sure big gas Tank if fu
before starting
It Takes 3/4's of a Tank of gas
per 12½ hours.

⑫ Must watch once the water come
over the oil will be 3 to 5 minu
behind

184   D. Gary Young | The World Leader in Essential Oils

D. Gary Young Memorial corner in the Muscat distilling facility.

③

⑬ The oil will fill the seperator every ten minutes and must be removed.

⑭ Watch - when oil drops into bottom of seperator bowl before it reaches the return tube that goes to swan the oil must be taken off by opening red valve on bottom

⑮ Once oil is removed the place in freezer in office to freeze any water in the oil.

⑯ Oil then should be taken out of freezer after 24 hrs poured through filters and placed in bottles for shipping.

⑰ Make sure prop Lot numbers and codes on each bottle before shipping

⑱ It is absolutly important to make all entries in the distillery Log book
Time - Temp - outside temp
Time you start
Time the oil passes over and the volume
Record the oil volume each time you take it off.
Record temp and time when you stop and total oil recovered.

④

⑲ Must check the transfer oil level on the jacket and add oil before starting the next cook. IF the is Not kept Full it will burn the oil and ruin the chamber

The first two distillers that Gary brought to Oman are well-maintained and kept in the Gary Young Memorial corner of the building along with a few other things that hang on the wall.

Dr. Suhail proudly displays Gary's first instructions about distilling that were written on March 11, 2010.

His notes are very detailed, with obvious mechanical understanding of the process. Gary was very adamant about keeping precise records to establish the exactness of resin distilling.

Putting the oil in the freezer is a simple way to separate the residue water from the oil, which has been used for many different oils.

D. Gary Young | The World Leader in Essential Oils 185

The largest known frankincense tree in the world, estimated to be 800 years old, in Salalah, Oman.

Gary teaching the Diamonds among the ruins of Fort Sumharam during the 2013 Diamond Retreat.

Wadi Andhur, an ancient way station on the Frankincense Trail, which Gary discovered in 2009, where distilling vats are still identifiable.

Gary seemed to have a knowing or a sense about things; and when he was told something didn't exist, it wasn't there, it couldn't be done, it was just a legend, he became more determined. He had read about Wadi Andhur, and for 16 years every time he returned to Arabia, he looked for the ruins, without success. He was told by archaeologists at the historical museum that a way station did not exist, but he continued to search in different areas, with a feeling that he would find it if he kept looking.

In 2009, while exploring in the Al-Hasik Mountains, a feeling of tremendous anticipation grew as he climbed upward. He knew there had to be a way station somewhere in the mountains for the caravans traveling through to Ubar because the distance was so far. Finally, as he reached the high plateau, the way station emerged from the rocks, hidden from the view of anyone passing below.

Gary found this stone with an engraving of a flying serpent, carved by protectors of the frankincense trees to frighten resin poachers away. This very heavy stone is approximately 2,000 years old.

D. Gary Young | The World Leader in Essential Oils

A local harvester cuts the tree, so the resin can flow.

John Whetten, with his camera, and Karen Boren, researcher and technical writer, are having fun during the filming of the frankincense documentary.

Gary took this picture of Marco Gentille and John Whetten in the brokerage house in Aden, Yemen, from where tons of resin are shipped all over the world.

Yemen—Going into the "Forbidden Zone"

Hundreds of years ago, Queen Sheba ruled the Hadhramaut, located in modern-day Yemen, which is rich with the history of frankincense and myrrh. Gary was fascinated with Queen Sheba and this ancient civilization, which was the center of the land of frankincense through which the caravans passed.

Gary was determined to see the remains of this ancient civilization because he wanted to see and document the different frankincense and myrrh species still growing in the Hadhramaut, as well as in the surrounding countries, while traveling the ancient frankincense caravan trail from Oman through Yemen, Saudi Arabia, Jordan, and Israel.

In 2009 Gary flew to Sana'a, the capital of Yemen, to continue his research and hopefully obtain permission to travel to Shabwah, a major trade center of the ancient caravans. Unfortunately, Shabwah is in the heart of what is called the "Forbidden Zone," inaccessible to even most of the people of Yemen, let alone to any foreigner, especially an American.

While waiting, Gary explored Aden and visited many resin brokers, who were a wealth of information. He learned that only very small amounts of frankincense and myrrh resins are harvested in Yemen, and most of the resin that Yemen exports is *Boswellia papyrifera*, which is imported from Ethiopia and then shipped to other places in the world. He saw different categories and qualities of resin and how they were mixed to make the different grades very convoluted in their distinction.

Specific grades went to China and other areas of the world, but the mixed variety and lower quality were shipped to America because the broker said that Americans didn't know the difference, a sad commentary for most American brokers and buyers.

The sweet myrrh tree (*Commiphora erythraea*) on the island of Socotra.

Myrrh tree (*Commiphora myrrha*) in Yemen.

The *Boswellia elongata* tree that grows on Yemen's Socotra Island.

The minister of antiquities had been assigned to travel with Gary to help facilitate his needs while traveling in the country. Gary told the minister that he wanted to go to Shabwah. The minister was very surprised by Gary's request and told him it was impossible because Shabwah is in the middle of terrorist territory and is very dangerous. However, Gary was determined and insisted that the minister try to get permission.

Letters, conversations, and persistence continued for about two weeks, finally resulting in the permit he wanted. Dressed in native attire and with his heavy, black beard, he looked like a native of Yemen. The quiet excitement mounted as the minister picked him up at the hotel in Atac, and the journey began.

After three hours of driving, Gary entered Shabwah, the first outsider in 42 years. It was a glorious experience to see the caravan gateway through which the camels passed into Shabwah's taxation area. In those days, all caravaners had to pay 25 percent of the value of their goods to be able to continue on their journey. To avoid taxation meant death, and Queen Sheba was unmerciful.

The minister of antiquities said it was impossible to go to Shabwah; however, Gary was persistent and kept sending the minister back to the government with different reasons for giving him the permit.

After receiving his permit, Gary traveled with a military escort into the interior of Yemen to the "Forbidden Zone." The ancient city of Shabwah, which was the home of Queen Sheba, can be seen in the background to the left.

Ruins of the ancient city of Shabwah in today's "Forbidden Zone" in the heart of Yemen.

Dwellings of Shabwah's ancient inhabitants.

A 3,000-year-old incense burner from Shabwah was gifted to Gary by the minister of antiquities.

Gary is standing near the ancient gateway of Shabwah through which caravaners traveled that led to the taxation way station.

Ruins of the storage vaults, distillation vats, and the queen's palace were very identifiable. While digging down on the outside foundation of one of the buildings, Gary found an old resin burner, which the minister said was about 3,000 years old. As Gary handed it to the minister, the minister gifted it back to Gary, knowing of Gary's great love for the history of his country.

It was a glorious experience filled with so many unknowns and much danger, but Gary felt very blessed to be able to see this ancient city. Returning to Sana'a, he continued on his journey to the Island of Socotra, where he photographed and documented another seven species of frankincense.

His travels were a saga of many dangerous situations, unusual solutions, and determination. Some of Gary's personal experiences were so dramatic that he was compelled to write them in his journal that evolved into his historical novel, *The One Gift*, which depicts life on the camel caravans and the commanders who led them. It is an adventure of intrigue, excitement, romance, tragedy, and the portrayal of indomitable perseverance.

This novel is truly a wonderful insight into life, death, and amazing accomplishments against all odds in this historical time period. During June 2014 it was listed as No. 1 on the Amazon best seller list. Visit: TheOneGiftBook.com

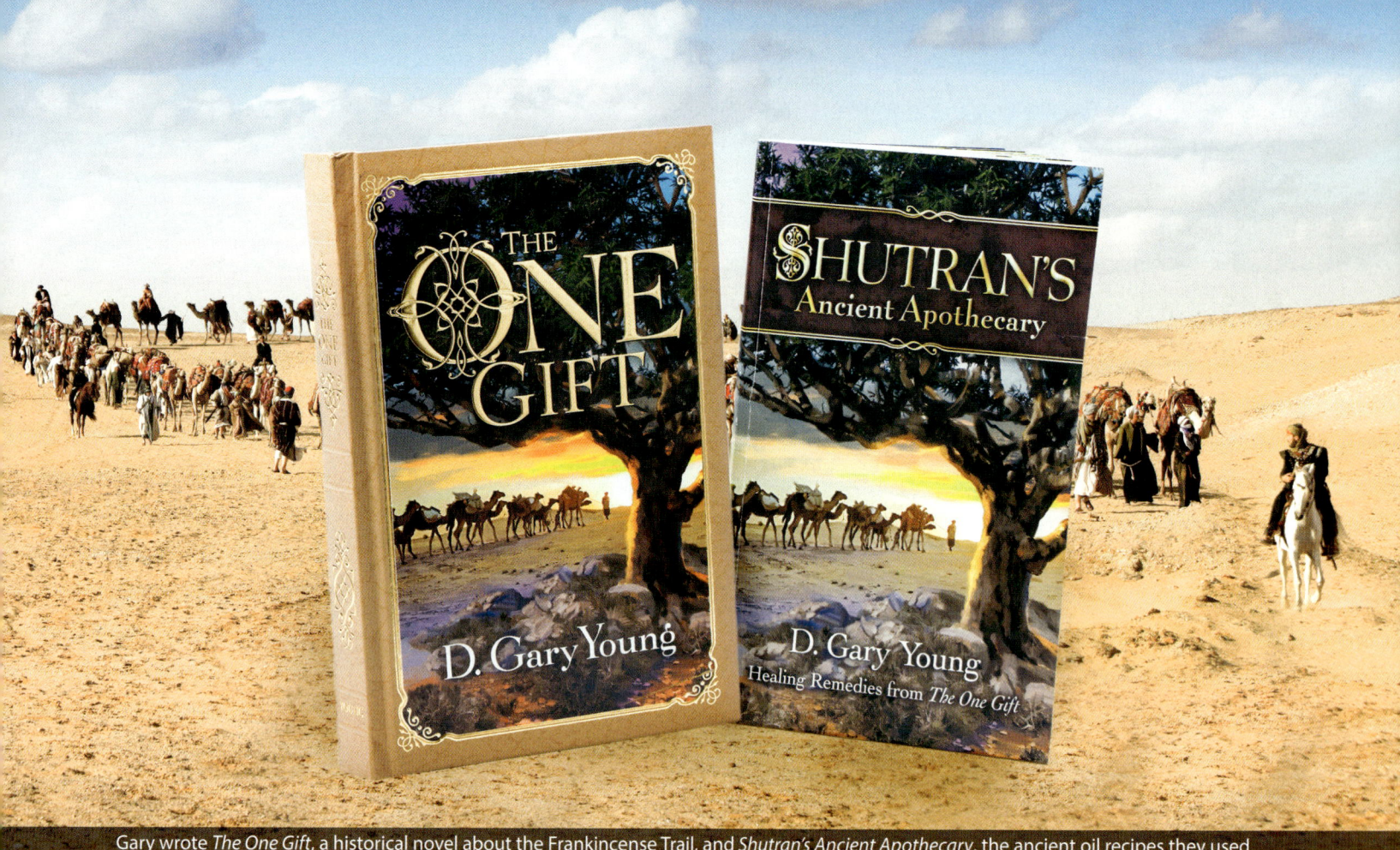

Gary wrote *The One Gift*, a historical novel about the Frankincense Trail, and *Shutran's Ancient Apothecary*, the ancient oil recipes they used.

The talk around the fire at night was a time for stories of desert marauders and heroic tales of adventures of the caravan on the Frankincense Trail.

The Rub' al Khali, or Empty Quarter, is the foreboding desert of intense sun, freezing nights, wind, endless sand, and dangers of the unknown.

Shutran, the caravan commander in Gary's novel, *The One Gift*, was brought to life during the filming of the frankincense trail documentary, 2010.

About 100 Young Living members and employees filmed the frankincense documentary with Gary.

D. Gary Young | The World Leader in Essential Oils

Caravaners arrived in Petra and carried the resin sacks into the Treasury House.

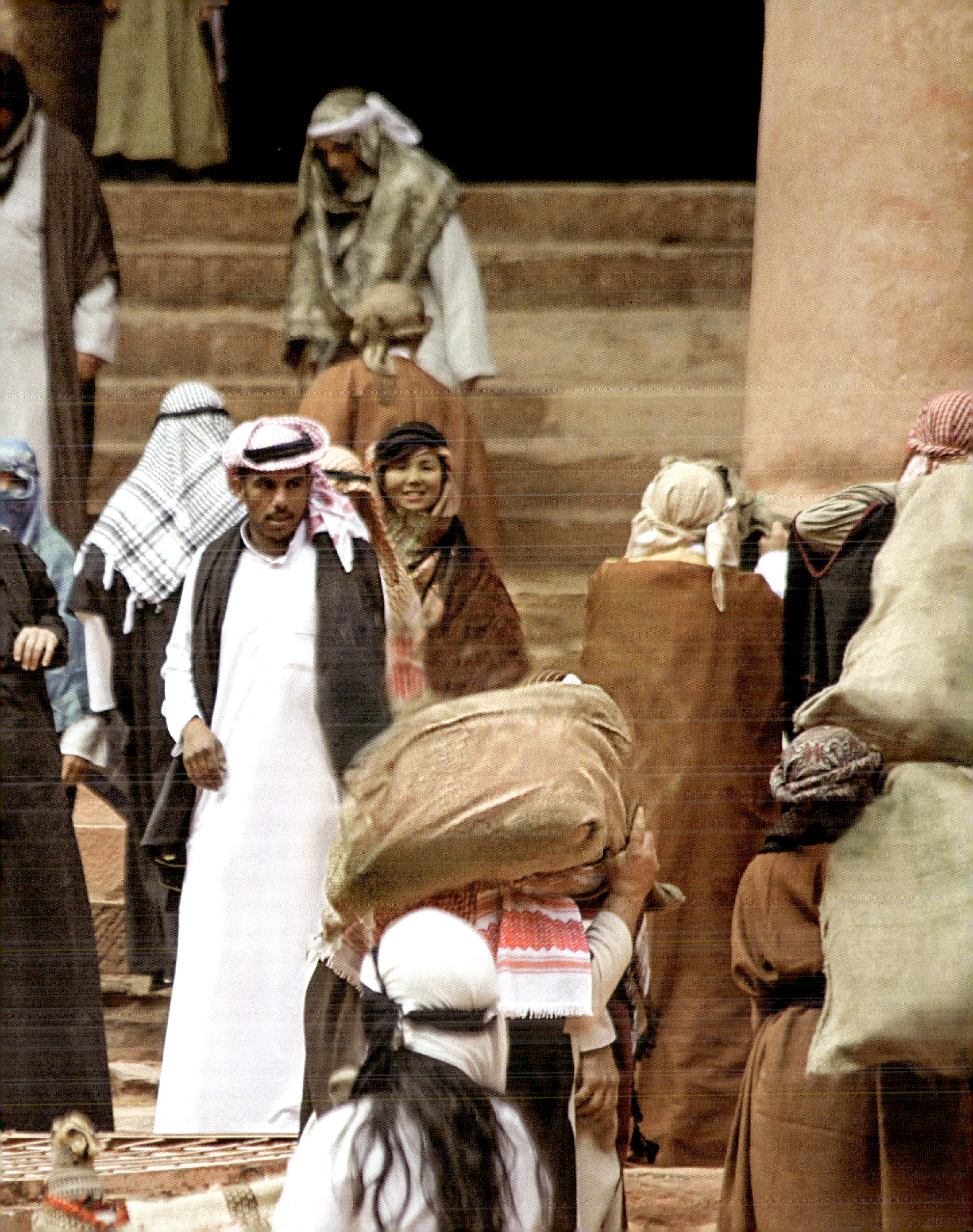

GARY'S JOURNEY

THE HORN OF AFRICA

The owner of Jubba Airways helped Gary get his visa to Somalia as well as the domestic flights to Hargeysa and Bosaso and then his return to Nairobi.

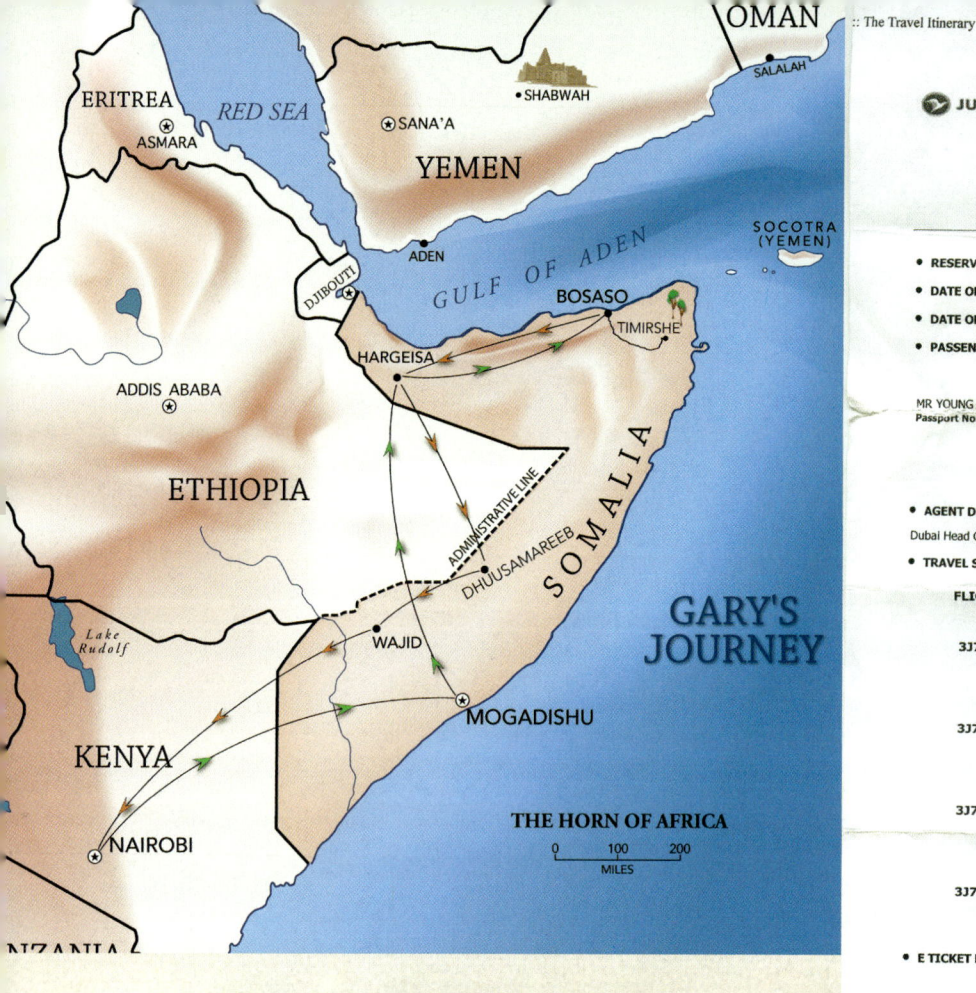

JUBBA AIRWAYS
RESERVATION CONFIRMED

- RESERVATION NUMBER (PNR): 10478141
- DATE OF BOOKING: 31 Oct 2013
- DATE OF ISSUE: 31 Oct 2013
- PASSENGER DETAILS

Passenger Name(s)	Fare	Charges	Paid Amount	Balance
MR YOUNG DON GRAY	1000.00 USD	0.00 USD	1000.00 USD	0.00 USD
Passport No. -				
TOTAL IN USD	1000	0.00	1000	0.00
TOTAL IN			630.00 USD + 1358.00 AED	0.00 AED

- AGENT DETAILS
Dubai Head Office (JBW) +971 4 2226869 reservations@jubbaairways.com

- TRAVEL SEGMENTS

FLIGHT	ORIGIN / DESTINATION	DEPARTURE / ARRIVAL	CHECK-IN FROM	CLASS	STATUS
3J708	Nairobi - Hargeisa	Fri, 01 Nov 2013 07:00 / Fri, 01 Nov 2013 11:10	Fri, 01 Nov 2013 04:00	Business Class C	OK
3J705	Hargeisa - Bossaso	Sat, 02 Nov 2013 09:30 / Sat, 02 Nov 2013 11:00	Sat, 02 Nov 2013 06:30	Economy Class Y	OK
3J706	Bossaso - Hargeisa	Fri, 08 Nov 2013 08:30 / Fri, 08 Nov 2013 10:00	Fri, 08 Nov 2013 05:30	Economy Class Y	OK
3J707	Hargeisa - Nairobi	Sat, 09 Nov 2013 09:30 / Sat, 09 Nov 2013 16:00	Sat, 09 Nov 2013 06:30	Business Class C	OK

- E TICKET DETAILS

Passenger Name(s)	Segment	Flight	E TICKET NUMBER
MR YOUNG DON GRAY	NBO/MGQ/HGA	3J708	5354210563036/1
	HGA/BSA	3J705	5354210563036/2

DAWLAD.PL EE SOOMAALIYA.
WASAARADDA AMNIGA & DDR
(Office of minister)

PUNTLAND STATE OF SOMALIA.
Ministry of Security & DDR.

Ref: WW/A/DDR/346/13   2/11/13
TO:- Immigration Department   BOSASO.

Sub.;- Entry Visa Permission

The Ministry of Security and DDR Has authorized an Entry Visa for the Fallowing persons that requested to Visa in puntland Abdishakur Miree

Name	Nationality	Passport
1-Don Gary Young	USA	039704835

Therefore the Immigration offices of the airports & ports are requested to facilitate His/her requirements

This visa is permitted according to the Law And Valid for One Moth

Abdirizak Hared Ismacial
Deputy Ministry Of Security & DDR

JUBBA Airways
Name: Young Don Gray
From: BSA
To: HGA
Flight:
Class:
Date: 8-Nov-13
Gate / Board Time / Seat No.

ECONOMY CLASS

198 D. Gary Young | The World Leader in Essential Oils

Somalia—A Trip Into the Unknown

In August 2013 Gary had become curious about *Boswellia frereana* frankincense because of its historical prominence and all the stories told about it by another essential oil company that had been claiming for six years that frereana grew exclusively in Oman. Having spent so much time in Oman, Gary knew that *Boswellia frereana* did not and never had grown in the geographical area of Oman. The other company was unknown to any official in Oman, and its claims were upsetting to His Majesty the Sultan of Oman.

So Gary decided to distill the frereana resin to analyze the compounds in the oil and determine possible uses. The compounds found supported its ancient aromatic use as a perfume, which has carried over into present times. The frereana resin is also softer than carterii or sacra, making it more desirable for chewing, which is very common in the Arabian countries.

Boswellia frereana essential oil is an interesting comparison to the oils of *Boswellia carterii* (Frankincense) from Somalia and *Boswellia sacra* (Sacred Frankincense) from Oman. Gary was very curious and since he was considering putting Frereana Frankincense essential oil into the Young Living inventory, he was more determined to see the trees for himself.

There was so much mystery associated with this oil, and the information seemed to come from one person writing about what another person wrote. Gary wanted to see and know the truth for himself. He had been trying for eight years to go to Somalia and had flown to Nairobi several times expecting to go see the trees, but there was always a roadblock—too dangerous, terrorist attacks, uprising, state of anarchy, chaos, turmoil, kidnapping risk, too difficult to get to the trees, or just too far away—and so the stories came and went.

In October of 2013, while giving a Young Living presentation in Dallas, Texas, Gary met a former U.S. Special Forces military officer, who said he personally knew the president of the largest clan in Somalia, who he knew would help, opening up a new opportunity for Gary to make that journey.

A week later Gary flew to Nairobi, where he was met by the clan president, who was currently living in Nairobi. He helped Gary pass quickly through Nairobi immigrations and customs, where an unknown adventure was about to begin.

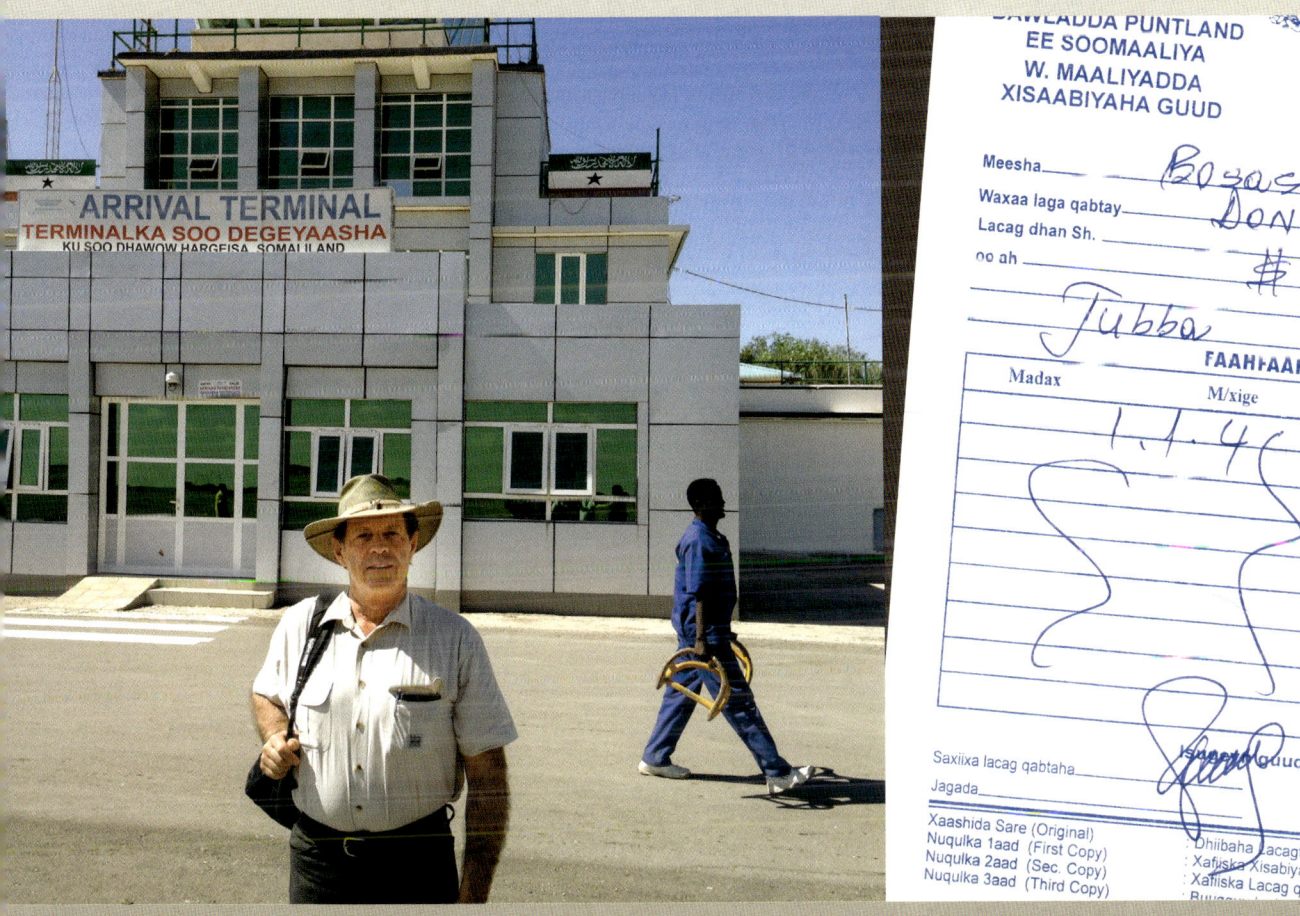

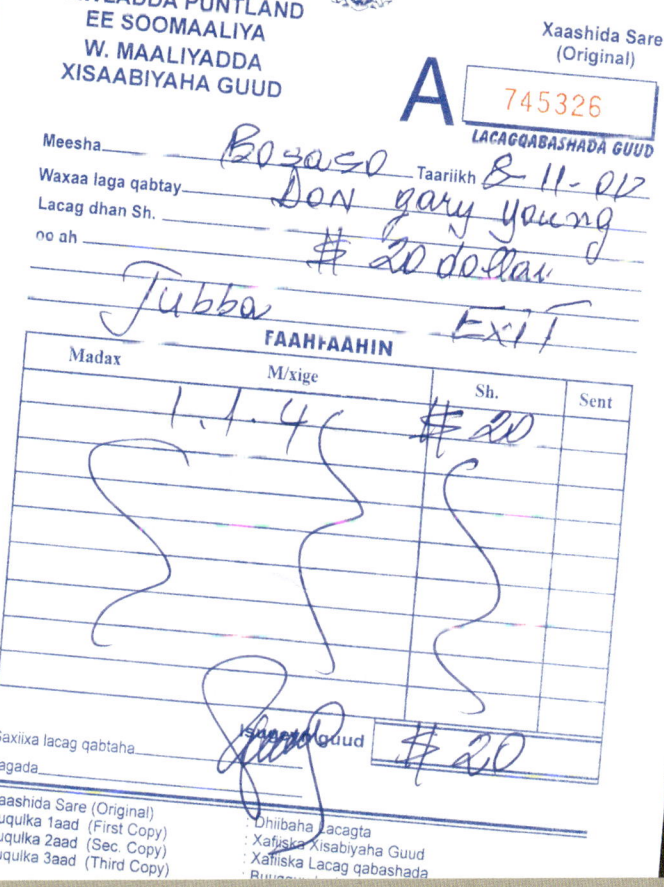

"A Fascinating, but Unnerving Adventure" in Gary's own words:

"The clan president was very helpful and answered many of my questions as he drove me to the hotel. The next morning he took me to meet the president of Jubba Airways, who was born in Somalia and said he could help me with my travels in his country. When I told them what I wanted to do, they said that it might take a few days to get the visa for Somalia; but I said that didn't matter to me if, indeed, I really would be able to fly there. I had made it this far, so I was not going to turn back and would wait as long as it took.

"But to my surprise, they called that evening and said they would be able to get my visa the next day. The night seemed long; but when morning came, we drove to the immigration office. With my passport stamped, the president drove me to the airport and said that there would be someone waiting for me when I arrived.

"When I boarded, I felt a mixture of excitement and anxiety, which seemed to stifle my breathing for a moment; but with a little self-talk, I was able to calm down; and an hour and a half later, we landed in Mogadishu, the capital.

"I sat quietly on the plane while the cleaning crew prepared for the next flight to Hargeysa (also spelled Hargeisa). Some minutes later an airport security officer boarded the plane; and when he saw me, he stared at me with a very angry look. He made a call on his radio and speaking in English said there was one American on the flight. I was uneasy and felt the hair on the back of my neck stand up, realizing that I had no place to which I could retreat for a defensive position. I felt very vulnerable and started asking myself what I was doing here.

"I turned my head to look out the window, wanting to deflect his energy. As soon as he left the plane, the other passengers started boarding; and we were soon in the air again. The flight to Hargeysa was about two hours sitting in not the greatest comfort, but I was getting closer to my goal. When I got off the plane, two Jubba Airways employees were waiting for me and quickly walked me through customs and then helped me change some money so that I could go to the market to buy some frankincense resin and get back to the hotel before dark.

"They said they would be back at 8 a.m. to pick me up; however, my departure was delayed a couple of times, so the driver didn't pick me up until 1 p.m. I was sitting in the VIP lounge at the airport waiting to board when a security officer came through and asked to see my visa. He rejected the one to Hargeysa and said I had to have a separate visa for Bosaso (also Boosaaso). I didn't know I needed two different visas for the same country. Feeling dejected, I walked back to the waiting room, wondering what I should do.

"To my amazement, the same employees who had helped me get this far came to my rescue. They led me through a side door out to the plane and told me just to get on board. I was a bit shocked when I saw the plane with several bullet holes in the fuselage that had been patched with a black caulking compound that looked relatively fresh. This plane definitely belonged in a bone yard; it wasn't even good enough for a museum.

"When the flight crew lowered the stairs, they fell off and hit the ground. I wanted to laugh as I helped them reposition the stairs. As I entered the plane, I knew I had made a mistake. I really began to question my senses and wondered why I was doing this to myself. The inside of the plane was far worse in appearance than the outside.

"Was a simple grove of trees really worth the price I was paying? If I died, would this information really mean anything to anyone? How would Mary and the boys feel? I felt my stomach come up in my throat and thought I was going to lose my almost-digested breakfast all over the plane. I took a deep breath to calm myself.

The patched bullet holes in the airplane in which Gary flew to Bosaso.

"The pilot came and started the engines, and the plane shook like it had tremors as it taxied to the runway. As the plane took off, all my thoughts went to my home and family. I felt I was drowning in overwhelming emotion as hot tears moistened my cheeks. I began mentally talking to myself and thanking God for my protection and that of my family so far away. Gradually, a feeling of peace and calming came over me.

"As we started the descent into the emptiness of the desert of the remote port city of Bosaso, I again began to question the purpose of coming to Somalia. I felt relief as the wheels touched down, skidding through the dirt and creating a huge dust storm; but I didn't care—I was on the ground. I could feel the tension and oppression in the air with soldiers everywhere. I knew there were only two flights a week out of here, which made me feel trapped like being held hostage.

"I was greeted very kindly by a gentleman who spoke perfect English, which didn't seem to fit in with the culture; but nevertheless, I was very grateful. He escorted me outside where three vans were waiting with soldiers who were there to guard and protect me. It was a strange feeling, making me wonder if something unusual was going to happen. I was taken to an enclosed compound that was locked down at night. I slept on a mattress on cold concrete equal to the cold water, but I was not one to complain. I surmised they were really just trying to take good care of me.

"He told me that I was the first foreigner in a very long time to come there and that everyone knew about the 'high profile American' who had just arrived. This gentleman was the president of a smaller clan of native people, but they were the ones who lived near the groves and harvested the resins. When I told him that I had come to see the frankincense trees and collect some resin to take back for research and identification, he quickly told me that he could get resin for me but that it was impossible to go to the groves.

"The groves were 400 kilometers inland to the mountains, the dirt roads were horrible, in some places were completely washed out, and traveling would take several hours with extreme risk. I told him that I didn't come this far to not see the trees; and if the vehicles could go there, the time and risk were not a deterrent.

"Seeing my determination, he reluctantly agreed but said we had to leave in the middle of the night so that no one would see us. For some reason, he said we would have to wait

The young girls were so surprised to receive these wonderful books from the American stranger.

a day or so to get everything ready; so I spent the waiting time walking through the market buying resins and watching the women clean and separate the frankincense "tears" by size and color for quality grading.

Boswellia carterii has three grades, but *Boswellia frereana* has five grades, since it comes in much larger pieces of resin. The lady who interpreted for me told me that the women who have been doing the cleaning for many years looked healthier and happier than those in the village who just worked in the shops. It was most interesting.

"I bought pencils and notebooks for the children in one of the local schools that I had asked to visit. The school was dilapidated and had little to offer. My meager gifts seemed like such a small token, but they were so happy and grateful.

"It was pitch-black when we left in the middle of the night. It seemed eerie as we drove in silence down this very bumpy road, while the driver constantly looked for road signs along the way that were obscured and in many places completely washed out. After a miserable 10 hours, we could see the village on the horizon with the light of the dawn.

Stopping at a small village on the way to Timirshe to stretch their legs, the guards were close by and always watching for any unusual activity.

In some places finding the road was guesswork.

It was amazing to see a *Commiphora gileadensis* (Balm of Gilead) tree growing next to the frankincense trees.

Gary talked with the president of the clan that guards the frankincense trees and harvests the resins.

"The village people greeted us with a big fanfare, welcoming the first foreigner they had ever seen. They were kind and loving and offered what little refreshment they had. I enjoyed our short visit, but I was anxious to get to the trees.

"I had been telling everyone about why I had developed my frankincense chewing gum; and here I was, in the home of the *Boswellia frereana* trees. It seemed that everyone I met, since landing in Bosaso, was chewing gum—frankincense gum. It was most fascinating and confirmed some of my feelings about the resin.

"The groves were 5 or 6 kilometers beyond the village, and I didn't want to wait any longer. We drove up a 300-yard-wide wadi (dry riverbed) where *Boswellia carterii* trees were growing on the rocky side hills, and I gathered a little resin from a few trees that had been cut earlier. I was most surprised to see a *Commiphora gileadensis* tree (Balm of Gilead) growing right next to the frankincense.

The villagers of Timirshe had never seen a foreigner before, but they were very receptive and excited to meet Gary.

Boswellia carterii (left) grows out of the soil, while *Boswellia frereana* (right) grows out of the rocks. Yet both trees often grow near each other.

Boswellia carterii (center) can be found growing among the *Commiphora* shrubs from the myrrh family.

3

Different Species of Frankincense

All three essential oils have different chemical profiles with some similar uses and yet very different applications. They may be used for flavoring, perfume and cosmetics, spiritual enlightenment and awareness, and physical support and strengthening. One interesting and not well-known fact is that they all seem to use the resin as chewing gum. Amazingly, these people have fewer dental problems, and older people seem to have all their teeth that are strong and healthy.

All the oils are desirable and have usage for those who understand the value of pure Frankincense. Here you can compare the GC analysis of the most prominent Frankincense oils and their resins.

Boswellia sacra

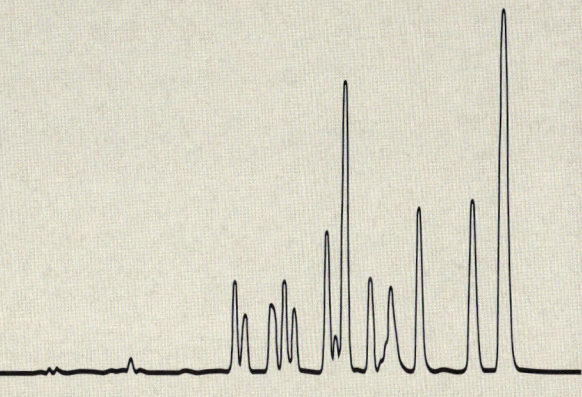

Boswellia sacra resin GC analysis

Boswellia carterii

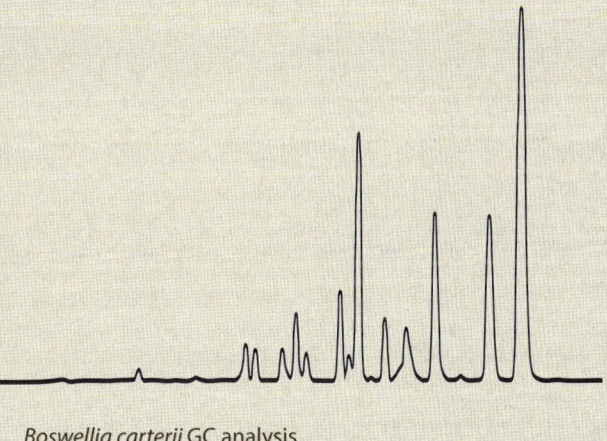

Boswellia carterii GC analysis

Boswellia frereana

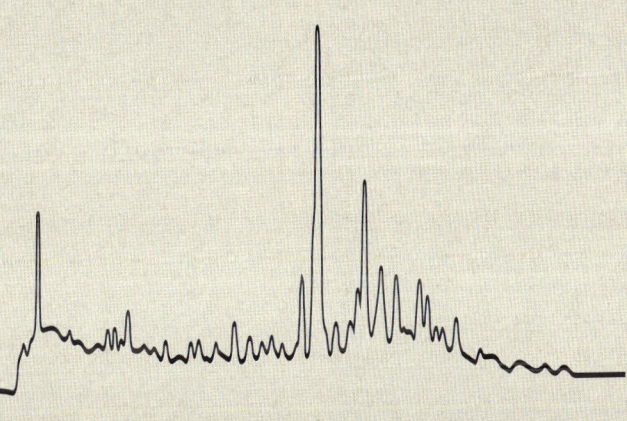

Boswellia frereana GC analysis

D. Gary Young | The World Leader in Essential Oils

Boswellia sacra resin and tree.

The largest *B. sacra* tree growing in Oman.

Boswellia carterii resin and tree.

B. carterii is thin and compressed.

Boswellia frereana resin and tree.

B. frereana is more trunk and bark with fewer branches and flowers.

The Truth About Boswellia Frereana

"There is so much conflicting information about where the two species of frankincense trees grow, and now I was seeing it for myself. It was extremely interesting to see that carterii trees grow out of the soil, and frereana trees grow out of the rocks; and yet they grow practically side-by-side, usually about 20 feet apart.

"I learned that frereana resin is difficult to gather and takes a long time because it usually takes 12 bark cuttings for the resin to really start to run, and then it is so voluminous that it runs down the entire length of the trunk. The resin is luminescent with white stripes that are exquisite. It takes about eight months to harvest because the resin pieces are so big, which is why pure frereana commands a much higher price than the carterii and myrrh resins. Frereana can be harvested only once a year, and in Somalia, only every other year.

"I collected several pounds of frereana and carterii resins to bring home, so I could distill and analyze them both to see the compound ratios in the pure oils, a bit of historical research. I also brought home different grades of carterii and frereana, so I could distill them and see the difference. I asked many questions and enjoyed the stories about the history and customs of those whose families had been the harvesters and guardians of the frankincense trees for hundreds of years.

"I thought about how I became fascinated with the exquisite, white hojari resin, the sacred frankincense of Oman, when I first walked through the marketplace in Salalah. After all my travels, it was curious to me that *B. sacra* grows mostly in Oman and Yemen, but no *B. frereana* grows anywhere in Southern Arabia. Naturally, only Mother Nature can explain that. It seems strange, because we know that anciently, carterii and sacra grew in the area known as the Hadhramaut, which was under the control of Queen Sheba. *B. carterii* and *B. frereana* today grow in other areas that are now different countries. *B. sacra* grows mostly within the borders of Oman and Yemen, and the Omani hojari is unique and certainly difficult for others to acquire.

Climbing trees and taking pictures was a passion of Gary's.

Gary chewing *Boswellia frereana* resin, typical of the local people who generally maintain good dental health into old age.

The most prized *Boswellia sacra* trees grow in Oman and small, isolated areas of Yemen. The hojari resin was highly prized in ancient times, and some historians believe that this was the frankincense taken to the Christ Child. Its resin is delicately formed and is exquisitely white and almost transparent.

Boswellia frereana grows out of rocks.

"But now I had achieved my goal, and I could talk and write about *B. frereana* from my own experience, my own knowing. I had walked through the groves, touched the trees, felt the resin as it ran from the trees, talked with the harvesters—those who gather the resins—and collected a sufficient amount—about 50 pounds—of resin and was ready to go home. But getting out of Somalia caused me a bit of uneasiness, wondering if going out would be as difficult as coming in had been for me.

"The journey back was full of unusual surprises: men with weapons who followed me in disguise in the market in Hargeysa from whom I hid, a shootout as I entered the airport that could have resulted in several drastic things, and even a battle with Kenya immigration officials who were forcing vaccinations on foreigners coming from Somalia.

"The vaccinations seemed to be a moneymaker for those in authority, and I believe that I was the only passenger who won that battle, even though it caused me to miss my flight and endure the frustration of having to spend more time in Nairobi.

"But when the wheels finally lifted off for the flight to Paris and then home, a sense of freedom came over me. My nine days in Somalia and three days getting out of Nairobi was a once-in-a-lifetime adventure, one that I didn't need a second time. My discoveries were priceless and I am forever grateful for my experience and for my safe return."

Gary was so enthusiastic about his trip, the discoveries he made, and the many possibilities of helping the people he met there that he wanted to build a frankincense distillery in Somaliland. However, the challenges were complex, many roadblocks kept surfacing, and it was hard to make progress. Cultural differences, the instability of the country, and difficulty in communicating made it a huge challenge to understand ideas and plans that were suggested.

Gary made the comment, "There is so much need everywhere I go that I would have to live more than a thousand lifetimes to do the work that is needed." He was, however, successful in being able to provide the money to build a school for the village children.

Through many unusual circumstances, Gary had an uncanny ability to meet the right people to secure our frankincense oil. We signed an agreement with this Somalia-based company to purchase *Boswellia carterii* resin that was to be sent to our partner distilleries.

This multigenerational, family-owned frankincense farm is one of the largest resin collectors and exporters of frankincense and comply with the legal requirements regarding the harvesting and exporting of frankincense resin. They are a perfect business partner, as they align with our mission of seeing oils in every home and giving back to their communities, which includes paying school fees for the children of their workers and supplying clean water, food, medicine, and a vehicle for the village in case of emergencies.

Gary was always persistent in finding solutions and building relationships, which resulted in our current supply chain. Because of our partner distilleries in Spain and Turkey, our members now have the opportunity to see the frankincense resin distilled.

The harvest in the winter is often a challenge, but the chips yield the greatest volume of oil.

Gary pulled the trailers loaded with chips 125 miles from the Highland Flats farm to be distilled in St. Maries, regardless of the weather conditions.

THE HIGHLAND FLATS TREE FARM AND DISTILLERY

Gary and I came across a field of balsam fir trees in 1998 in northern Idaho near Naples, close to Bonners Ferry on the Canadian border, while we were driving around looking for fields of wild tansy that he could cut and truck back to St. Maries for distillation. On the edge of a Christmas tree farm, he noticed a pile of trees that apparently was going to be burned. He stopped abruptly and ran to the field to investigate. He learned that many farmers were bulldozing and burning the overgrown Christmas trees because the demand was diminishing every year, and the trees had grown too big to be sold. In addition, the spruce weevil had attacked the trees, making them impossible to sell even for nursery stock.

Gary asked if he could "take the trees in exchange for clearing their land so that it would be usable for other crops." They eagerly agreed because it was costing them between $400 and $600 per acre to have them cleared and burned. The farmer thought it strange and perhaps even a little crazy, but he was happy to let someone else take them away. It was a win-win for both.

After the first distillation of the balsam trees, there was no doubt that he had made a remarkable discovery and that he had to bring this oil to Young Living.

That began the new operation of cutting and chipping trees for distilling. It was an immense project with a complex learning curve. Determining the best way to distill to get the most oil out of the trees was challenging, but exciting. The difficulty was chipping the trees, getting the chips into the trucks, and then getting them hauled to St. Maries. It would have been so easy to harvest the trees in the summer, but the trees didn't yield as much oil when the temperatures were warm.

Conifer trees send the oil up their branches to protect themselves from freezing in the cold—a bit like antifreeze. When the temperatures are warm, the oil goes back into the roots because it is not needed for the trees' protection. So what did Gary discover? "The colder the temperature, the better the oil."

The first harvest began in early 1998 when winter temperatures dropped to -25°F for anywhere from two to five days, and was very dry. Then it would start raining when it warmed up to 30°F. Out in "the bush" miles away from food and protection from the harsh conditions, cutting and chipping the trees was miserable. The chipper that worked well for tansy wasn't strong enough. Yes, for little trees, but most of the trees were too big and overgrown for their purpose.

At lunchtime Gary and the crew would drive into Bonners Ferry to buy some food and then hurry to the local self-service laundromat to dry their heavy winter clothing while they ate, a blessing that probably only they could appreciate.

The first camp trailer—a welcome lunchroom out of the cold wind and blowing snow.

The camp takes form as the walls go up while Anna-Maya Powell and Kathleen Gardner figure out how to make lunch. Their husbands, Jim and David, worked long hours helping Gary build the farm in the early years of winter harvest.

These are the first wall tents, where members ate lunch and dinner at the tree farm. The firewood was stacked in the left tent, the middle tent was used for the kitchen and the dining room, and the right tent had a potbelly stove and a porta potty.

If there were any mechanical problems, someone had to drive 20 minutes to Bonners Ferry, 30 minutes to Sandpoint, 1½ hours to Coeur d'Alene, or 2½ hours to Spokane, one way. The snow and ice on the roads made traveling slow and dangerous; and the process of finding replacement parts, getting back before dark, and fixing the equipment out in the field with the blinding snow and cutting wind was very difficult.

But the oil was exquisite in smell and brought an excitement that drove Gary to find its secrets. What could this oil do for mankind? In 1999, 120 acres were purchased through a land auction, and a new Young Living farm was established.

A New Logging Camp

The next year a warming trailer and a larger chipper were a big improvement, but not enough. Many Young Living members came to help with the harvest, which was a tremendous help; but staying in the hotel in Sandpoint was not an efficient solution for the needs at the farm.

The idea of a logging camp began swirling in Gary's mind, and the next year a tent went up for a makeshift kitchen to serve lunch, and "honey buckets" were stationed nearby to meet everybody's needs, if they didn't mind baring their bottoms to a freezing cold seat.

The floor in the dining room tent was very close to the frozen ground, making it hard to get their feet warm. During lunch, everyone hoped their gloves would dry out; however, if the gloves and coats were hung too close to the stove, they would melt. But complaining wasn't an issue. Everyone was grateful for the new improvements.

But all this work wasn't just for balsam fir. Gary found different trees in the area that he also wanted to distill, including cedar, tamarack, pine, and for the first time, blue spruce, with its amazing properties. Gary felt a lot of excitement, but it was a huge challenge with so many unexpected problems. However, he was determined and knew there was an unseen force pushing him that was greater than the problems that would come—and he was ready.

Upgrading from a regular track-hoe bucket to a grapple made loading trees into the chipper much faster and safer.

When everything goes well, it takes about 45 minutes to an hour to fill a semi-trailer.

Hot meals were fabulous and the wood stove warmed everyone's hands, but the floor was not heated, and many feet were still VERY cold.

Gary's "Taj Mahal" logging camp, as it became known, began to expand.

Everyone loved Marci King and the wonderful meals she made on the wood-burning stove.

The rural environment of the logging camp is peaceful and uplifting and free from the noise of the busy city.

The hot tubs with essential oils and the sauna are very popular places, and the cabins are quiet, comfortable, and warm.

The learning atmosphere at camp is fun and stimulating.

D. Gary Young | The World Leader in Essential Oils

The Unstoppable Mustang Man

Going back to his boyhood experiences of logging with horses, Gary decided to haul some of his horses from the Mona farm up to the tree farm to log the ravines and areas where farmers just wanted their trees thinned, which wasn't possible to do with machines. This brought even greater excitement as Gary gave members the opportunity to either drive a team skidding the logs or the cleanup wagon that carried the broken-off branches to the chipper.

As a boy growing up on the farm logging with his father, Gary learned to drive horses first, then small trucks, and then operate equipment. These experiences served him well when he was homesteading in northern British Columbia, Canada, logging and ranching for a living. Then after his accident, looking for a way to support his family, he convinced the owner of a trucking company to retrofit one of the trucks with a hand brake and clutch so that he could drive and work.

It was fascinating to all who watched him pull into the truck yard, swing his wheelchair out of the truck, maneuver himself around to unload, then swing the wheelchair back into the truck, pull himself up into the cab, and drive out for the next load. It was an amazing feat of determination. He worked beyond normal working hours for six months, saved enough money, and went into partnership with a son and father team to buy a logging truck.

After about eight months of hauling logs, he asked his partners to buy him out; and with that money and the sale of his pickup truck, he was able to make a down payment on his first semi, a white Western Star, and became an independent contractor, hauling logs to the sawmill in Blue River and Avola, British Columbia.

By this time, he had progressed from the wheelchair to crutches and a walker, reverting only occasionally back to the wheelchair. Even though his pain was constant and often intense, he was working and making good money. Unfortunately, after only three months, IWA (International Woodworkers Association) went on strike throughout the entire country of Canada, and all the mills were shut down.

Because Gary was an American, he went to Lynden Transport in the State of Washington seeking work, and they contracted him to haul freight from Sumas, Washington, to Mile 1202 Beaver Creek on the Alaska Highway. After seven months making a trip each week, he transferred to Fairbanks, Alaska, and began hauling on the Alaska Pipeline.

Gary's logging business before going to Alaska, 1975.

On the haul road for the Alaska pipeline, 1976.

Gary stacked and hauled trailers that had been wrecked back to Fairbanks, for which he was well paid.

Thompson Pass, a 2,805-foot-high mountain gap northeast of Valdez, Alaska, averages 551.5 inches of snow per year.

Unloading a crane from Gary's truck at Prudhoe Bay.

Off-highway hauling, near Stewart Lake in northern British Columbia, 1972.

Taken at the Arctic Circle at Old Man Camp, October 1976, 20°F.

The hovercraft transports Gary and his truck across the Yukon River. Notice the shiny horse hood ornaments on the front of his truck.

Semi-trucks moved equipment in convoys because of the dangerous conditions in case anyone had any problems.

At age 27 Gary was the youngest owner-operator to haul on the pipeline and was known by everyone as "Mustang man." He was unstoppable and unbeatable. He hauled huge equipment weighing 70 tons over ice and snow in raging snowstorms, up and down steep mountain roads with temperatures reaching -40° to -70°F, which would have stopped most drivers. Dead Horse camp in February 1976 recorded the coldest days when temperatures dropped to -90°F without any wind chill for two nights and then warmed to -82°F the third night.

In Gary's own words:

"Two other drivers and I, Sid Budden from California and Frank Bromigen from Minnesota, drove in circles for three days and nights on the helicopter landing site, stopping only long enough to refuel in order to keep our trucks from freezing up. The haul road had been closed; but if we stopped, it was unlikely that the trucks would start again and would have been parked until spring.

"The first winter, 1975-76, over 1,500 semis were left on the slopes from wrecking and freezing up, several drivers died, and many returned to the lower 48 states, defeated and broken because they lost their trucks and trailers. It was one of the coldest winters ever recorded.

"When I made the first trip north, there were 52 semi-trucks dispatched to follow the 'cat train,' which was like a caravan of earth-moving scrapers, road graders, off-highway trucks pulling fuel trailers, camp trailers, cook trailers, D8 and D9 bulldozers that leveled the tundra as they moved forward, and the road patrol that was always there to call for help if needed. Out of the 52 semi-trucks dispatched from Fairbanks to Prudhoe Bay, only 13 drivers returned with their trucks.

"Alyeska Security officers brought us food from camp, so we could keep our trucks moving. When the temperature moderated to a 'balmy' -60°F, they opened the road and let us return to Fairbanks. But the temperatures dropped again, and the devastating cold caused many accidents and problems; so the union closed the haul road again from Fairbanks to the Yukon River and requested all drivers to return to Fairbanks until the severe cold front passed and the temperatures warmed up.

"Trucks were freezing up and drivers were freezing to death. I found a company driver for Bayles and Roberts Trucking Company who had frozen to death in his sleeper north of Cold Foot Camp. Another driver, whose truck froze up north of Dietrich Camp, was found 100 yards from his truck, frozen on the road as he tried to walk back to camp to get help 1,000 yards from where his truck quit.

If the engine stopped, it couldn't be started, and some trucks just deteriorated away in the harsh, winter conditions.

Terrible accidents were unfortunately commonplace and generally there was no recovery of the truck.

"Another time, five of us were hauling equipment one mile across the ice bridge on the Yukon when the lead semi-truck broke through an air pocket in the ice. The driver got wet up to his waist as the freezing water rushed in his cab. Alyeska Security was on site in minutes and pulled him from the cab, wrapped him in thermal blankets and rushed him to the helicopter site 5 miles away, in 5-Mile Camp, for emergency evacuation; but he died from thermal shock on the way. I was the fifth truck behind him and saw it happen.

"Neil Armstrong, the traffic administrator, asked if I was going to return to Fairbanks after they off-loaded me because of the road closure. I told Neil that I was here to work and couldn't afford to sit in Fairbanks and wait for the cold to pass. The union had no jurisdiction north of the river, and so I hauled and shuffled equipment between the camps for the two weeks during the extreme cold closure, again with crippling temperatures falling to -70°F.

"When I started in 1975, it was reported that over 3,500 semi-trucks started on the project. Some of the semis were company owned, but the majority of the semi-trucks were driven by owner-operators who were privately contracted to haul on the pipeline. So many drivers came from all over the States hoping to make a small fortune because the pay was so high for this demanding job; but most of them had little, if any, experience in this type of winter with such extreme conditions. Unfortunately, of the 3,500 who started, there were only 3 who finished the contract in 1977 when the pipeline was completed.

"Many times I did the mechanical repairs on my truck and forged through treacherous situations, where most would stop to wait out the storm. On the famous 'Ice Cut' just south of the Franklin Bluff Camp, I was hauling a D9 sideboom pipelayer on a 4-axle drop center lowboy. As I neared the top of the hill, I spun out with chains on both axles. I had no brakes on the lowboy and was sliding backwards toward a sheer drop-off of over 100 feet. I left the truck in gear hoping to slow down the speed of the slide when the drive shaft twisted in two, jack-knifing the trailer into the bank and bringing the semi and trailer to a stop just before the drop-off.

"It was about -60° that night when Alyeska Security patrolling the road found me and called into camp to have two cat bulldozers hauled down to winch my rig up on top of the hill. Parts were brought in for repairs, and I was eventually on the road again; but the whole ordeal resulted in a frost-bitten forehead, throat, toes, and fingers that later caused me to lose all of my toenails, several fingernails, and the hair on the right side of my head from touching the frame while working on the truck."

Sourdough Truck Stop, 1976.

Laying pipe at Franklin Bluff, 1976.

It is hard for most of us to imagine such experiences. Gary's ability to drive a semi-truck, operate heavy equipment, repair them mechanically, and conquer the formidable forces of Mother Nature in such an extreme environment might help explain why Gary would say that hauling chips and/or equipment from Highland Flats to St. Maries was "all in a day's work." Whatever the situation, no matter how difficult, he always looked for the solution or the answer, and he always found it. It was never too cold or icy if there was a job that had to be done.

That same indomitable perseverance and determination could be seen throughout Gary's life. He was about finding solutions and making the best decisions. He never lost sight of the goal or gave up his dream.

That did not mean that he wasn't flexible. There will always be changes. Sometimes the weather changes the time of harvest and distillation. Sometimes the political environment of a country will change. Government policies change, import and export laws change, and sometimes it just doesn't make financial sense to continue farming or conducting business activities the current way. Gary always made changes if he felt that it would improve the process to ensure the success of the project.

Only 125 Miles to the Distillery

Learning to log with his father while growing up in the mountains to the time of his accident prepared him well for his new challenge of logging conifer trees. Although he had never distilled chips before, he knew trees, and it was easy for him to organize and give directions. He had to know which trees to cut down and then how to chip, haul, and distill them, a skill that few people have.

After the chips were blown into the trailer, they were hauled to St. Maries, which was a dangerous undertaking. Gary and his friend Eldon Knittle were the only two who were brave enough to pull doubles (two trailers hooked together and pulled by one semi-truck), carrying 110,000 pounds of chips. The trips would take four to seven hours, depending on the severity of the weather. The road from Plummer to the Benewah turnoff is very windy with a lot of hairpin turns, but at least it is paved. The Benewah road up to the farm distillery is a 6-mile dirt road with narrow turns and sharp drop-offs, so drivers had to be extremely cautious.

Gary had several CDL drivers who were employees or volunteers; but as the trucks started swerving on the snow and ice and it looked like the second trailer was going to pass the first one, hearts beat faster and faster, knuckles turned white gripping the wheel, while drivers were frozen to the edge of the driver's seat with their hair standing straight up on the back of their necks.

They made the trip only once and refused to drive again. Seeing life pass before them was a heart stopper. "It was too dangerous. It was crazy. It was insane to drive those heavy trucks on those scary, narrow, and treacherous roads with snow, ice, and ferocious, blowing wind," they said. These drivers hurriedly slithered away, apologizing in an effort to hide their embarrassment. Some commented, "I've been driving trucks for 30 years and just discovered I am not a truck driver when it comes to these roads and conditions."

Gary made the drive every day and sometimes twice a day so that he could keep an eye on the logging, chipping, and distillery crews. His average downtime during the harvest was 4 hours every 24 hours, including fueling, eating, and sleeping. Gary felt they were really blessed in the 16 years they had been trucking during the winter to have lost only two trailers and had just minor damage to the four trucks.

So it was left to Gary and Eldon, but there was still tremendous worry and anxiety felt by those who knew the risks of driving back and forth. However, there didn't seem to be any other way if Young Living was going to have the oils. There were many challenges going back and forth.

Putting chains on and taking them off happened several times during just one trip between the Highland Flats Tree Farm and the St. Maries distillery.

The legal weight is 110,000 pounds (52 tons), but the ice and snow in the chips at times made them heavier, weighing between 55 and 65 tons. This makes it easier to understand the magnitude of the 75-ton link-belt cranes that Gary hauled on the pipeline.

Often times, Gary would work all day harvesting and loading, and then he would jump into the semi-truck, arriving in St. Maries at midnight. But that didn't mean the trip was over and everyone could go to bed. Not a chance! That was just the halfway point of the trip.

The chips had to be unloaded on the landing and covered with a tarp before they froze into one big lump. They were left only once in the trailer, creating a very miserable time for the several people who had to work two days with pitchforks, axes, and anything else to chop out the frozen chips. So after that experience, as soon as the trucks arrived, everyone hurried to get them unloaded, which took about three hours. Once in a while Gary was able to get something to eat or catch a quick hour or two of sleep. Most of the time, though, he would help unload and then jump back into the semi and head back to the tree farm so that the trailers would be there in the morning in time for everyone to start loading again. So who got any sleep? It wasn't Gary.

Putting chains on and taking them off was done more than once during the heavy winter storms. Sometimes the second trailer had to be left at the bottom of the last hill.

Driving at night on snow and ice was very dangerous.

The treacherous roads never stopped Gary and Eldon from hauling the chips to the distillery.

Members come from around the world to brave the cold to be part of the Seed to Seal experience.

This made it easier for the semi to make it up to the distillery. The usual five-minute drive when the road was dry turned into one or two hours of slipping and sliding. One bitter night, the second trailer slid and turned over at the bottom of the last hill before going up to the distillery, smashing the trailer, and spilling the precious chips in the snow all over the frozen ground. That was another miserable night. When things like this happened, it was easy to ask if the oils were worth it.

Gary made a trip with a Young Living Diamond who had come to be a part of the harvest. When they came to a turn in the road, the ice on the road had frozen so that the truck would not steer nor stop sliding until both trailers and the semi-truck were in the ditch leaning against the trees that held them from rolling all the way over. That night was spent with excavators, loaders, and skidders winching the trailers and truck back up on their wheels and out of the ditch; certainly an awesome and perhaps frightening experience for a member who had never had exposure to winter snow and ice.

Most people would have given up, but Gary had a mission and nothing would stop him. Having hauled on the Alaska Pipeline for two years from 1975-77 when the pipeline was being built, he knew the severe difficulties, frustrations, destruction, complete loss, and even death that came with the harsh Alaskan winters. He grew up in the mountains and understood the cold and the dangers. He had a solution for everything and was a marvel to everyone working with him, watching him fix equipment, and solving the problems. For Gary, it was just part of life.

One winter evolved into another as the oil grew in demand and the logging camp expanded. More tents went up, cabins were built, electrical lines were strung, water lines were put in, bathrooms and showers were built, and washers and dryers started churning. The kitchen was expanded, and a beautiful, antique, wood-burning stove was bought for hearty cooking and delicious meals, and the enlarged dining room served a larger number of people. Even the internet was installed to meet members' needs.

Bigger chippers were bought and another tree sheer, another skid steer, an excavator, and more equipment kept being added. The operation grew with more people coming to the harvest to be a part of Seed to Seal, as the demand for conifer oils continued to increase.

Dr. Richard Carlson meticulously testing the oils in the St. Maries laboratory, built in 2012. Gary wanted to have GC reports during the distillation for analysis, so that the recovery of all the oil constituents could be immediately confirmed.

Balsam fir chips were the first to be trucked from Highland Flats and distilled in St. Maries.

Relaxing in the floral water hot tub was a favorite place after working hard in the fields all day. When the new spa addition was built with three new hot tubs, many more members could enjoy this luxury.

Construction started on the Highland Flats distillery in May 2013, with a deadline to be in operation for winter harvest the first week of January.

Gary and his family spent Christmas working through the holidays to be ready when the first group of members arrived, and they weren't disappointed.

The Highland Flats Distillery

The entire Highland Flats operation was a challenge for everyone, and Gary wondered if the trees could be grown in St. Maries to be able to eliminate the horrific drive back and forth. In 2010 Gary thought he would sell the Highland Flats Tree Farm and grow the same trees in St. Maries; but, unfortunately, the soil was different and the conifers from the Canadian border wouldn't grow in St. Maries. So Gary continued trucking the 125 miles down Highway 95 through Coeur d'Alene, up the hills, around the narrow hairpin turns, and up the Benewah dirt road to the distillery that with the harsh winter conditions was sometimes a two-day trip.

As the years continued to add up, the harshness of working with equipment in cold temperatures and the stress of just getting the job done definitely took a toll on Gary's physical and emotional strength. The rising cost of fuel and the wear and tear on the trucks continued to increase the operational costs. Gary started asking himself if there was a better way, and ideas again started swirling in his mind. He looked at the terrain and what could be done. Millions of trees would be burned to ashes, destroying God's precious oils, if he left, besides the loss of oils needed for the growing demands of Young Living.

A new distillery was the only answer. Gary saw it all. The vision was decisive and in 2012 he began drawing the blueprints and laying it all out. Over a year's time, the ideas evolved until he had on paper what he wanted. This was his opportunity to build exactly what he wanted after 30 years; and in May of 2013, the plans were ready. In August the excavation began, forms went up, concrete was poured, and the 500-horsepower boiler was bought and delivered.

Digging out the reservoir at the Highland Flats Tree Farm.

Gary lifted a 7-ton beam for the hoist because the roof was put on when he wasn't there, and no one thought about placing the beam until it was too late. He had to either lift the beam up or take the roof off, and the latter wasn't an option for Gary.

The cookers are 9 feet in diameter and 12 feet deep.

The 6,500-liter chamber was lifted and set into place during freezing winter temperatures.

Trenches were dug and water lines were laid in the ground. Walls went up, the roof was nailed on, and the steel structure was bolted together for the 12-ton hoist. The cookers, condensers, and separators were built in the fabrication shop at the Mona farm and trucked to Idaho.

In December of 2013, excitement was high with the anticipation of completion, and on January 4, 2014, Gary distilled the first batch of balsam fir chips in the newest 21,000-liter steam extraction chamber. The distillery building is 135 feet long and 52 feet wide and houses the distillery office, new steam generators, extraction chambers, condensers, separators, decanting/filtering, bottling and labeling room, and a laboratory for the GC (gas chromatograph) instrument, giving the ability for instant analysis of the newly distilled oil.

A training and conference room that seats 75 people classroom style is located next to the lab, and a full fitness gym that is 36 feet by 26 feet is there for those who want to get up early in the morning and go work out.

The camp has several cabins and bunkrooms, with a total of 48 beds, a laundry room, a full kitchen, a dining room, and a lounge/entertainment room equipped with wireless Internet, so members can stay in touch with loved ones and continue to run their businesses from this remote farm. The spa with three tubs and two saunas is the perfect place to visit, share stories, or just relax and enjoy the energy of accomplishment that everyone feels who comes to be part of the Seed to Seal process.

The floors of the distillery are heated, and the building is completely insulated, including the 52-foot-by-85-foot truck bay. For the first time in the history of winter harvest, semi-trucks can be driven inside and the trailers unloaded in a heated room, preventing the chips from freezing and allowing the snow and ice to melt out of them before being loaded into the cookers.

The condenser to the far right has a glass covering over the end so that the oil droplets can be seen as they pass through, flowing into the separator. It appears black with small holes, but when you look closely, it is easy to see the droplets. Gary developed a new separator design for his distillation process. He had quartz crystals cut to specific dimensions in a marble shape. Then they were put in the separators so that as the oil passes through, the crystals tumble, increasing the separation of fine molecules that are often lost. The crystals also intensify the frequency of the oils. The GC analysis from the laboratory has shown as much as an 18 percent increase in the recovery of these fine molecules.

Glass Covering

The first members to help distill at the Highland Flats Farm were also inducted into the construction crew.

New members won't have the experience of unloading trailers in the bitter cold. Now when the semi-truck pulls into the heated bay, the trailer self-unloads with a walking floor trailer, making this part of the harvest much easier.

A 12-ton plug of distilled blue spruce chips, which produced 14 liters of oil, is being hoisted from the chamber.

The hot steam is warming to the outside temperatures.

Everyone wants a picture in the distillery, making lasting memories of their experiences in Seed to Seal.

Because Gary grew up with horses, he had a great love for them, which added more depth to the harvest experience. He took everyone back in time by logging and skidding the trees out of deep ravines and steep sidehills with his Percheron teams, which protected the land from the damaging effects of modern machinery. The horses are as powerful as they are magnificent looking, and they effortlessly skid the huge trees out to the chipper.

Riding the logs while skidding was a skill Gary learned as a child with his father logging in the mountains. It looks easy until you try it.

Winter harvest was a wonderful time for Gary to teach his sons.

The Young Living logging camp is fabulous for members who have never experienced the winter harvest and distillation.

Automation—History in the Making

In January 2014 history was made as the newest Young Living distillery became operational, but there was something else new—a dream. This distillery became the first automated, large-scale capacity, computerized distilling facility ever built in the world for essential oils. There are other automated distilleries for alcohol and non-essential oil commodities, but no automated essential oil distilleries exist on the scale of Young Living's Highland Flats distillery, with three 21,000-liter and one 6,500-liter extraction chambers.

The computer programming allows the operator to set the temperature in the chamber as well as the cooling water in the condenser, which triggers the temperature sensor to send a signal to the steam valve solenoid that regulates the steam flow, allowing consistent temperature ramping to ensure there is no homogenizing or reflux of the oil during the extraction process. This way the cooling water temperature can be maintained in the condensers and separators, facilitating greater oil recovery.

Homogenizing or reflux occurs when, in the middle of the distillation process, the temperature falls so low that the steam carrying the oil upwards to the condenser starts to turn back to a liquid state, and the oil drops out and falls to the bottom of the chamber. If this happens, the oil cannot be recovered.

In the automation process, Gary also wanted to include a web video camera to be able to control and monitor the distillery from any place in the world by phone. When the system is operational and perfected, it will be installed in all Young Living distilleries—another fabulous leap in raising the industry standard and our Seed to Seal standard. Gary's dream for many years has now come to fruition.

At the landing, you'll hear the deafening roar of the monstrous 350-horse-power chipper as it swiftly devours the trees and spits the chips into the 48-foot semi-trailer with a conveyor-type moving floor that automatically empties the trailer at the distillery. The machine can chip trees 26 inches in diameter at 1 foot per minute and can chip two, three, and four trees at a time, taking only 45 minutes to fill the trailer, and then it is off to the distillery.

The chips come from many different tree locations where the Christmas trees are overgrown and slated to be cut and burned by owners wanting to clear the land for other ventures. The going rate for clearing the land in 2019 is between $3,000 and $5,000 U.S. an acre, so these owners are very grateful to us because we save them a lot of time and money, and we benefit from being able to produce oils from trees that would have ended up as ash on the ground.

Excitement fills the air when one of the semis full of chips arrives at the distillery, and everyone hurries to unload and fill the distilling vats. It is fun to see how both young and old enjoy the opportunity to jump up and down in the chambers to compress the material, filling the cooker to the top. It's a moment of celebration when the lids are tightened, and the steam begins to whistle through the chamber.

The steam softens the chip fiber, releasing the oil vapor from the fiber canals and carrying them upward with the steam to the top of the chamber and into the condenser. The steam is then converted back to a liquid state, the oil and water begin to separate, and the oil droplets start to bubble to the surface of the separator. Throughout the distillation samples are taken and tested with the GC instrument to determine the quality of the chemical composition of the oil.

The automation system is complex, but Gary loved it.

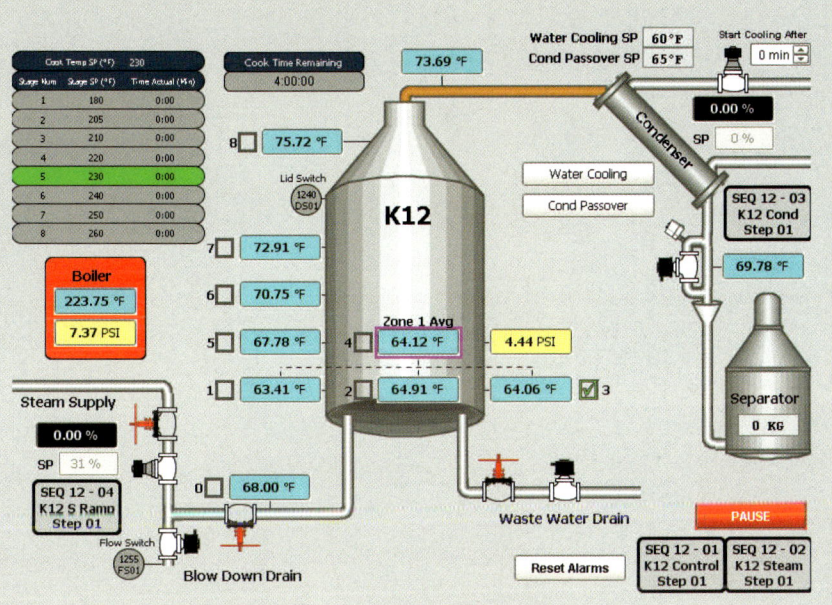

The computer interface for the automation system.

Computerized distilling was only in Gary's imagination until Highland Flats.

When the distillation finishes and the oil sample is approved, the oil is poured out and taken to the decanting room to be filtered and cleaned. Then it is poured into a 500-gallon stainless steel batching tank, where it is stirred slowly for 14 to 30 days, allowing the oil molecules to harmonize and mature.

All plants have what is called a "green note," which is the chlorophyll that naturally occurs in the plants. As the paddle automatically turns, the chlorophyll gradually flashes off, leaving the beautiful, mature aroma of the oil. From there it goes to be bottled and labeled.

Gary knew the demand for the conifer oils would keep growing; so shortly after the distillery went into operation, cookers were dedicated to particular trees and therefore did not have to be cleaned after every cook.

Every type of tree has a different distilling time. For example, it takes 3.5 hours for balsam fir, 4.5 hours for blue spruce, 3 hours for pine, and 3 hours for cedar. The more variables there are, the more testing is needed to determine the best temperature and distilling time for each different tree to produce the best oil quality and yield.

It takes 12 tons of chips to produce 6 to 12 gallons of oil per cook, depending on the age of the trees. One 32-foot semi-trailer can fill 2.5 extraction chambers with raw material, so it takes two semi-trailer loads of raw material to produce 16 gallons of oil, which varies depending on winter temperatures and the age of the trees. Throughout winter harvest, as temperatures changed and information was gathered with each distillation, it became evident that the colder the temperature, the greater the oil production.

Each year of harvest, new discoveries are made, and knowledge is gained, making the art of conifer distillation very exact. It was discovered that the floral water from the distillation can be repurposed as cooling water, increasing efficiency.

Members can soak in hot tubs to which various conifer oils are added to enjoy a relaxing time and soothe their aches and pains after a hard day at work. These "miracle waters," as some call them, are a favorite attraction. Two infrared saunas are available for "sweating out those toxins." Being part of the Seed to Seal process is an amazing experience for everyone.

From the time our plant material enters the cooker and the oil is extracted and poured into little brown bottles, the oil never comes in contact with anything other than stainless steel or glass. This is unlike small producers in developing countries who use carbon steel, copper, and aluminum, which leave a heavy metal residue in the oils that will alter the ketones, thus changing the oil.

Brett Packer, manager of the Highland Flats farm and distillery, carefully watches the oil production.

In the laboratory at the St. Maries Farm, Kevin Pace is fascinated watching the GC instrument run an analysis on the oil immediately after distillation.

The filtering, bottling, and labeling room. Oils that are not bottled are poured into stainless steel containers to be transported to Utah.

Don Schuler fulfilled his bucket-list wish to drive a team of horses—an opportunity available to anyone at winter harvest.

Members come from around the world to winter harvest to participate in our Seed to Seal process.

Everyone was so surprised when the Blue Spruce oil bubbled up like pink champagne into the separator.

GARY'S IDAHO BLUE SPRUCE SAMPLES							
Components	IBSF1312-4 15 min	IBSF1312-4 30 min	IBSF1312-4 1 hour	IBSF1312-4 2 hour	IBSF1312-4 3 hour	IBSF1312-4 4 hour	IBS #25 hr
Santene	0.16	0.13	0.18	0.18	0.16	0.24	2.00
Tricyclene	1.22	1.05	1.48	1.09	0.98	1.	1.40
Alpha-Thujene					0.15		
Alpha-Pinene	27.27	28.11	21.07	27.45	20.03	18.82	21.05
Camphene	7.52	7.03	7.28	7.78	7.06	7.56	7.48
Sabinene	1.88	1.46	1.67	1.14	1.06	1.27	1.47
Beta-Pinene	9.92	9.45	8.84	8.79	7.72	7.75	9.69
Myrcene	5.44	4.60	5.66	4.64	4.85	5.62	4.45
Delta-3-Carene	6.93	6.57	6.75	6.23	5.96	6.17	7.44
Limonene	22.03	23.95	20.87	24.96	22.61	20.72	20.53
Gamma-Terpinene	0.38	0.34	0.55	0.39	0.49	0.60	5.17
Terpinolene	1.81	1.85	2.40	1.68	2.15	2.36	2.46
Camphor	4.92	5.00	5.52	3.88	4.75	4.46	2.60
Exo-Methyl-Camphenilol	1.39	1.48	1.91	1.26	1.58	1.58	1.11
Borneol	1.19	1.34	1.88	1.23	1.62	1.62	1.17
Terpinen-4-ol	0.45	0.49	0.83	0.47	0.71	0.77	0.53
Alpha-Terpineol	0.47	0.48	1.12	0.52	0.94	1.09	0.64
Citronellol	0.08	0.06	0.48	0.06	0.39	0.52	0.23
Bornyl Acetate	4.27	4.92	6.72	6.17	9.51	8.30	8.40
Beta-Caryophyllene	0.02	0.02	0.04	0.02	0.05	0.12	0.05
Delta-Cadinene	0.07	0.08	0.17	0.12	0.31	0.28	0.22
Tau-Cadinol	0.02	0.004	0.04	0.03	0.14	0.05	0.13
Alpha-Cadinol						0.10	
Tau-Muurolol	0.01	0.01	0.02	0.02	0.11	0.12	0.10
Crembrene	0.57	0.27	0.62	0.40	1.86	1.85	1.85
Crembrene (different isomer)	0.17	0.06	0.19	0.09	0.57	0.65	0.63
Manoyl Oxide	0.02	trace	0.04	trace	0.10	0.10	0.13
Phylloclanolide	0.03	trace	0.07	0.04	0.20	0.20	0.23
Rimuene	0.02	trace	0.03	0.02	0.10	0.10	0.11
Crenbrenol	0.11	0.05	0.25	0.13	0.83	0.81	0.87

Steam Generators

Every aspect of distillation can make a difference in the oil quality: the design of the distillery equipment, the temperature and quality of the water used for steam production, and the quality of steam produced by the boiler or steam generator. Then, of course, the seed quality, the soil pH and nutrients, planting and cultivating, time of harvest, Brix testing, curing time if needed, and so many more intricate details all affect the quantity and quality of the oil produced.

In the summer of 2018, the Highland Flats farm replaced the steam boiler with two steam generators, which is very progressive in our distilling operation. The results will be analyzed to determine how we move forward with the other farms.

The steam boiler is a large reservoir of hot water that requires a lot of heat to produce the necessary steam, which must be monitored to maintain the correct temperatures and pressures.

- **Reduced Safety Risk**—The design and operation of steam generators is inherently safe with no possibility of a hazardous steam explosion, so it reduces the safety risk of those in the distillery, is less stringently regulated, and has lower insurance rates.

- **Lower Emissions**—The EPA regulates the trace amounts of harmful pollutants that are products of combustion (POC's). Nitric Oxide (NO) and Nitrogen Dioxide (NO_2)—commonly referred to as NOx and Carbon Monoxide (CO)—get the most attention and are usually a result of incomplete combustion. The steam generator burners are designed with a Flue Gas Recirculation system (FGR) and high-efficiency burners that help control the temperature, oxygen concentration, and the time of elevated temperatures, which are necessary to minimize the formation of these pollutants, to stay within environmental regulations.

- **Less water waste**—The steam generators require 90 percent fewer blowdowns than steam boilers, which reduce water usage and heat loss.

- **Steam Quality**—The steam generators are designed to separate the moist steam from the dry steam to ensure that only dry steam is delivered to the extraction chamber. This "drier" steam works especially well for extracting essential oils from the coniferous materials, and yields have grown from approximately 13 kilograms of oil to 17 kilograms of oil per distillation.

- **Better Fuel Efficiency**—Steam generators heat the water as needed for the process, at which time approximately 30 gallons of water are heated and converted to steam. Although the burners are fired for less time, they still deliver sufficient steam to the cookers. In comparison, the steam boiler is required to heat approximately 3,000 gallons of water and work continuously to maintain steam temperatures.
- **Redundancy in steam supply**—Two steam generators can be installed in the space of one boiler enabling constant distilling while one steam generator is shut down for maintenance. With a single boiler, the failure of just one component could bring the distillery operation to a halt. Having two steam generators greatly reduces the risk of the distillation process stopping because of mechanical issues.
- **Responsive**—Steam generators automatically adjust to the changing needs of the steam with different plant material. If only one steam generator is necessary, then only one will operate. If the demand requires both generators, then both will run according to the load.
- **Fast start**—The steam generators can go from a dry, cold start to full steam in less than 10 minutes, which is far less time than it takes to heat up a boiler that starts cold to reach full steam. This means that the steam generators can be started as harvested material is being unloaded from the truck. With the boiler, the heating process would need to start well before the harvested material arrived at the distillery. Any delays or stoppage at the harvest site, or in transportation, would result in the boiler creating steam that has nowhere to go and a lot of wasted fuel.

Installing steam generators at the Highland Flats Tree Farm is very progressive in our desire to find more efficient ways to produce steam. As we gather data from the distilling, we are able to determine if we want to go this way at the other farms.

Brett Packer works with contractors and other distillery operators to bring the new steam generators on line. The huge single steam boiler was replaced by two, much smaller, steam generators in the summer of 2018.

Highland Flats Reforestation

Reforestation has always been important to Young Living. Many members come each year to be a part of spring planting to replenish the trees harvested during the winter. We even have members who come to winter harvest and then return in the spring. It is rewarding to be part of the planting and then come back a year later to see the growth.

Our reforestation program is fabulous for everyone and ensures that for years in the future, we will have trees to distill for oil. The annual planting average is anywhere from 65,000 to 85,000 trees. Each year as the trees grow taller, a sense of satisfaction permeates the air. This cycle of life is a joy to be a part of in a productive and blessed way.

Gary was excited to take his family with him to walk the fields and see the amazing growth of the two-year-old balsam fir trees.

4-year-old Douglas fir trees in left foreground; 1-year-old balsam fir trees in background and to the right.

Members from different countries and cultures become great friends working together during spring planting in the reforestation project.

In the spring of 2015, 85,000 new balsam fir saplings were planted as part of our commitment to replenishing the earth.

The illumination of the northern lights is a magnificent gift to all those who come to the Young Living Northern Lights Farm in the depth of winter.

DISTILLING UNDER THE NORTHERN LIGHTS
Fort Nelson, British Columbia

In 2012 Young Living began growing at an amazing speed, and the need for oils was increasing dramatically. Black Spruce oil was a major component in several important oil blends, but the supply produced at our partner farm in Quebec, Canada, during the last 20 years was declining because the driving distance from the distillery was over 12 hours one way. Acquiring the trees was difficult and the road back was not easy; so less distillation was taking place, and the supply of oil could not increase fast enough to meet the needs of the growing number of Young Living members. As Gary assessed the situation, he realized that if he wanted to have Black Spruce oil for Young Living, he would have to find the trees and build a new distillery.

However, black spruce trees grow in northern Canada, where the winters are severe and the area is far from any major industry, with little access to the machinery and materials that it would take to build a distillery. But Gary felt he had no choice, so he started looking. Luckily, Young Living had its own small plane, so it was easy for Gary to fly over thousands of acres of land in northern Canada from Saskatchewan to Alaska. He finally found the perfect farm with virgin soil that had never had chemicals on it and had only a few roaming buffalo that were like the guardians of the property.

The farm is 8 miles outside of Fort Nelson at Mile 308 on the Alcan Highway, which made the access very easy. Papers were signed, the land was bought, and Gary broke ground on July 29, 2014, with the intent to beat the onset of winter. Not only did he clear land for the distillery, but he and his crew cleared land for the new fields that were planted before the ground froze in early October.

Six bison protect the farm.

Gary discovered wild yarrow growing on the farm, but there was not enough to make it affordable to harvest, so the new planting included yarrow, German chamomile, and einkorn, which to our knowledge have never before been grown in this environment. However, with the long summer daylight hours and temperatures reaching into the 90's in early June, Gary felt it was worth it to give these crops a chance.

He felt a lot of excitement when he discovered thousands of acres of wild ledum, goldenrod, and conyza (Canadian fleabane) growing in the area around the farm, although in short supply worldwide. Another discovery was the abundance of white fir and a new species of balsam fir that he was anxious to distill, which he thought could be added to the Young Living array of conifer oils.

248   D. Gary Young | The World Leader in Essential Oils

Could Gary have imagined as he drove down the two-lane dirt road called the Alcan Highway while hauling on the Alaska pipeline that 35 years later, he would be moving his own equipment to his own farm on that same highway that was now paved and well-marked?

Breaking ground for the Northern Lights distillery was momentous for Gary, July 29, 2014.

Gary drew the plans, purchased and/or rented equipment, cleared the land, excavated and dug out the footings, built the roads, and hired the crews. Jim Powell, Scott Schuler, and Chip Kouwe, who had worked with Gary at the Highland Flats farm, answered Gary's call for help immediately. They started very early in the morning, and because the summer days were so long, they worked until 11 at night to get as much done as possible before the winter wind and snow came.

Even Jacob, Josef, and I helped before returning home for school. Jacob is a terrific excavator operator, having been taught by his father in Ecuador; Josef is learning to operate the D6 bulldozer; and I took lots of pictures and brought food and water.

There were only a few weeks before winter would arrive, so working 14 to 16 hour days was not unusual, especially with sunrise at 3:30 a.m. and sunset at 10:30 p.m. Everyone worked fast to take advantage of the long daylight that winter would turn into a very few short hours.

Gary always said he could take a D8 bulldozer apart and put it back together blindfolded, but with computerization—not likely.

There was so much ground water, a culvert had to be put in to make the road stable going into the farm.

A lot of construction equipment was moving at the same time. It was a race against time to beat the onset of winter.

This fabulous working team moved a lot of dirt in a few short weeks: Dave, Jim, Scott, Mark, Chip, Jacob, Gary, and Josef worked from early morning to late at night. I drove back and forth to town to bring food and water, so everyone could keep working, and took a lot of pictures.

Gary was constantly on the phone coordinating so many of the moving parts.

Since construction began in August 2014, 556 cubic meters (727 cubic yards) of concrete were poured. The outside dimensions of the building are 150 x 72 feet, which includes the distillery, truck bay, shop, and two-story laboratory.

Ben Howden, a top leader in Young Living, had been a contractor in British Columbia for several years. When Gary asked for his help, he and his wife Carol moved to Fort Nelson. Ben called his son Cory, who had 25 years of experience in construction and cement work, and asked him if he could come and help. Cory was working in the Philippines, but within a few days, he arrived with his family and took the responsibility of construction superintendent in the race to get the distillery up and running before winter. Carol, Ben's wife, and Marnie, Cory's wife, cooked three healthy meals each day, so the men could work fast with little interruption and have the nutrition to sustain them in the cold, harsh, winter temperatures.

The forms went up and the men started pouring concrete. For weeks it went back and forth between forms and concrete. But winter came fast and the temperatures dropped anywhere from -27°F to -44°F in mid-November. Working in the freezing temperatures was a challenge, even to the point of having to shut down a couple of times. Several Young Living members braved the cold to come and help with the construction.

Gary and I went to an equipment auction, where Gary bought several large pieces of equipment. It brought back fun memories of the early days when buying equipment at auctions for the St. Maries and Mona farms.

Between the terrible cold, government regulations, and required permits, the construction was slower than expected. But finally, the last pipes were connected; three cookers were loaded; and on March 9, 2015, the boiler was fired—and the newest distillery went into operation.

The Northern Lights Farm offers so much opportunity, especially with Young Living's 5x5 business plan. Wood chips will be reused in a biomass incinerator system to produce steam for the boiler and generate electricity for the distillery. If excess electricity is generated, this green energy will be supplied to the local energy grid. The pellet plant recycles the excess chips, which are a fantastic alternative fuel source, making good use of the plant material after it's distilled. The Northern Lights Farm is a wonderful educational experience for everyone who comes to visit as well as for members who participate in the harvest.

When the cookers finally arrived from Utah, they were off-loaded by the side of the road, waiting to be installed in their new home.

Ben's wife, Carol, and Cory's wife, Marnie, cooked three meals a day for everyone and brought lunch out to the hungry crew.

254   D. Gary Young | The World Leader in Essential Oils

While digging out the reservoir for the distillery water supply, wells were also drilled, and filtration systems and holding tanks were installed. Pipes were laid 10 feet deep to get below the frost level and then covered with 4 inches of insulating foam before being covered over with dirt.

Cory Howden, construction superintendent, discusses the construction progress with Gary.

It was a huge push and even though winter came too soon, the construction went forward in spite of the tremendous cold.

This 350-horsepower boiler was trucked from Virginia with a smaller 100-horsepower boiler for a backup.

256   D. Gary Young | The World Leader in Essential Oils

Winter temperatures averaged -20° to -30°F and on occasion even fell to -50°F.

The first of the three cookers was carefully set in place by Gary.

Ben Howden, Dillon Rioux, Clay Southwick, Greg Howden, Cory Howden, Wes Michiels, Gary Young, and Lee Boyton were happy with the progress being made. When the boiler and cookers were installed, they could feel life coming into the distillery.

Bitter cold temperatures made the construction very difficult.

At -30°F, the dirt froze and wouldn't come out of the bed, causing a rollover and snapping the driveshaft. Gary spent the night welding, so they could winch the bed upright to put it back into operation as quickly as possible. The extreme cold created problems that were difficult and miserable to fix.

It was a fabulous day when the walls were up, the roof was on, and the heaters were installed, which eased the misery from the snow and bitter cold.

Finally enclosed, the distillery was ready for operation in March 2015.

Cutting trees at -20°F in the snow was cold and challenging, but that's when the chips yield the greatest volume of oil.

A feller buncher cuts and holds 5 to 12 trees at once, and when the grippers are full, it moves the trees to where the forwarding machine can pick them up and move them to the landing site for chipping. This machine has been invaluable in the severe winter conditions.

New equipment had to be purchased to be able to forward the heavy trees to the chipper.

The logs are chipped on-site and then trucked to the distillery.

Members are eager to help as Gary loads the chamber.

There are two 12,000-liter cookers, one 10,000-liter cooker, one 20,000-liter cooker, and one 3,500-liter cooker, 2015.

Tanya Pariseau from Yellowknife, in Northwest Territories, and Joanne and Larry Haley from New Brunswick traveled great distances to see the first black spruce distillation.

D. Gary Young | The World Leader in Essential Oils

Black Spruce Speaks

By D. Gary Young

I am here now, here to fulfill my mission as told by the ancient people. No one would hear me; but after thousands of years, I have been released to do what I was created to do for the children of this world.

The ancient people call me "Black Spruce of the Northern Lights" because my branches touch the dancing colors in the sky, intertwining Mother Earth's strength with the mysteries of the heavens. I bring light to the darkness of the mind, release spiritual blockages, and free the bondages that some humans call emotions, which can lead to the deterioration of life. I live in an extremely harsh environment, with challenging growing conditions, climate changes that drop to 80°F below zero, and howling winds with a wind chill of up to minus 120°F.

Summer temperatures reach 90°F, with long daylight hours that never see darkness in some areas of the northern hemisphere, in dramatic contrast to the short daylight hours in the winter that don't see the sun for weeks at a time.

I live with the extremes of Mother Earth, so I can deal with the extremes of humankind. I am one of the least explored by modern man because I am looked upon as dwarfed and ugly. I am considered a nonproductive scrub tree with no value, but I can help others find their value when they are dwarfed emotionally.

Wild animals do not sleep beneath me, as my skinny branches offer little shelter from the freezing wind and snow. Yet as they gather around me, they feel my energy, which increases their circulation, warming them. I am not here to be a shelter for protection or a crutch to bear the burdens of the world. I am here to give strength that teaches self-reliance, which helps all creatures become secure, as am I.

I am here to help the human race build a relationship with the Creator, not looking to the Creator as the protector but to understand that He made all living things to have the power to be strong, adding purpose to creation, not taking energy but giving back.

Humans are co-creators with the Master of the universe and must come to understand their God-given power over all the elements, as He gave to me; to own their greatness; and to become what they were created to be. My roots can attach to anything, and I never blow over because I am so strong. My molecules bring strength to the human core so that people can feel grounded and never be defeated by the problems they encounter. Man must be able to anchor to any condition at anytime, anywhere and be able to adjust and adapt. This is what keeps me alive and will help humans find success as they partner with the Great Spirit in their journey of life.

Hold and cherish my essence. Let it help you grow, learn, and explore your God-given potential to know who you are and have the power within you to change the world with just your thoughts and to be a living example of your creation.

The Ancients treasured our sister White Spruce, which will soon come to teach another dimension of truth and knowledge. Be ready, for she works fast and is not as patient as her brother. I work more on the physical, but she works on the spiritual to help you become independent in preparing you for your partnership with the Great Spirit.

Our brother Blue Spruce is universal and grows in many different regions of the world. Our earthly powers work well together to help you find balance as you seek your highest potential in your journey through life.

The ancient people of the North look down and give thanks that we have joined together with the Great Spirit for the support and well-being of His people and Mother Earth.

The first distillation of black spruce was on March 9, 2015.

The first distillation of black spruce was a marvelous wonder as we watched the oil droplets bubble up into the separator. The action was intense, as if the oil was speaking to us.

We had an awesome feeling of triumph as the drums of Black Spruce oil from the first distillation were delivered to the warehouse. There was a buzz of excitement as word went out that Black Spruce oil was back in stock.

The Northern Lights distillery is a beautiful work of art, with a new, state-of-the-art water-cooling and recycling system. While Gary was building the Highland Flats distillery two years earlier in northern Idaho, he was constantly thinking about his design. When the distillery went into operation, he kept watching and analyzing the flow of the distillation, which brought a new idea to him. In his mind, he could see a way to make the process better and more efficient, so he designed and built his innovative idea into the new Northern Lights operation, which has worked very well. Modification has been made on our distilleries around the world, along with the renovation of our distillery in France.

Our Northern Lights distillery has a large, heated truck bay; so the trucks can come in and unload in the warmth, just like in Highland Flats. However, this bay is larger to accommodate the 53-foot walking floor trailers that transport the chips from the logging site. There are two 12,000-liter, one 10,000 liter, and one 20,000-liter extraction chambers, with production now running at about 530 liters each week. There is also one 3,500-liter extraction chamber for small sample distilling. From the distillery, the oils go to the filtration and decanting laboratory and then to 500-gallon batching chambers before being bottled and packaged.

The Northern Lights distillery includes a large laboratory and research center with a state-of-the-art GC instrument with dual 50m and 60m columns for analytical and scientific testing and documentation. Sample analysis is always completed as part of the distillation process, and sometimes multiple samples are tested during various stages of distillation to ensure that oil component percentages and other oil characteristics are optimal.

A training room that seats 100 people is used for educational seminars and is where high school and college students from around the world will come who want to study and learn distillation, organic plant chemistry, and essential oils analysis.

The number of members coming to participate in the harvest is growing each year. The lure of the northern lights and true winter conditions is very exciting to anticipate.

The growth of new helichrysum at our farm in Split, Croatia, was truly rewarding for Gary and Dominik Bekavac.

CROATIA—DISTILLING IN 19 DAYS

Croatia, the land of a thousand islands, is a paradise of aromatic plants, a beautiful land of valleys, hills, lakes, and thousands of acres of farmland on which many aromatic plants are growing. It is not only the land of helichrysum (*Helichrysum italicum*) but also of many other crops that will be distilled at the Young Living facility located on the outskirts of Split, Croatia.

In May 2015 Young Living purchased a two-story commercial building totaling 16,580 square meters (180,000 square feet), which includes several offices, conference rooms, warehouse space, and two large bays for the distillery. The boiler was shipped from France, the separators from Utah, and the four 4,000-liter and one 6,000-liter chambers were built in Split. Dominik Bekavac, the farm manager, had four 1,000-liter extraction chambers that he was already using, powered by a woodburning firebox, bringing our total distilling capacity to 26,000 liters.

Everything was assembled in our new facility, and distilling began June 19, 2015, exactly 19 days from when Gary started to assemble everything and refit the building so that they would be able to distill during the short 55-day harvest time allowed by the government—a most amazing accomplishment.

After the crops are harvested, they are trucked to this new facility, where the Seed to Seal process continues with distilling, laboratory testing, filtering, and decanting. Then some of the oil goes to another area of the building, where it is bottled, labeled, and shipped to our European distribution center. Bulk oils are shipped to the warehouse in Utah for bottling, labeling, and further distribution to other countries throughout the world.

This building houses the distillery, a large curing area for the plant material when delivered, and a large amount of storage for material waiting to be distilled. The enclosed boiler room; decanting, bottling, and labeling rooms; and a laboratory with a GC instrument for testing the oils are also on the main floor.

Management offices and education training rooms are on the second floor. Rooms on the lower level are for the spa with the floral water hot tubs, which will be a fabulous addition for our members and visitors, as well as rooms for massage, Raindrop, and other skin care and cosmetic applications.

On the main floor, the manufacturing plant bottles Lavender, Peppermint, Lemon, Helichrysum, Vitex, and Bay Laurel. The warehouse and distribution center services 21 regions and countries, which include: Albania, Austria, Balkans, Bulgaria, Estonia, Greece, Hungary, Lithuania, Macedonia, Montenegro, Poland, Romania, Russia, Slovakia, and Ukraine.

For the first time, members and visitors alike from Europe, Russia, and the Adriatic countries can see and experience the entire Seed to Seal process on their continent and participate at harvest times each year. This will surely prove to be a wonderful opportunity for thousands of our members on this side of the world.

Thousands of new starts were germinated and then transplanted in the fields.

Domesticating Helichrysum

Our farm is growing about 100 hectares (247 acres) of helichrysum and contracting with many other farmers who have small acreages of helichrysum. It is a short drive from the farm to take the harvested crop to the distillery. Young Living Adriatic d.o.o. (proper business identification like an Inc. or LLC) was registered at the end of January 2015, giving Young Living Croatia the right to obtain more farmland, a project growing more every day. Croatia is a country very rich with aromatic plants that we are planning to cultivate with partner farms and certified growers that will be distilled in the new facility.

It seems that whenever Gary went into a new country to begin a farming project, the people were skeptical and even critical; but that changed when they saw him driving the tractor and tilling the ground or working with the construction crews, welding and fabricating the framework for the extraction chambers. Even teaching the boiler operator how to install the 100-horsepower boiler, shipped from France, was no doubt amazing to everyone after having seen only small firebox boilers.

The people were astounded as they watched him work alongside the field and construction crews. The electrician put his arm around Gary's shoulder and in very broken English said, "You are the best. You do not tell us how, you show us how. This is not normal for a business owner."

Helichrysum grows the best in extremely rocky soil, so Gary bought a 305-horsepower tractor and stone crusher, which was shipped from Germany, that had tremendous power and made the ground preparation much faster.

Our members are thrilled to have a new farm where they can come and work by helping with the weeding and care of the plants.

Gary always walked the fields checking on the health and growth of the plants, and he was very pleased with the weeding.

D. Gary Young | The World Leader in Essential Oils

Helichrysum, thriving in the rocks and the humid Mediterranean climate, is almost ready for harvest.

Zoran Mustic, Young Living general manager, and Domagoj Bekavac, our farm manager, join with Gary in the excitement of the success of the distillery.

Josef helped turn the fresh helichrysum for curing to prepare it for distillation, June 2015.

The first distillation of helichrysum took place 19 days after the building was purchased.

Always checking to make sure everything is ready for distillation.

The beautiful stainless steel extraction chambers and separators were manufactured in Split.

Members from around the world attended the ribbon cutting and official opening of the distillery in Split.

The Young Living distillery, manufacturing and distribution center, and corporate offices in Split, Croatia.

Young Living staff and members join in the celebration of the ribbon cutting in Split, October 6, 2015.

Bottling department in the Young Living Croatia headquarters.

bne INTELLINEWS

Croatia Reaps Bitter Harvest From Illegal Plant Trade

Guy Norton in Zagreb November 17, 2014

Croatia reaps bitter harvest from illegal plant trade Guy Norton in Zagreb November 17, 2014 A group of concerned citizens on the Adriatic island Krk held a demonstration at the toll bridge connecting their island home to the Croatian mainland on November 12 to air their concerns about the increasing environmental and financial devastation being wrought by the illegal harvesting of wild plants.

Front and centre of the good-natured protest by an assorted group of olive growers, wine producers, bee keepers, sheep farmers, war veterans and eco-warriors were concerns that the Croatian Ministry of Environment and nature protection has dismally failed to combat a growing wave of illegal harvesting of wild plants on the island, which is threatening not only environmental destruction, but is also imperilling the livelihood of traditional agricultural producers on Krk.

The main bone of contention with the protesters has been the picking of the plant Helichrysum arenarium, better known by its poetic name of Immortelle. A litre of essential oil from the plant which thrives on the rocky Croatian coast and islands can command as much as €1,700, as it is in growing demand in the cosmetics industry, especially in France, which accounts for 90% of Immortelle oil exports. The rising cost of the oil has led to an explosion of interest in harvesting Immortelle and it has been claimed that experienced pickers can earn as much as HRK10,000 (€1,250) a month – almost twice the official average wage in Croatia.

While traditionally the harvesting of the plant has been carried out under official licenses granted to companies and individuals by the government, the lure of short-term profits has attracted a growing band of illegal pickers who the protesters on Krk claim are leaving a trail of destruction behind them. Licensed harvesters are required to abide by a strict code of conduct that involves seeking the permission of landowners before cutting off the flower heads and upper stalks of the Immortelle, which are later boiled and distilled to produce the prized essential oil – around 7,000kg of fresh flowers are needed to produce a single litre.

Illegal pickers in contrast have been guilty of criminal trespass and have simply ripped up Immortelle by the roots, destroying any chance that the plants will regrow and leading to soil erosion on the environmentally sensitive Croatian archipelago. In August this year, for example, wildlife rangers on a visit to the uninhabited island of Prvic, which is a strictly protected botanical and zoological reserve with no public access, intercepted a band of pickers who had been illegally harvesting Immortelle.

Meanwhile, on inhabited islands like Krk, gangs of pickers from nearby mainland towns such as Ogulin and Karlovac have been illegally camping out in environmentally sensitive areas of the island that form part of the EU's Natura 2000 protected habitats network, leaving behind rubbish, knocking down traditional dry stone walls and frightening livestock in their search for Immortelle.

Unenforced

In response to the environmental destruction being wrought by roving bands of illegal pickers the environment ministry announced a complete ban on harvesting Immortelle on the Croatian archipelago in September.

http://www.bne.eu/content/story/croatia-reaps-bitter-harvest-illegal-plant-trade

---

> *...have simply ripped up Immortelle by the roots, destroying any chance that the plants will regrow and leading to soil erosion*

The Battle to Find Helichrysum

It was a sad realization for Gary as the events surrounding helichrysum in Croatia unfolded. Gary first purchased land in 1996 but lost it all during the war that separated the states of Yugoslavia. In 2014 Gary realized that it was imperative to establish a farm for helichrysum. He traveled to Croatia eight times in a few months to establish a partner farm, purchase a building for the distillery, truck the boiler from France, and ship equipment and parts from the U.S. for what became the largest distilling operation in that area of the world.

Until 2014 helichrysum was harvested without restriction from June to December, when the government decided that the wildcrafted helichrysum was being depleted and dying out. So the harvest was limited from June to July for 45 days and then again from October to November for another 45 days, making it very difficult for so many farmers because their little wood-fired distilleries were too small to distill any sizable crop in such a short time. Many wildcrafters are now not able to harvest and distill enough to make the money they depended on in the past.

Because it is still legal to harvest on private land, much fighting and poaching took place. Paid by unscrupulous foreign companies, poachers went to the islands and invaded private property at night to steal the helichrysum plants, just ripping them out of the ground, stuffing them in bags, and running. They cut fences, endangering herds of goats and sheep that were freed to wander out onto the highways and be killed. Even worse, some farmers were beaten and hospitalized.

This caused the Croatian government to make a new law in 2014 restricting the wildcrafting harvest to 45 days two times a year. Then in 2015 the ruling was again changed, allowing for only one harvest for 55 days from June 18 to August 15. Presently, the wildcrafters are fighting with the government to extend the harvest. In 2014 one region that was wildcrafted produced 40.5 tons of helichrysum raw material. In 2015 the same region harvested only 5 tons.

The government decided to auction the helichrysum by the kilo in different regions, with the bidding starting at 1 kuna per kilo. Within the week the price had gone up to 7.6 kuna per kilo ($1.00 = 6.69 HRK). In addition, a Croatian VAT tax of 25 percent has to be prepaid but can be redeemed at the end of the year. A Croatian Ministry of Forestry tax also has to be paid.

Some unscrupulous brokers have hired black market laborers to poach the helichrysum before the mandated harvesting time and then smuggle it over the border into nearby towns to avoid paying the Forestry and Croatian taxes so that they could offer their helichrysum for a cheaper price. In the first week of June, according to newspaper reports, more than 70 people were arrested and the helichrysum confiscated. These were people promising early delivery of oil in July.

Due to the shortened harvest time and small distillers, there was a shortage of oil in 2015. A small amount was still available, but many companies either went without or had to rely on a synthetic and manipulated substitute for their oil.

Therefore, knowing the source of your oil will become more and more important. Gary was blessed to be in the right place at the right time doing the right thing; and with a total of 26,000 liters of distilling capacity, Young Living is able to produce enough oil to meet our needs.

Croatia offers an exciting future for Young Living and for those who go into partnership with us. This beautiful country, rich with aromatic plants, will become a bright light in the essential oil world and for those looking for Mother Nature's pure, unadulterated gifts. Young Living looks forward to a long and prosperous relationship with the people of Croatia.

Unhealthy soil and too much water produce poor plants.

Bandido wasn't just a saddle horse; this Friesian champion and Gary were one as they explored the ranch together.

SKYRIDER WILDERNESS RANCH

Tabiona, Utah— In Gary's Words

"For the past few years, I had been thinking about buying a ranch as my own getaway—a place to rest. I was always looking and at one time was considering a ranch in Montana but didn't have time to fly up to look at it. Then in the fall of 2014, while hunting elk, I was told about an elk ranch in Tabiona that had been repossessed by the bank and had been sitting empty for about five years.

"I became curious and felt a bit of excitement, and I decided to take a look. Mary and I flew to Duchesne, where we were picked up by the real estate agent. It was beautiful and serene, and the rugged mountain terrain and gentle sloping valleys were so engaging. I felt a peacefulness as if going back in time.

"It seemed strange, but as we came closer, I was amazed at the majestic construction set back against the mountain overlooking the valley. I could see that the lodge had not been taken care of and was in a rather deplorable state. The grounds were full of weeds, and tons of rocks had been pushed up against the windows, completely blocking the natural light.

"It was supposed to be an elk ranch, but the elk were skinny and were all bulls, which presented a slight problem that I would have to solve. The land was wide open and flat—perfect for farming—perfect for many things. If this were mine, I would have my safe haven away from people and the cement city, and I could create and build as I desired. The excitement of the newness reminded me of how I felt when I signed the papers for my section of land in Canada that was part of the homestead act, but the circumstances were very different.

"When we walked through the doors into the huge kitchen, we found our eyes following the immense stonework of the fireplace up toward the ceiling. Around the corner on the other side of the stone wall was yet another huge fireplace, built to warm the spacious living room that had a wonderful, alluring energy. Massive logs spanned the ceiling that was about 25 feet high, and beautiful handcrafted scenes of the great outdoors and the animals that ruled were eloquently carved in the walls.

"The original owners built it as a hunting lodge but never finished it for financial reasons. Drawers were missing handles, tile work was not finished, and many cabinets had not been installed. But the possibilities were enormous for me and for Young Living, and the ideas were spinning in my head. It was perfect—my sanctuary where I could work and build as I wanted, envelop myself in the spaciousness of the isolation, breathe pure air, and drink unpolluted well water. The realization of my dream was before me, and, of course, true to my nature, I wanted to share my dream with my Young Living family.

"I made the bank an offer that was less than half of what they wanted. Naturally, the bank wanted more than what I was willing to pay, but they also wanted the property off their books. They tried to make a deal with me, but I was unwavering with my offer: "Take it or leave it." Within 24 hours, they took it, and on March 12, 2015, I purchased the 3,748-acre ranch at my price. Everyone marveled, but it was meant to be. In that same year, I also purchased several other pieces of property adjacent to the ranch that I could farm, bringing the total to 4,500 acres.

"I looked out over the fields and the majestic mountains that spanned the Duchesne River at 6,500 feet to the mountain tops at 10,000 feet, and I could see all the potential that God's paradise could bring to our Young Living family, from corporate activities to member retreats.

"In my mind, I could see the new Elk Barn Inn with its gigantic kitchen, sleeping rooms, and big dining and meeting areas on the top floor, with the elk pens below with the baby elk. I could see that old-fashioned barn dance in the horse barn and my horse saddled to take me to the mountain. I needed a garage for Mary and then a gym on the second floor.

"I could see the einkorn swaying in the wind, and the new distillery was busy with members who were there for the harvest of the crops that would eventually be planted.

"It was all mine, mine to create and build as my vision grew. My eyes welled up as my feelings of gratitude went to my Father. This was home, to enjoy my final opportunity where I could fulfill the dreams of my creation, and live a life of peace and happiness, and ride up to God's living room and feel His presence for whatever time was left that He was going to give me.

The lodge was unfinished and had been empty for five years. There was no landscaping and the grounds were weedy and unsightly. But Gary envisioned only the beauty and created a magnificent retreat in the mountains.

Beautiful rustic craftsmanship in the kitchen in the lodge.

A barn dance was the best, especially in the new barn.

The ranch wasn't complete without a horse barn—and of course—a Cowboy Christmas barn dance for the community, December 2017.

D. Gary Young | The World Leader in Essential Oils | 281

It took weeks and many hands to move tons of rocks to prepare for planting. | These ferocious bison are very quiet and peaceful at the ranch.

Gary loved the elk so much, he gave them all names and treated them like his pets. Hunting? Not his friends.

When the Utah Division of Wildlife Resources came to inspect the elk barn, they were so impressed, they asked Gary if they could use his barn as a model for other wildlife ranches and facilities.

European members enjoyed their retreat at the Skyrider Ranch. No one could imagine such amazing and beautiful accommodations in this remote area far away from city life. What a fabulous time of learning, sharing, and camaraderie; exactly why Gary built it.

Gary designed this magnificent kitchen and dining hall that he knew would eventually serve thousands of members.

In December 2017 Gary invited the community of Tabiona to a cowboy Christmas held at his ranch. Over 300 people enjoyed the feast at Elk Barn Inn.

"The ground was an immense field of weeds and rocks, even though it was flat, but I just knew this would be a fabulous place for einkorn to grow. I decided to prepare the ground; however, it was very rocky, meaning tons of boulders, rocks, and scrubs had to be moved. Many corporate staff members came to help clear the land and prepare for the first planting. The work was tedious, making sore and aching muscles, but the camaraderie created meaningful and treasured memories.

"In May the seed came from our farm in France, enabling us to plant 100 acres for trial planting and growing. Normally, einkorn does the best with late fall planting; however, because of the late fall rains, I wasn't able to get a crop in the ground before the cold temperatures and winter came. I didn't want to wait another year, so I felt it would be better to experiment with spring planting and see how the einkorn would do.

"As I expected, it grew extremely well and was tall and healthy, so after the first harvest, we prepared 1,000 acres for the next spring planting. Because the einkorn had grown so well at the ranch, I wanted to expand the acreage not only on our land but hopefully also with other farmers in the area. Thousands of acres of hay were growing in the valley, and I believed that many of these farmers would love to plant einkorn for us."

The view from the lodge overlooking the einkorn fields is breathtaking.

Skyrider River Ranch – Tabiona, Utah

Gary was always looking for more land close to his Skyrider Wilderness Ranch, and amazingly enough, 12,250 acres became available just a couple of miles from the current ranch, which he bought on January 8, 2018. Various small parcels of land, added to the purchase, brought the total acreage to 19,000. The property spans 4.5 miles of the Duchesne River, with beautiful farming land on both sides that gradually move up the mountain terrain.

Young Living is donating 11,600 acres of unfarmable mountain land for the D. Gary Young Wildlife Sanctuary, the largest conservation easement in Utah. The community, the state of Utah, and the members of the neighboring Ute tribe are happy for the protection this will provide the wildlife, and the prevention of any kind of urban development will protect Gary's vision of the great outdoor wilderness.

Visitors can enjoy canoeing, fishing, and hiking and photographing the elk, buffalo, deer, and maybe even a cougar if they have a telephoto lens. Wonderful Native American petroglyphs carved into the rock on the mountainside offer an amazing photography opportunity. The beautiful red rock terrain, also found only in this area, is breathtaking to see.

Many member organizations enjoy week-long retreats where they share their Young Living experiences and strengthen their business-building knowledge and skills while basking in the beauty of the Skyrider Wilderness Ranch, a special place—Gary's final resting place that he loved so much.

About 1,000 acres have been prepared for test plots of crops like melissa, goldenrod, conyza (Canadian fleabane), yarrow, lavender, and hemp; and another 2,500 acres will soon be added. We want to determine the best crops for distillation and eventually build a distillery where members can join the harvest and be part of the Seed to Seal process. More einkorn will be planted and we hope to partner with farmers in the Tabiona Valley in growing this ancient grain.

Dogsledding— Gary's Last Great Adventure

I asked Gary why he wanted to dog race in Alaska. The twinkle in his eyes really told me all: something new, something different, something on his bucket list, a dangerous challenge, a getaway from the cement city, and an opportunity to be alone in the beauty of Mother Nature—to be with God.

In Gary's words:

I'll never forget Mary's reaction, a day or two after Christmas, 2016. I turned over to her in the morning and said, "Honey, I'm going to go to Alaska and race dogs."

After a quiet moment, she said, "Have you lost your mind?"

"Well, maybe so, but I have to go to Alaska to try to find it."

"What on earth possessed you to want to do that?"

"It's been on my bucket list for over 40 years, when I lived in Fairbanks from 1975 through 1977. The start of the Iditarod was close, and there was a frenzy in the air. Women were going shopping in dogsleds instead of a car. You'd see 15 to 20 dogsleds and maybe one or two cars at the shopping center. I loved watching them take their kids to school in a dogsled.

I whispered to myself, "I want to do this. I'm going to do this someday."

But I made the mistake of saying "someday." I haven't found a calendar yet that has "someday" in it. So, if you want to do something, put a date on it. When you get to that date and things haven't worked out for you, then move the date. You're in charge of your destiny, so direct it.

Well, last year I woke up and decided that someday had finally come. Mary wasn't too happy with my decision, so I decided we would put it to a family vote in a very diplomatic way.

I said to Jacob, "Hey, son, what would you think if Dad went to Alaska and raced dogs?"

"Dad, that's so cool."

"Josef?"

"Go for it, Dad."

Three against one; what could she say? So, I took off for Alaska with a hole in my heart, post-ventricular contractions, post-atrial contractions, pleural effusion, pulmonary hypertension, and a myriad of other problems. Was I crazy? Probably.

Mary quizzed me in her realistic way, "Honey, what if something happens?"

I smiled and said, "I couldn't think of a better place for it to happen. I'll be closer to God. I'll be in beautiful country, in His living room. Nothing is going to happen."

I called a friend of mine who had raced dogs for years and asked him if he had time to take me out and see what I could do. So I flew up to Alaska on January 11, knowing absolutely nothing about dog racing.

We hooked up a team of eight dogs, and I jumped on a sled and followed. We went out through the bush, came back, and then we went out that afternoon for a second little 10-mile jaunt and came back. I thought, "Is this all there is to dog racing?"

At 2 a.m. my friend decided I needed a midnight ride, so we harnessed 10 dogs this time and went for 20 miles. He took me around this real sharp corner because he knew that I needed an experience of rolling a dogsled, and did it ever roll.

He told me, "If you roll over on a dogsled, don't let go because those dogs won't stop until they get back to the kennel, and it's a 20-mile walk back."

So I rolled but hung on as the dogs dragged me through the snow, in and out around the trees, until so much snow piled up that the sled stopped them. I got up, pulled my sled upright, and we took off for home.

I was anxious to know, "What do you think?"

Gary trained for the Alaskan dogsled races at his ranch in Tabiona.

"Gary, you're a natural-born musher. I'm going to sign you up for a race."

It seemed like no big deal, and since I had my ranch where I could practice, I bought eight dogs and brought them to Tabiona and then borrowed a sled. We cut a trail with the snowplow, and then I started to run with my dogs. I made a total of five runs, but on the third run, I rolled again and broke three ribs. I made two more runs after that and then flew back to Alaska to get ready for my first race.

snowmobile, the one I'm thinking I would have to follow. Her dogs lunged and she flipped over. I gasped and thought, "I can't do this. They'll laugh at me." Then I heard the announcer call number 28 and my name.

Ready or not, they pulled the pin, releasing the sled, and with the power of 12 dogs, I felt I was levitating as I went through the starting chute. The trail immediately crossed a road, and even though I had my foot on the brake trying to slow my dogs down, it felt like we were going 110 miles an hour. When the sled hit the berm in the road, we launched several feet high and cleared the road. While flying through the air, I was thinking to myself, "Don't crash now," and when the sled hit the ground, I was relieve to still be upright; but the dogs didn't slow down for a second. It was so exciting.

The start of the Tustumena 200—Gary's first race.

Waiting for my turn, I was feeling a little bit nervous, because all the people in this race knew what they were doing, and I was just pretending like I knew what I was doing. I watched this 20-year seasoned musher in front of me and thought, "If I do exactly what she does, I'll be okay." I was holding onto my sled, anchored to my snowmobile, with 12 dogs lunging at the line, excited to go. I could feel their passion— their destiny—their love of running.

The musher in front of me was set to go, and I felt a burst of excitement when they pulled the pin to release her

The Tustumena 200 is one of the most difficult races in Alaska.

What I didn't know until I got to Freddie's check station 50 miles later, everyone was betting that I wouldn't make it halfway. So when I pulled into the station, there was a big celebration. "Mr. Young, you made it," they said, and I was trying to figure out why they were so excited that I made it. I didn't know they were betting against me.

D. Gary Young | The World Leader in Essential Oils | 289

Arriving at the Homer check station of the Tustumena 200, 4 a.m.

I took care of my dogs and tried to catch a few winks, but it was soon time to go again. It didn't take long to get the dogs hooked to the harness, and off we went into the snowy mist.

We came to a steep hill that descended into what was called Deep Creek. The musher ahead of me went around the corner at the bottom and headed for the bridge. Although the lead dogs made it across, the sled jammed into the side of the bridge and snapped the lead ropes like a bowstring, and 10 of the 12 dogs went into the river.

The dogs were floating downstream toward the ice that was frozen solid across the river below. Patrick jumped off his sled, ran across the bridge and down the river bank with snow up to his waist to get to the lead team. I could see the sled was about to pull away from the bridge, which meant disaster because the dogs would be lost under the ice.

Even though I had just broken three ribs a week before, the adrenalin was rushing, and I had to do something. I set my snow hooks and jumped off and ran. I grabbed the tow line and pulled and pulled. I wanted to scream and let go, but the fear of those dogs drowning gave me strength. It didn't matter how much I hurt, I couldn't let them go under that ice.

As I pulled back to keep them from floating away, the sled stopped moving. Patrick was able to reach the lead team and pulled them up on the snowbank. Then he pulled one way and I pulled the other way, and we lifted the other eight dogs up on the bridge, and they made it across. Patrick was a 20-year seasoned musher, and he had just put his team in the river—and I had to cross that bridge?

I had an advantage because we were stopped, so I walked my sled and slid it around to where I could get it onto the bridge, and we went across. I wanted to build a fire to dry out the dogs, but Patrick just laughed and said, "They're huskies.

We're just going to run it." He checked all the harnesses and off they went. My dogs were shaking, but in just a few minutes, they were steaming. It was amazing to see this, especially in 10 degrees below zero; just a nice, brisk evening.

When we made it to Maclaren's, the halfway point, I had a funny experience. The official, Jane, came with her clipboard to check me in and look at the dogs to make sure they were all okay. She was very friendly and asked, "Mr. Young, how long have you been training for this race or for how many years?"

"I haven't."

"What do you mean?"

"This is only the seventh time I've been on a dogsled."

She dropped the clipboard in the snow. "No, no, you're kidding me," she said as she picked up the board. "That's amazing. Why did you pick the hardest race in Alaska to be your first one?"

"Well, no one told me it was the hardest."

We chatted as she checked the gear in my sled to make sure I hadn't ditched anything to lighten the load to be able to run faster. There were mandatory things like snowshoes, an axe, a cooker, food, and a sleeping bag that had to be in the sled.

She laughed and said, "I understand you had problems at the Deep Creek crossing. We had three other teams go into the river. Are you going back?"

"Yeah, I have to go back to finish."

She informed me that four other mushers had already scratched and said they were not going back.

I had two goals. One was to finish the race, and the second was to take the same dogs home that I brought—and nothing was going to stop me.

You're never too old to try something you've never done before. Was I scared? Yeah, there were a couple of times I was dang scared, and probably the scariest was when I didn't know if I was going to get across that bridge. I didn't know what I was doing, and so many times I knew the dogs were talking to me and laughing because they knew I didn't know what I was doing.

I created my own system, which I called "a one-ear hill, a two-ear hill, and a three-ear hill." When the first dog disappeared, I called it a one-ear hill because it was steep. If two ears disappeared gently, then I knew it was a moderate hill. If three ears disappeared slowly, it was a rolling hill. When it was a one-ear hill, I knew I had better be on the brake and try to slow them down.

Just before the dogs went over the top of the hill, they would look back at me, and I was sure they were laughing and saying, "Let's see if we can lose him on this one," and they would just run faster, and over that mountain we would go. I put my arms under the handle bar and stood with both feet on the drag brake trying to slow it down, but we were just dashing in and out around the trees and down the hill. I closed my eyes because I couldn't see anything anyway and knew I was going to die. I didn't know where the dogs were going, but as they raced up a hill and disappeared over the top, my stomach would go in my throat. What was on the other side that I couldn't see?

The ultimate exhaustion—80 hours without sleep in the bitter cold. Harnessing the dogs for the final 30-mile run of the Willow 300.

It was a triumphant moment when I came to the finish line at 4:20 in the morning, 200 miles later. I felt like a frozen popsicle, like I was mummified, and I hadn't slept. As I came around the corner, there were lights and a lot of people, and I didn't even know who was there to greet me, a nobody. But then I saw two young boys running just outside the chute; yes, Jacob and Josef; and in the crowd was this little woman who I could barely see, but I could tell by her walk and her clothes. Wow, my heart was so full, and I felt my very being warming.

Little things can mean a million to you, but there wasn't anything in the world that had more value to me at that moment than seeing my family at that finish line.

I had achieved my two goals and felt such exhilaration in my accomplishment that I had to race again, so I jumped into the Willow 300 race a week later. Many people tried to discourage me, but the challenge was in my blood.

The finish line of the Willow 300 was very close.

If you think about the worst that can happen, you have to put it out of your mind, expect the very best, and go for it. You need to quit worrying about the dark, a turn in the road, a hill, or a river. There are a lot of times you can't see where you are going, but that doesn't mean you quit, you stop, or you turn around and go back toward the light because darkness is falling. There's nothing blacker than being in a black spruce forest with no stars shining. It's so black you can't see the end of your nose.

My first race taught me to trust the dogs and my own instincts, so I was more mentally prepared for the Willow. Naturally, the terrain was different, but it didn't seem as treacherous, perhaps because I knew more what to expect. However, there were long, lonely stretches with freezing, blowing winds that never seemed to end.

I kept hearing Mary's words, "You don't have to do this." No, I don't have to do it, and I could quit, but that would be a huge disappointment to me and to everyone who was cheering for me. I hurt everywhere, especially my legs, and I felt the cold to my bones, but I just kept seeing the finish line in my mind and those I loved who would be there.

It was daylight when I crossed the last stretch over the frozen lake, and my family and staff members were waiting and cheering me across the finish line; what a celebration.

The lady who checked me in this time said, "Mr. Young, there are not many people who run two races back to back, and certainly not a rookie."

I chuckled and replied, "Nobody told me." Since I base my information on myself and not on what other people do and say, I just did it. This was how I grew up—the ruggedness of the mountains and the harshness of life. I loved it then and it is still my passion.

I always had dogs growing up because we ran cattle, sheep, and horses. After my third dog was killed by a grizzly bear on our ranch in Canada, I never really developed a strong relationship with another dog. I didn't want to feel the pain again from that kind of a loss.

Being with these dogs brought back so many memories and brought back the love that I had always had for the animals. These huskies are intelligent and fun to be with if they trust you and if you allow them to feel your heart. It was a remarkable experience, which I will remember as one of the greatest challenges and memories of my life.

Although I thought this would be the ultimate getaway for me, I wanted to share my adventure with my family and my Young Living family. I had all kinds of marketing ideas to raise money for our foundation and bring awareness about Young Living to a different culture of people. After all, the dogs would benefit from our products just like humans. It was exciting as our members joined in and supported me in my quest. We raised about $40,000 for the rebuilding of Nepal, which was our fundraising target for which I felt much gratitude.

I learned so much from this experience that gave me greater insight into myself and my purpose for doing the things I do. It became a great teaching tool, from which I hoped others would learn and benefit.

There will always be problems in life, so what is going to be your focus? Are you going to focus on building your business and success and on sharing with people and helping people change their lives, or are you going to focus on the hill that looks too steep, the river that you might fall into, or the darkness of the unknown?

Focus on where you want to go and don't let anyone take you off your path. Let the Spirit guide you as you follow your dreams and reach your highest potential.

There was a lot of excitement with everyone cheering as Gary approached the finish line of the Willow 300—realizing his dream.

The Ultimate Dogsled

After Gary had finished two dogsled races, he had a good understanding about the event he found exhilarating and about the equipment that to him was very old in its design and functionality. Dogsledding dates back hundreds of years, but the design of the dogsled has remained almost the same. Although today's sleds are made from lighter, modern materials, they have the same ancient frame design.

Gary dreamed of racing in the Iditarod and began creating a new design for a faster, more efficient sled. He started looking for a company that could engineer his ideas and build it and was happy when he found a team of designers and engineers who thrived on turning ideas into real working products. They developed solutions where every aspect of the race was considered and brought into the design of the sled.

Mushers carry frozen meat and use methanol to heat 3 gallons of water for an hour to thaw out the food. A new cooking system was developed that contains the heat from the burning fuel to boil water in a lightning fast 7 minutes from ice, so a musher would gain an extra 50 minutes between runs.

After feeding and taking care of the dogs, putting them down for a rest, and preparing for the next run, mushers will often have only a little time to sleep in the frigid -40-degree weather. A carbon fiber sleeping compartment on the sled that is insulated, lightweight, comfortable, and sets up in literally seconds allows the musher to sleep anywhere along the course, out of the wind, out of the noise, and as cozy as one can be in a dogsled race.

Current sleds have painfully inefficient storage, so a hard-shell gear compartment at the base of the sled under the sleeping compartment was engineered to make a place for everything. In addition, the gear was spread out wide and shallow to make everything easily accessible and to maintain a low load, providing more stability.

Sleds sit fixed on straight runners and are steered mainly by the musher's commands to the dogs with the musher dragging the sled side to side. The sled tilts and can flip, and "steering" is dangerous and fatigues the musher, who is constantly fighting both dogs and sled.

To solve this, the sled was designed with two rigid carbon-fiber side frames connected by pivots, giving over 30 degrees of side-to-side articulation. Also, a wider runner made the sled more durable, more stable, and provided better float.

Gary had a sled that was as comfortable as a Cadillac but cornered like a roadster, held all his gear, and made stops easier and faster than any sled in history. Sadly, Gary was never able to make that next race in his modern, most high-tech, engineered sled that was ever built for this industry.

The new dogsled that Gary designed is on display in the Young Living headquarters' museum.

Hieroglyphics depicting the presentation of blue lotus oil, the most prized oil in all of ancient Egypt.

IN SEARCH OF ANCIENT KNOWLEDGE

The Ancient Secrets of Egypt

The more Gary learned, the more he was driven to go to Egypt, the heart of the ancient world of essential oils. His experiences were amazing and the knowledge he brought home convinced him even more that there was so much that had been lost to the modern world.

Gary traveled throughout Egypt exploring the pyramids, tombs, temples, and museums and visiting government offices. He even wandered through the marketplace looking at all the essential oils, dried herbs, resin burners, beautiful oil containers, etc., to get ideas. The information was voluminous. He felt very comfortable "walking back in time" as history told its story, opening up still another chapter of discovery.

In 1991, during Gary's first trip to Egypt, he was fortunate to meet Dr. Radwan Farag, dean of the biochemistry department at the University of Cairo, who had been conducting research on essential oils for years. As of 2015 he has published nearly 200 research papers. Dr. Farag willingly shared his knowledge with Gary. He was a wealth of information and a wonderful mentor.

Gary tells an interesting story when he visited the Temple of Isis on the Island of Philae: "One of the guards came to me and said, 'I know what you come here to see' and indicated that I should follow him. It was very strange and I thought the guard just wanted money, so I joined a tour group to get away from him. But the guard was persistent and tapped me on the shoulder a second time and repeated himself. I tried to get away from him by going a different direction, but he came around the corner and met me face to face and for the third time said, 'Come quick; follow me. I show you what you come to see.'

"By then I was annoyed but had also become a bit curious, so I followed him. He had an old metal key to a heavy iron gate that he quickly unlocked, pulled open, and motioned for me to hurry inside. As soon as I went through the gate and started up the stairs, the guard walked in and locked the gate behind him.

Dr. Radwan Farag visited Gary's lab in Riverton, Utah, 1995.

"It was very unnerving, but I didn't feel I should go back; so I followed him up the stairs into an open area on the roof and over to a room with no door. As the guard motioned for me to enter, I could see the sunlight illuminating the hieroglyphics on the wall showing the ancient ceremony of the 'cleansing of the flesh and the blood' using essential oils. It was a glorious moment of discovery for me that became the foundation for the 'emotional clearing' that I have used in my teaching."

Dr. Farag was amazed at Gary's experience and translated the idea of the ceremony for him. He was fascinated with Gary's interest in essential oils and in his development of growing aromatic plants for distillation. In 1995 Dr. Farag came to Utah as a guest speaker for Young Living's first convention and to see the tiny Young Living operation. He was helpful and encouraging and remained a friend since that time.

Gary visited a distillery in Fayum, Egypt, to see the distillation of chamomile, 1991. Note: Gary's hands to the right.

A guard, who kept following Gary, tapped him on the shoulder and said, "Come quick, follow me. I show you what you come here to see."

In 1991 at the Temple of Isis on the Island of Philae, Gary stands at the doorway of the room where he learned about the long-lost Egyptian ritual that was known as the cleansing of the flesh and the blood.

Two Egyptian priests stand at the head and foot of the person undergoing the three-day cleansing ritual that included the use of essential oils. This hieroglyph is found in the Temple of Isis in an upper room that is rarely shown to the public.

This is an ancient clay essential oil extractor that dates back to 350 BC, now displayed in the museum in Taxila, Pakistan. The guard in the museum told Gary there were no distillers, but there was an old type of "water purifier" made of clay in a glass case at the back of the building.

Discovery in Pakistan

When Gary and I went to Oman in 1995, Gary decided to go to Hunzaland to interview the old people and to see if he could discover their secrets to longevity. He had heard that there was a museum in Taxila, a small town outside of Lahore, Pakistan, that had some ancient clay distillers. We had to fly to Lahore on the way to Hunzaland, so it was not much out of the way. Gary really wanted to see these early clay distillers, so that was even more of a reason to go there. It was an exciting moment when he spotted them at the very back of the museum. The guard allowed Gary to take pictures so that he could share his discovery with everyone at home.

The Old World

The ancient world of Egypt, Israel, and Arabia, which comprises many countries of today, contains many distilleries; artifacts of essential oils; and apothecaries filled with salves, beauty creams, and medicines. It was part of their culture, and the oils were prized commodities used only for royalty and those of a higher social status. Essential oils were obtained in many different ways, as was evident by the different types and methods of extraction that could be determined from the ruins and what was left of the distilleries. It was extremely interesting and educational for Gary, as he was constantly following legends, rumors, books, maps, and stories that he heard from the people in the countries he visited.

Gary talked with both the old and young people in Hunzaland.

Masada, on a high mountain plateau on the west bank of the Dead Sea

In 1990 Gary traveled to Masada, where he found the ruins of an ancient distillery that was easy to see in the rocks.

It was amazing how his explanation brought it to life. All of this certainly went into his data bank for his plans to build a distillery.

The ruins of Ein Gedi in Israel near the Dead Sea are estimated to be from between 2500 and 2000 B.C.

Ein Gedi was an ancient way station and depository where frankincense, myrrh, and balsam were distilled. Many ointments, tinctures, and skin creams were made in the apothecary, guarded behind the stone door.

Israel—The Ancient Balm of Gilead—Liquid Gold

Gary traveled to the Middle East many times between 1991 and his death in 2018 to learn more about the trees that grew anciently in this region. He traveled to Jerusalem to study Biblical archaeology at the Hebrew University and spent his weekends driving throughout Israel following stories of legends told to Gary by his professors, who had become interested in Gary's essential oil research. Driving, stopping, looking, asking questions, and following clues that were given him, he finally found the ancient Ein Gedi distillery in the Judean Mountains west of the Dead Sea in 1996.

This heightened his curiosity and gave him a whole new awareness about the balm of Gilead, frankincense, and myrrh trees that once grew in Israel until about 1921. The original trees were first brought by camel caravan to Israel as a gift by the Queen of Sheba and given to King Solomon as an offering of peace and her desire to learn from him of his great wisdom. Sadly, as history evolved, and the great era of the caravans and the desire for the resins and oils diminished, the distilleries became defunct; and no one cared for the trees, eventually leaving them to die out.

But for Gary, Ein Gedi was a great discovery. He could see the vats, the water channels, the apothecary, and the great stone door that was still in place. His mind was filled with visions of all the activities that took place in this ancient distillery; and he could see it in detail as if it were just yesterday when the caravans were delivering the sacks of resin for safe keeping or for the extraction of the oil.

In Gary's historical novel, *The One Gift*, the camel caravans seem to come to life while carrying the frankincense, myrrh, and balsam resins and oils as they traveled from the heart of the frankincense groves in Arabia to Israel, Egypt, India, and other far areas of the world. The story culminates in Ein Gedi, where the ancient distillery looks down from the hills to the Dead Sea and where the oils of the balm of Gilead, known historically as liquid gold; frankincense; and myrrh were extracted, and various ointments, salves, and tinctures were made.

The great stone door protected the distillery.

Gary took this picture of Marcella Vonn Harting and me in front of the distilling tub and entrance way into the apothecary, 1999.

This tub was filled with resin and water for the typical, but rudimentary, method of distilling at that time.

Israel was a historical feast for Gary to which he often returned in search of the undiscovered. In October 2012, while visiting Israel and Jordan, his hope was to find some balsam trees perhaps still growing somewhere in the area. He was told about a gentleman who had a small farm east of Jerusalem who supposedly was cultivating a few balsam trees.

When Gary found the farm, he was surprised to learn that several years earlier, this man had become interested in the aromatic plants and trees from the desert and wanted to bring back the balm of Gilead (*Commiphora gileadensis*) tree that produced the most prized essential oil in ancient Judean history.

He had a small farm and two large greenhouses close to the Dead Sea, where he was growing a variety of desert plants and working to expand his balm of Gilead tree project as well as growing *Boswellia sacra* (sacred frankincense).

Resin runs from the cut bark of the gileadensis tree.

Keeping meticulous records has always been very important to Gary.

Four-year-old *Commiphora gileadensis* (balm of Gilead), often referred to as balsam, is growing well.

The fruit of the *Commiphora gileadensis* tree.

The aroma of the rare balm of Gilead was captivating.

The distiller for balm of Gilead, or liquid gold, as it was called anciently.

Gary was ecstatic to finally find the balm of Gilead tree, which he had studied so much and just knew that somewhere there would still be some trees growing. It seemed amazing that this farm was so close to the ruins of Ein Gedi, where these ancient resins had once been distilled.

The history of resins and distillation is the greatest in ancient Arabia, and yet this history had been covered with the dust of ages and lost to mankind.

Gary's desire to travel the Frankincense Trail sent him exploring all facets of this once-flourishing industry. He wanted to learn as much as he could about the famous resins of frankincense, myrrh, and balsam (balm of Gilead) and traveled throughout Arabia looking for clues.

When he found the balm of Gilead tree—the *Commiphora gileadensis*, he was immediately interested in this ancient oil and wanted to bring it to his Young Living family to enjoy this little bit of history as well.

This small farm was just that—a very small farm with one tiny cooker. With the size that we are today and the continuing growth, it was not feasible that enough oil could be produced to meet even the orders of one week. However, Young Living is looking for possibilities to make this happen with the right partner farm located in a safe area of the country with all the right conditions.

In this area of the world, in this very place, the demand for the oils for the supreme physical and spiritual benefits they provided was at a pinnacle, but at the same time, the oils were being lost to the world.

The exploration, research, and dedication of D. Gary Young has brought much of this lost knowledge back to the modern world. That which we learn today teaches us that there is so much more to discover. His vision of what history can teach us today rewards all those who are beginning their journey down this road of discovery.

Beautiful, two-year-old sacred frankincense trees (*Boswellia sacra*) growing near the Dead Sea.

The nursery is doing very well, and many new *Commiphora gileadensis* trees are ready to be transplanted. Josef was happy traveling to new places, visiting the farms, and discovering new things with Dad.

Louis was very focused as he received instruction from Gary about distilling vetiver. Mary Lou Jacobson from the office was there to conduct an audit.

Gary checks the ylang ylang distiller in Madagascar.

308 D. Gary Young | The World Leader in Essential Oils

After visiting the ylang ylang groves in Madagascar, Gary knew that ylang ylang would thrive on the farm in Ecuador.

Madagascar

Gary went to Nosy Be, Madagascar, to visit several ylang ylang plantations. He carefully watched their production and felt that these trees would grow well in Ecuador. In 2011 he was able to find a greenhouse in Guayaquil from which he bought 24,000 trees and planted them on 10 acres at the farm.

They grew very well and quickly produced an abundance of flowers, but because the flowers are so delicate, the volume has to be smaller for distillation, which meant more cookers. With continued demand for this oil, more acreage was planted, and today ylang ylang is a major crop at the farm.

Pickers are paid by the weight of their baskets.

5 SEED TO SEAL® PARTNERSHIP PRINCIPLES

We dedicate significant resources to all our corporate-owned farms, partner farms, and Seed to Seal-certified growers to support their production quality and success. Authenticity is important as part of our wellness journey and is the core of who we are. All Young Living corporate-owned farms and partner farms are committed to producing 100 percent pure, genuine, therapeutic-grade essential oils.

1. **Established Relationships:** We hand-select well-known suppliers of premium botanicals and build relationships with them for decades.
2. **Seed to Seal Specifications:** All corporate farm managers, partner farms, and Seed to Seal-certified growers sign declarations that they will follow our strict specifications.
3. **Legally Binding Contracts:** All farm owners and managers are required to sign legally binding contracts..
4. **Stringent Laboratory Testing:** If a product does not meet our standards, it is rejected and returned to the supplier.
5. **Ongoing Audits:** We verify the quality of our oils and our supply chain members as part of our commitment to bring our members the highest quality products possible.

The aroma enveloped Gary while inspecting the fields of oolong tea, an ingredient for Young Living's Slique Tea.

YOUNG LIVING PARTNER FARMS AND CERTIFIED GROWERS

Gary traveled the world in search of new plants and visited other farmers and producers of essential oils. He saw the value of creating partnerships and being able to work together to improve crop growth, harvesting, and the extraction process of the oils. Since Gary's first partnership in 1997 in Quebec, other farmers have become partners, and since 2016 the number of partner farms has accelerated.

Young Living is the only essential oil company in the world that sources 100 percent of its oils from its corporate-owned farms, partner farms, and Seed to Seal-certified growers. This gives us complete visibility and enables us to oversee the production of our oils—from seeding and cultivating to harvesting and distilling.

These partnerships have been invaluable in providing 100 percent pure oils that help secure the volume that is needed to meet the demand of our members, as well as bring new oils to Young Living from crops grown in totally different climates and terrain.

Young Living's Sourcing team has become very sophisticated as they meet with independent growers in different countries to determine partnership possibilities. Young Living corporate-owned and partner farms produce thousands of liters of essential oils a year that are bottled and shipped all over the world.

There will always be some oils in the world that we cannot grow on our own farms, so Young Living has developed partnerships with farmers around the world. We invest in their operations and help them become more efficient. We build stainless steel extraction chambers, purchase farm equipment, teach better distillation practices, and support their operation with our technological and financial assistance.

Years ago Gary put in place a whole new standard in the essential oil industry for farms and distilleries to use food-grade stainless steel. Before that, distilleries were built with carbon steel, which certainly would have had a negative effect on the oils.

Through our partner farms, Young Living is able to support local, independent growers while maintaining our commitment to quality. To work with Young Living, our partners must meet very specific requirements and pledge to adhere strictly to our Seed to Seal quality commitment. We closely monitor the quality of the botanicals and test the oils they provide.

We also purchased essential oils from Seed to Seal-certified growers, who must abide by our stringent Seed to Seal quality standard, and we often travel to the farms to audit their production. If any oil fails to meet the Young Living standard, the oil is rejected and returned to the growers or distillers.

Our Seed to Seal quality commitment, to which we strictly adhere, is the foundation of our business. Our Seed to Seal commitment guarantees that our partner farms and certified growers have met our requirements and is the standard by which we are known throughout the world.

Global Farm Operations in 2019

Corporate-Owned Farms

St. Maries Lavender Farm and Distillery	St. Maries, Idaho, USA	1992	Lavender, Melissa, Goldenrod
Young Living Lavender Farm and Distillery	Mona, Utah, USA	1995	Lavender, Clary Sage, Goldenrod, Juniper, Blue Yarrow, Einkorn, Evergreen Essence
Simiane-la-Rotonde Lavender Farm and Distillery	Simiane-la-Rotonde, France	1996	Lavender, Clary Sage, Rosemary, Lavandin, Einkorn
Highland Flats Tree Farm and Distillery	Naples, Idaho, USA	1999	Idaho Blue Spruce, Idaho Balsam Fir, White Fir
Finca Botanica Farm and Distillery	Chongon, Ecuador	2006	Ylang Ylang, Palo Santo, Mastrante, Lemongrass, Eucalyptus Blue, Dorado Azul™, Ocotea, Oregano, Ruta Graveolens, Chocolate
Arabian Frankincense Distillery	Muscat, Oman	2010	Sacred Frankincense™, Myrrh, Sweet Myrrh
Skyrider Wilderness Ranch	Tabiona, Utah, USA	2014	Einkorn grown and harvested from which the following are made: Gary's True Grit Einkorn Flour, Pancake and Waffle Mix, Rotini Pasta, Spaghetti, Granola, Einkorn Flakes Cereal, Einkorn Crackers, Einkorn Berries
Northern Lights Farm and Distillery	Fort Nelson, BC, Canada	2014	Northern Lights Black Spruce
Dalmatia Aromatic Farm and Distillery	Split, Croatia	2015	Helichrysum, Sage, Juniper, Bay Laurel
Skyrider River Ranch	Tabiona, Utah, USA	2017	Research and testing plots in progress
Mera Ocotea Farm	Mera, Ecuador	2017	Ocotea

Partner Farms — Contract Signed

Canada—Quebec Partner Farm	Grondines, Quebec, Canada	1997	Goldenrod, Canadian Fleabane, Tsuga, Ledum
Australia—Outback Botanical Reserve and Distillery	Darwin, Australia	2007	Blue Cypress
Taiwan—Cooperative Farm and Distillery	Dianio, Taiwan	2012	Jade Lemon, Hong Kuai, Xiang Mao, Camphor Wood
Hawaii—Sandalwood Reforestation Project	Big Island, Hawaii, USA	2014	Royal Hawaiian Sandalwood (Began suppling Young Living in 2012)
Australia—Ord River Sandalwood Farm and Distillery	Kununurra, Australia	2016	Sacred Sandalwood
South Africa—Amanzi Amahle Farm and Distillery	Cape Town, South Africa	2017	Eucalyptus Radiata, Tea Tree, Grapefruit, Lemon, Orange
Spain—Vida de Seville Distillery	Almaden de la Plata, Seville, Spain	2018	Cistus, Frankincense, Myrrh (Began suppling Young Living in 1996)
Australia—Melaleuca Gihndagun Farm	Tatham, Australia	2018	Tea Tree
Washington, USA—Labbeemint Partner Distillery	White Swan, Washington, USA	2018	Peppermint, Spearmint (Began suppling Young Living in 2016)
Philippines—Happy Pili Tree Farm and Distillery	Bicol Region, Philippines	2018	Elemi
Mexico—Finca Victoria	Tamaulipas, Mexico	2018	Grapefruit, Lime (Began suppling Young Living in 2014)
Italy—Bella Vista Farm and Distillery	Condofuri Marina, Italy	2018	Bergamot (Began suppling Young Living in 2014)
Turkey—Hediye Rose Farm and Distillery	Senir, Turkey	2018	Rose, Frankincense, Myrrh
Brazil—Painted Stone Farm and Distillery	Itacoatiara, Brazil	2018	Copaiba (Began suppling Young Living in 2009)
Argentina—Esmeralda Farm	Tucumán, Argentina	2018	Lemon (Began suppling Young Living in 2014)
China—Ningxia Wolfberry Farm and Processing Plant	Ningxia Province, China	2019	Wolfberry Pureé, Wolfberry Oil, Dried Wolfberries (Began in 1993)
Philippines—Kalipay Coconut Farm	Manila, Philippines	2019	Organic Coconut Oil

Gary and I visited this melaleuca/tea tree forest in Australia in 1997—the beginning of developing our partner farm relationships.

Australia—Outback Botanical Reserve and Distillery

Gary and I were excited to fly to Australia in January 1997. We drove to Darwin, located in the Northern Territories on the northern coast where the Australian blue cypress trees grow, to visit the blue cypress farm, owned by Vince Collins. This was the beginning of a great relationship and one of the earliest Young Living partnerships.

The trees were used for construction, but after a terrible typhoon destroyed so many homes in 1974, the government abandoned the plantations because it was obvious that it was more important to build brick-and-mortar houses.

Vince curiously decided to distill the blue cypress trees when he saw that they produced a lot of aromatic sap. In 2000 he petitioned the government for a patent for the process of distilling blue cypress trees that was finally granted in 2002.

Vince contacted Gary, and subsequently, Young Living provided the funds for the distillery. Vince began supplying Blue Cypress to Young Living, and since 2007 we have worked closely together. Many of our members have been to Darwin to see the plantation, wood chipping operation, and steam distillation of our Blue Cypress essential oil.

Resin of the blue cypress looks like crystal drops.

Vince proudly shows the exquisite blue cypress oil.

The aroma from the forest of the blue cypress trees fills the air for miles.

Quebec Partner Farm

In 1997 Gary contacted Pierre and Lucie Mainguy in Grondines, Quebec, who had been distilling aromatic crops since 1988. Gary asked if they would distill black spruce trees and said he would help them expand their distillation facility to increase their capacity. Pierre unexpectedly passed away a year later; but since 1998 Lucie and her children have continued to partner with Young Living not only for Black Spruce essential oil but also for Ledum and Canadian Fleabane oils. She invites all Young Living members to visit her farm and distillery, so she can show them her own Seed to Seal process and the extraction of the essential oils.

Lucie's small distillery for black spruce, ledum, and conyza near Montreal.

Discussing production in Lucie's laboratory.

Black spruce chips ready to be distilled.

Early distillers are on display at the entrance of the frankincense distillery in Spain that Gary and I visited in 1996.

Spain—Vida de Seville Distillery

In 1996 Gary and I visited the frankincense distillery in Spain, which had been in business for almost a century, located in Almaden de la Plata, about an hour north of the city of Seville. Gary was fascinated with the extraction of the frankincense oil from the resin that was very different from the distillation of aromatic plants, and he wanted to understand the process. He became friends with Fernando, the owner, who invited him to come to Spain to see his operation.

The distillery was very clean with high-tech equipment, which was amazing to see in such a remote area of the countryside. During the 12 hours of the distillation of the frankincense resin, Gary and Fernando talked about the possibility of creating a partnership, which became official when the papers were signed in 2018.

Gary's mechanical aptitude made it easy for him to see and understand what was necessary for the distillation and how to build and operate the equipment. The design was in his mind, so he was ready when it came time to build in Oman.

Besides frankincense, the oils of myrrh and cistus are also produced in this facility. Cistus is wildcrafted and has a very sticky sap, and for 42 years, the workers have harvested cistus in the traditional manner in the Sierra Norte to maintain the integrity of the plants for future growth.

This partnership allows us to sustainably keep up with the demand for these popular essential oils. They burn the biomass to power the boiler for the distillery, which supports their conservation practices to further sustain the land and produce the highest-quality essential oils.

In 2010 Gary returned to the distillery in Spain to solidify his understanding of resin distillation in anticipation of building his own distillery in Oman.

The chamber is filled 1/4 with resin and 3/4 with water for greater agitation to the breakdown the resin, releasing the oil.

George and Gary seal the distilling chamber.

Filtering the frankincense oil.

D. Gary Young | The World Leader in Essential Oils

Freshly cut cistus waiting to be distilled.

Hundreds of tiny cistus seeds come from a single seed pod.

The villagers from the nearby town of Almaden de la Plata work in the distillery.

Because of its delicate leaves, the distillation of cistus has to be done in a smaller extraction chamber.

Dr. Ginn Lee had many new oil samples from his research distillery for Gary to smell in Taiwan, 2011.

Taiwan—Cooperative Farm and Distillery

In 2011 Gary flew to Taiwan to investigate the aromatic plants of this beautiful, semitropical country. He met retired professor Dr. Lee, an agriculturalist who owned a small distiller and had been farming all his life. He and his son Tiger, a young engineer, joined forces to further their agricultural projects with Young Living. Young Living purchased a 500-liter extraction chamber (distiller) and a wood chipper to help improve the farm's efficiency; and by the summer of 2012, they had distilled 130 aromatic plants and trees. Gary chose 13 oils of which, Red Hinoki and Red Lemongrass, were produced for the 2013 Young Living convention Exotic Oils Collection. Red Hinoki, called Hong Kuai in Mandarin, is known for its rich, woody aroma and is high in sesquiterpenes that deliver oxygen molecules to the cells.

This aromatic tree is native to the 9,000-foot elevation rainforest that caps the tall peaks at the center of the Taiwan Island. However, the trees are harvested only near sea level in the large rivers that start as heavy streams in the steep mountains. Monsoon rains cause landslides on the steep slopes of the red hinoki rainforest that eventually fill the small streams and large creeks, widening the rivers with red hinoki logs.

The fallen logs are taken to sawmills, where the scrap lumber is chipped and distilled for the essential oil. This essential oil is about 95 percent composed of heavy, bioactive sesquiterpenes and is known for its ability to build self-confidence and security prior to physical activities.

Red lemongrass has long been grown and distilled for making soaps, shampoos, and cleaning products. By 1940 farmers had planted 140,000 acres of red lemongrass, producing 50,000 kg (110,000 lbs.) of this essential oil each year. However, after the Japanese occupation, the need for red lemongrass was replaced with the need for more rice and fruit orchards. In 2013 fewer than 200 acres of red lemongrass were being grown on fewer than 20 farms.

Dr. Ginn Lee's distillery in Taitung, Taiwan.

One of the largest remaining red lemongrass plantations was found over 1,000 feet above sea level and is owned by the native Paiwan Tribe. The tribe had nearly 100 acres of red lemongrass ready to harvest and a new 1,500-liter steam distiller in the valley below. Agreements were made and they began harvesting and distilling this wonderful plant. Red Lemongrass essential oil, Xiang Mao in Chinese, has a beautiful aroma and is known for its ability to enlighten the mind and spirit for learning and focus.

For convention in 2014, the Young Living Taiwan Farm produced a third essential oil, Jade Lemon. This essential oil is expressed from green jade-colored mature lemons that grow only in Taiwan and China. Because more jade lemon is grown in China, our partner in Taiwan, Dr. Lee, is working with the growers in southern China to produce more quantities. Jade Lemon essential oil has the aroma of lemon and lime together, which is very pleasing to the mind and is exclusive to Young Living.

Our Taiwanese partners continue to collect wild aromatic plants, propagate them in their large greenhouses, and domesticate them on farming land for production. A new, high-capacity steam distiller was installed to increase production capacity at the farm.

A grove of jade lemon trees in Taiwan.

D. Gary Young | The World Leader in Essential Oils

Hawaii–Sandalwood Reforestation Project

Young Living and the Kona Sandalwood Reforestation Project in Kailua-Kona, Hawaii, have signed a long-term, exclusive agreement with licenses and permits from the state to support long-term sustainability. Young Living now has a secure source of this treasured essential oil that has become threatened by overharvesting and livestock grazing.

Gary was committed to the conservation and reforestation of sandalwood trees and was excited to have a partner who offers us this opportunity to help. Planning and implementing this project was something that Gary looked forward to doing with Young Living members all over the world, similar to the reforestation project at the Highland Flats Tree Farm in Idaho. The members have a rewarding time in Hawaii planting saplings at the farm, as well as enjoying the beautiful weather and scenery, where snow boots, coats, gloves, and hats aren't necessary.

Josef is fascinated by the huge sandalwood root, which is about 4 feet tall.

Young Living members learn about sandalwood distillation.

322   D. Gary Young | The World Leader in Essential Oils

Mariana Arévalo Madrid (age 7) from Mexico loved planting her sandalwood sapling, 2016.

Distillery operators are having fun with the members as they tour the facility.

D. Gary Young | The World Leader in Essential Oils

Australia—Ord River Sandalwood Farm and Distillery

In June of 2016, Gary met with the owner of the sandalwood farm in Kununurra, Australia, and was very impressed with such a beautiful oil and their commitment to high quality with long-term plans for sustainably grown sandalwood.

In October 2016 Young Living signed a long-term partnership agreement with them to supply its premium Indian (Sacred) Sandalwood (*Santalum album*) oil. The agreement is helping drive new product development and allows Young Living to immediately double its sandalwood oil volume to meet current and future demands. The new sandalwood oil complements Young Living's Royal Hawaiian Sandalwood (*Santalum paniculatum*) from our partner farm in Hawaii.

Since 1999 the Ord River Sandalwood Farm and Distillery has owned and operated the world's largest plantation, with 13,000 hectares of cultivated sandalwood trees in Australia's tropical north. Each year they harvest 15-year-old trees and then replant saplings to replace the harvested trees. They use an award-winning water-recycling facility in their distillation process for a renewable energy source with a biomass boiler (biomass is the distilled plant material that has no value and is usually thrown out).

The owners of this amazing farm are committed to maintaining the highest environmental and ethical standards in all aspects of their business.

This modern and highly technical distillery produces Sacred Sandalwood for Young Living.

The sandalwood plantation encompasses thousands of acres.

Australia—Melaleuca Gihndagun Farm

In July 2018 the Gihndagun Farm in Tatham, Australia, became a Young Living partner farm. Gihndagun (pronounced Gihn-dah-gun), which means "respect the earth," will provide *Melaleuca alternifolia* (Tea Tree) essential oil exclusively for Young Living. This is one of the most widely used and extensively researched essential oils in the world and can be used for everything from home cleaning solutions to skin care.

The Gihndagun Farm, located near the small town of Tatham 137 miles south of Brisbane, is Young Living's third partner farm in Australia. This family-owned and -operated company has more than 20 years of farming experience and puts skill and thought into every step of the production process. The farm is dedicated to sustainable growing practices and the highest quality of essential oil production.

The Gihndagun Farm covers 100 acres of rich soil that is cultivated with all-natural tree biomass, wood chips, and naturally derived fertilizer. Crops are irrigated with water that is captured and reused. The farm proudly upholds the Australian Tea Tree Industry Association's Code of Practice and is Halal certified.

To help achieve these rigorous standards, the Gihndagun Farm sends its tea tree oil to be tested at the nearby Southern Cross Plant Science (SCPS) laboratories, which is globally recognized for its essential oils program, before being sent to Young Living's laboratory for additional testing. Two SCPS faculty are also members of the International Organization for Standardization's (ISO) essential oil committee.

The Gihndagun Farm received a partner farm grant to research and implement new methods of sustainability in all facets of production. We are also working together with a new aromatic plant to produce a new oil called fragonia (*Agonis fragrans*), which will soon find its way into the Young Living market.

The tiny seeds are germinated in the nursery by soaking them in water for several days to soften the hard exterior coat. After about four months, the seedlings are transplanted into prepared fields at planting rates of 25,000 – 35,000 trees per hectare.

Over 100 acres are planted with seedlings that will grow to a height of 2 to 2.5 meters in 12-14 months before being harvested the first time. The trees are robust and regenerate quickly after the first harvest, and the yield improves over two to three years as the trees establish a strong network of roots.

Washington—Labbeemint Partner Distillery

In 2018 the Labbeemint Partner Distillery, with roots in beautiful White Swan, Washington, became a new Young Living partner. Labbeemint has been supplying the U.S. with the essential oils of peppermint and spearmint since 1940. For generations it has been owned and run by a family of mint farmers who take great pride in their operation and the quality of the oils they produce.

Labbeemint has always placed the needs of their customers first. Their quality standards align with our Seed to Seal standard. As a market leader in high-quality mint essential oils, they have a strong background in mint cultivation and distillation, making them perfect as our primary supplier for peppermint.

The operation of the Labbeemint distillation creates a strong and sustainable source of quality mint oils. Mint species are perennials and grow best in cold winters, forcing the plants to go dormant, which enhances the oil quality. With warm days, cool nights, and nutrient-rich soil, Labbeemint's location is ideal for growing mint.

As is typical of natural products, it is not unusual to have a slight difference in the aroma due to weather conditions that may vary each year. Our Sourcing team and farming experts have spent time working in the fields, distilleries, and laboratories to ensure the highest standard of production and quality.

Like all our partners, they were eager to embrace our Seed to Seal principles, because in every step of their operation, they mirror our same quality standard. This partnership supports our longstanding commitment to the purest essential oils and to sourcing from the world's most reputable growers. The Labbeemint partnership is a model for partners and suppliers who care as much about the environment, the people, and the final product as we do.

The distillery for peppermint, wintergreen, and spearmint.

The lush mint grows in accordance with our Seed to Seal specifications and produces beautiful, high-quality oil.

South Africa—Amanzi Amahle Farm and Distillery

In August 2017 the Amanzi Amahle Farm and Distillery in Cape Town, South Africa, became a Young Living partner farm, providing Young Living with the essential oils of Eucalyptus Radiata, Tea Tree, Grapefruit, Orange, and Lemon.

Scattered across the vast continent of Africa, the Amanzi Amahle Farm and Distillery has more than 29,000 acres of rich soil for growing aromatic botanicals. The farm has 35 years of experience in sustainable growing practices with an extensive farming network and potential for new crop development.

All aspects of the process from planting to distillation are monitored and maintained through quality control practices and testing. They scatter the distilled biomass back onto the land, among other sustainability methods.

The Amanzi Amahle Farm and Distillery plays a vital role in development of the essential oil industry in South Africa. They work with the farmers, investing financially in various farm needs, such as seed programs, and teach good sustainable practices for long-term production of high-quality essential oils.

Oranges are washed before cold pressing.

Weeding the rows of tea tree saplings is very tedious.

Distilling *Eucalyptus radiata*.

Eucalyptus radiata plantation.

D. Gary Young | The World Leader in Essential Oils

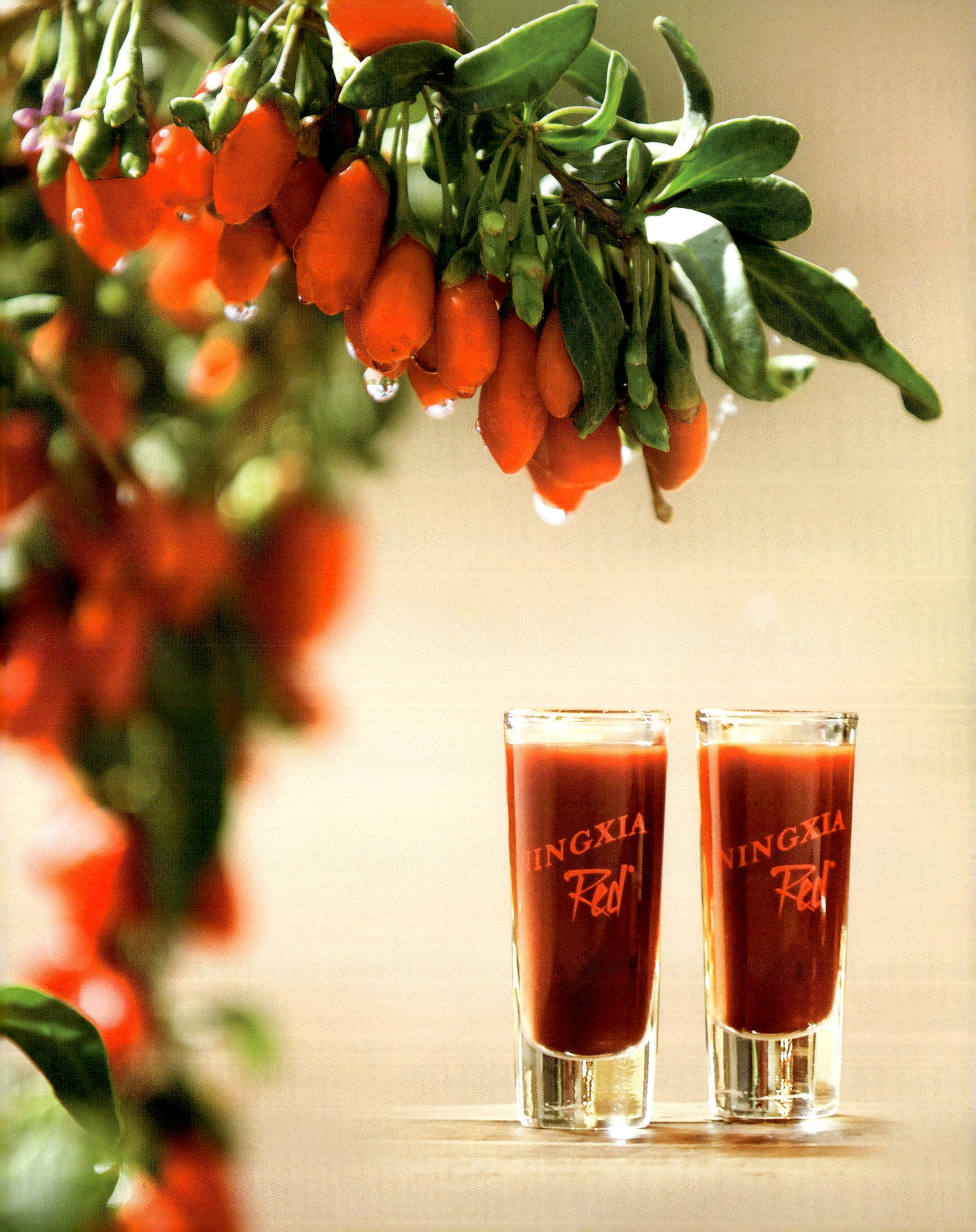
NINGXIA
Red
NINGXIA
Red

WOLFBERRY

In 1993 Gary met Dr. Cyrus McKell, one of my neighbors, who was the dean of the Botany Department at Weber State University. Dr. McKell had been doing some collaborative research with Dr. Songqiao Chao, a Chinese scientist and dean of the Science Department at the Beijing Technical University. Dr. McKell had invited Dr. Chao to lecture at Weber State University, and while he was in Utah, he invited him to go to the Young Living office to meet Gary and learn about essential oils.

Dr. Chao was fascinated with the oils and wanted to know more. At the same time, he asked Gary if he knew about Ningxia wolfberries. Dr. Chao had directed a research project with his students on the *Lycium barbarum* wolfberry species growing on the Elbow Plateau in Inner Mongolia. It had been noted that the people living in the area who were eating large amounts of wolfberries seemed to have greater longevity than those not eating wolfberries. Although there are many species of wolfberries, *Lycium barbarum* proved to have the greatest nutritional benefits compared to other species in China that showed very minimal or almost no extraordinary benefits.

Dr. Chao's daughter, Sue Chao, a biochemist teaching at the University of Utah, subsequently came to work for Young Living to conduct research, test the oils, and manage the laboratory. She translated her father's research and documentation into English for Gary to study. He became very excited and wanted the wolfberries for Young Living.

On a subsequent trip to China, Sue introduced Gary to Mr. Pan, a grower of this particular species on the Elbow Plateau in the Ningxia Province of China. They signed agreements and Gary began importing wolfberries—the first to import tons of the berries for commercial use. He started experimenting and formulated a wolfberry juice drink and different food supplements.

Those eating this superfood say they feel a greater flow of vital energy that supports their physical and emotional well-being. Wolfberries contain an abundant mixture of highly concentrated essential nutrients in perfect balance; and with essential oils added to the juice, they become even more potent and energy-sustaining for the body.

Testing high on the ORAC scale, in addition to all of the wonderful benefits, it's easy to understand why wolfberries have been used and treasured in China for centuries.

Gary traveled to China to learn everything he could about the wolfberries.

Harvesting and pruning wolfberries is very tedious and time-consuming. More than 3,000 pickers work during the harvest time, from June through October.

330   D. Gary Young | The World Leader in Essential Oils

Gary loved creating new recipes and had a lot of fun developing Wolfberry Crisp Bars, Josef's favorite snack.

The NingXia Red production line can fill between 120-130 bottles per minute.

Young Living's array of products made with wolfberries are enjoyed by everyone. Dried wolfberries make a great tea and are also a popular ingredient in recipes for muffins, cookies, and trail mix and go well with Einkorn Flakes Cereal. In China rehydrated berries are used as a garnish in many dishes.

D. Gary Young | The World Leader in Essential Oils

China—Ningxia Wolfberry Farms and Processing Plant

Gary was fascinated with his new discovery and wanted to learn everything he could about wolfberries. Through his research and testing, he knew the berries had great value for the human body and was the first to import tons of the berries for commercial use.

Gary traveled many times to China to meet the people who lived in the region where Dr. Chao had conducted his research to learn more about their secret of longevity. Over the years he and Mr. Pan developed a friendship and shared many ideas and plans for the future.

Mr. Pan has seven farms and a large processing plant that provides us with wolfberry pureé, dried berries, and wolfberry seed oil. This is also the first wolfberry company to pass FDA inspection.

Mr. Pan also developed a special organic fertilizer that protects the soil from pests and disease, which he uses on all his farms.

Gary had often talked about Mr. Pan becoming a Young Living partner, and in 2018 that became a reality. The farm is located in Jinfeng District, Yinchuan, Ningxia Province. It is remote and unpolluted from the contamination of dense urban life, making it better for growing healthy trees.

All of us at Young Living are very excited, and plans are being made for greater production and packaging for China and neighboring countries. We have many projects we are working on together and look forward to a very productive future.

The fields of wolfberry bushes extend beyond what the eyes can see.

Tai-an Pan and his wife, Qi-yan Pang visit the farm in Mona, Utah.

Gary met with Mr. Pan and his process engineers in China, 2001.

The beautiful, FDA-approved plant that processes wolfberries for Young Living.

D. Gary Young | The World Leader in Essential Oils 333

Philippines—Happy Pili Tree Farm and Distillery

The Happy Pili Tree Farm and Distillery is found in the Bicol Region of the Philippines and became a Young Living partner farm in June of 2018.

The pili tree (elemi) belongs to the same family of trees as frankincense and myrrh and is known for its smooth and aromatic bark and releases resin from its barks and roots. Located in the Bicol region, close to five volcanoes, the soil is extremely rich and fertile. The tropical climate—with many typhoons during the rainy season—helps the tree produce a higher volume of resin.

However, over the last few decades, deforestation had become rampant, and harvesters were damaging the trees without knowing that it is possible to keep the trees healthy and in production for future generations.

Trees were often cut down and used as firewood and the resin as fire starter. Harvesters did not have the needed training and were overcutting the trees, thinking that would help the tree produce the most resin, not realizing that this left the trees open to infection and pest invasion.

Rosalina Tan, a long-time organic farmer, sought to change the Pili industry in Bicol by implementing innovative organic processes and teaching proper harvesting and distillation.

Young Living offered Rosalina a grant to build the first commercial-scale distillery at their farm and to help educate the people about sustainable harvesting to ensure the betterment of their livelihoods. The farm protects natural resources and helps ensure long-term viability of high-quality Elemi essential oil, while providing fair wages to workers and keeping job opportunities and expertise within the local community.

With their commitments and mission to place people at the center of their process and a value of caring for the trees, Young Living is proud to be a part of this amazing project with Rosalina and her team.

Elemi has a spicy, incense-like scent that is soft and somewhat balsamic. It is nourishing to the skin and traditionally known to help reduce the appearance of fine lines, leaving the skin with a radiant glow. The fragrant influence is uplifting and comforting to the mind and immune-supporting.

Resin seeps out of the Pili tree.

Block of elemi resin being cut into chunks for distillation.

Rosalina Tan, a long-time, dedicated organic farmer, is always happy when working on the farm.

Mary Young; Rosalina Tan, Director of the Happy Pili Farm; and Jared Turner at the 2018 Young Living convention.

The Young Living Partner Farm Grant program paid for the construction of the second floor, where the distillery is located.

D. Gary Young | The World Leader in Essential Oils 335

Mexico—Finca Victoria

In 1998 Gary was asked to come to Guadalajara to teach a seminar about essential oils. He was thrilled with the response, realizing how culturally accepting the people of Mexico are about natural remedies. Having lived in Mexico in the mid-1980s, he was familiar with the country and its many resources. Every time he returned to Mexico, he became excited as he envisioned future farming possibilities and was continually exploring the countryside looking for suitable property.

In 2018 Young Living entered into a partnership with a farm in Victoria, Mexico, that produces citrus oils, specifically Grapefruit and Lime, which is a wonderful way to fulfill Gary's vision.

There are over 180 workers, including second- and third-generation family members who are part of the farm operation, which is certainly how Gary would want to see the local community supported. There is a lot of excitement as we move forward to strengthen agriculture education, offer seed donations to schools and families, and provide health and nutrition incentive programs, including possible internship programs with the local university.

A citrus fruit processing plant with zero-waste initiatives is also one of the goals of the partnership. The rinds and peels from the processed citrus fruit go through a dehydration process and are sold as dehydrated peel to the food and personal care industries. After the essential oil and juice are extracted, the pulp is sold to the beverage industry. The essential oil is known to cleanse and purify with a fresh and renewing aroma.

Workers fill their bags as they harvest the fruit.

Lime oil has a fresh and cheerful aroma that elevates the spirit and mind.

Grapefruit is ready for harvest.

Pure, organic lime oil is filtered to be poured into drums for shipping.

Italy—Bella Vista Farm and Distillery

The 40-acre organic Bella Vista Farm, founded in 1930, became a Young Living partner in 2018. It is run by third-generation family members headquartered in Condofuri Marina, the Reggio Calabria province in southern Italy. They produce the essential oil of bergamot, which is grown only in this small coastal region due to a specialized micro climate. Sustainable eco-friendly practices with clean water and sanitation help produce affordable clean energy. They use only non-GMO seeds and well water for irrigation and distillation. During the off-season they run entirely on solar power.

The Bella Vista Farm is a member of both Sedex and UN Global Compact, organizations dedicated to improving ethical and responsible business practices, labor rights, and sustainable development in global supply chains.

The fruit is cold pressed and collected in stainless steel vats ready for filtering and pouring into gallon drums for shipping.

The Bella Vista Farm and Distillery welcomes visitors from all over the world to enjoy its scenic beauty and rural peacefulness.

Turkey—Hediye Rose Farm and Distillery

In 1997 Gary was invited to attend a UNIDO conference in Eskisehir, Turkey, to speak about his farming methods and distillation process for essential oils production. Because we were already in Turkey, we decided to visit our growers in southern Turkey who were producing Rose and Oregano essential oils. During our visit we were able to see the rose farm and distillery, which gave us great insight into the delicacy of rose oil extraction.

Over the years the possibility of a rose partner farm was very important to Young Living. Subsequently, in 2018 a beautiful partnership emerged with a Mediterranean farm and distillery located in Senir, a small village in the southern province of Isparta known as the Land of Roses and Lakes. The farm is located 200 miles southwest of Antalya on the coast and has been growing and harvesting roses for over 160 years. The acres of roses are breathtaking, and because the petals are so delicate, they are picked by hand and must be distilled carefully. Approximately 27 pounds of rose petals produce one 5-ml bottle of oil.

Unknown to many, this partner farm also distills the resins of frankincense and myrrh, which is very advantageous to the inventory supply as Young Living continues to grow.

The region around Senir is an agricultural haven of flat farm land surrounded by beautiful mountains. The partner farm employs more than 50 local families year-round, which provides strong economic support to the village.

The sweet smell of roses growing in the fields can be enjoyed from every corner of the city. Almost every type of rose-based product, including Rose oil, is produced and exported from Isparta. The region provides 60 percent of the world's Rose oil production. In addition to the rose industry, the region is also famous for growing clove, lavender, thyme, apples, peaches, and cherries.

Today's distiller

Ancient frankincense and myrrh distiller.

Rose distiller

Rose petals being prepared for distillation.

Brazil—Painted Stone Farm and Distillery

In 2018 Young Living signed a new partnership with a farm in Itacoatiara, Brazil, in the state of Amazonas for the production of copaiba. This farm has an unusual history, as it originally produced firewood for charcoal but was subsequently bought by a company that took interest in protecting the forest through plantation management of natural resources.

The cultivation of pink wood (*Aniba rosaeodora*), laurel mamori (*Ocatea cymbarum*), lemongrass (*Cymbopagon citratus*), and priprioca (*Cyperus articulatus*) was gradually introduced over 10 years, respecting the environment with good practices of natural resources, making the process sustainable.

Priprioca is an Amazonian root used in cosmetics and, with its strong aroma (which is similar to vanilla) and woody flavor, is used in sweet and savory dishes. This is just one of hundreds of new varieties of plants yet to be researched in the Amazon that makes the region one of the most exciting in the world.

Itacoatiara, known as the Painted Stone City, is located on the north bank of the Amazon River, in northwestern Brazil. The name is derived from the indigenous writing of Tupi, which is painted on a stone at the entrance to the city. "Ilta" means "stone" and "coatiara" means "painted;" thus, Painted Stone. It is considered the fifth largest city in the Amazonas State, even though it has a low population density.

The climate is hot and humid with a year-round growing season. The reddish-yellow sandy soil is covered by dense foliage that looks like a solid ground forest with huge trees that are harvested in a sustainable way. The fields are planted with various types of vegetation and harvestable crops.

A new distillery was completed mid-2019, which provides good economic support to the area. Besides securing a continuous supply of copaiba, the prospects are immense for the discovery of new aromatic plants and essential oils.

The Young Living compliance team audits the copaiba harvest in Brazil.

Tapping the copaiba tree for oleoresin for the oil that has traditionally been used for many things from soaps to medical applications.

Local copaiba harvester and family.

A 100-foot tree can grow from this seed and produce about 40 liters of oleoresin.

Argentina—Esmeralda Farm

Our Tafí Viejo lemon farm in the region of Tucumán is beautiful to see. In November 2018 a new partnership was signed with the owners of the Esmeralda Farm, a family-owned business of three generations that has been in operation for more than 60 years. Approximately 345,000 trees grow on 1,300 hectares (3,212.37 acres) of farmland nestled in the shadows of the Andes Mountains, which help shield against freezing temperatures and encourage rainfall.

Their nurseries are certified by SENASA, which ensure that the plants do not get citrus greening, which attacks the plants before there are signs of disease. Other certifications include Global Gap, BRC, and Sedex.

The lemon industry is the main economic driver in Tucuman and employs tens of thousands of people, mainly women, during the harvest, which lasts four to five months.

Argentina has more than 50,000 hectares, 90 percent of which are located in Tucumán, devoted to the cultivation of lemons, yielding an average of 35 tons per hectare. Unlike the vast majority of regional economies, the lemon industry is profitable in Argentina.

In 1960 the region had only 1,630 hectares planted with lemons, but in the past 10 years, it has grown to produce 1.3 million metric tons of fruit per year. Argentina produces 2.5 to 3 million tons of citrus a year, making it one of the biggest producers and exporters of lemons in the world.

Because lemons are more delicate than most fruits, they are still picked by hand, which makes the harvest labor-intensive. The extraction process has evolved with technology, and most producers are using a cold-press system that makes use of the total fruit.

Lemons are put into a container of shallow water where rotating rollers with thousands of stainless steel points puncture the small oil sacs located in the outer part of the peel, releasing the essential oil with minimum disruption to the whole fruit. The oil and water are separated in a centrifuge at room temperature, and then each drum is analyzed for chemical and physical characteristics and recorded so that it can be traced to the time and place of production.

After extraction the natural insoluble wax compounds are put into cold storage to be separated by sedimentation, then filtered, dried, and sold to the commercial food industry as an excellent source of pectin or fruit fiber. The entire process meets the requirements of the quality standards for ISO 9001 and HACCP awarded by Bureau Veritas Quality International.

Lemon oil has many culinary uses and works well in household cleaning products for disinfecting, deodorizing, removing grease, and dissolving wax and grime as advertised in many commercial products. The fragrance is fresh and uplifting, mood-enhancing, and used for many physical and emotional applications.

The lemon trees grow strong and healthy in the humid climate of Argentina.

Philippines—Kalipay Coconut Farm ("Kalipay" means "joy" in Cebuano)

Young Living's partnership with the Kalipay Coconut Farm is very unusual and innovative. The product this farm produces is MCT, which stands for "medium-chain triglycerides," or medium-chain fatty acids. Located in Manila, Kalipay has been in business since 2006, and its parent company was created in 1963.

Coconut oil is recognized for its many uses and health benefits worldwide and is a very favored oil. This partnership brings the surety of a pure coconut oil to Young Living.

Kalipay Coconut Farm processes dried coconut from many coconut plantations throughout the Philippines. It works with the Philippines Coconut Authority, as well as with local farmers, to develop new technologies to both support the coconut industry and improve product quality.

In its state-of-the-art R&D laboratories, scientists work hard to formulate new products such as an organic oil spray that kills coconut scale insects. It has been reported by farmers to have complete eradication success in 7-10 days.

Its management system ensures the highest standards for product quality and care for customers, employees, and the environment. In addition, it has a foundation, which offers scholarships for various learning programs, education opportunities, work sponsorships, awards for excellence, welfare assistance, and community outreach programs to support various community activities.

Employees are hired locally and often remain loyal employees for many years. The company even uses monetary gifts as rewards for the children of employees who turn in good report cards.

The company is very resourceful and because the coconut fiber is so strong, after the meat has been scooped out, it is used to make many things such as medium-density fiber board for construction, unique furniture, ropes, floor mats and rugs, scrubbing brushes, toys, hydroponic planting soil, and even activated carbon for filters.

Peeling the husk off of a coconut.

Four legs are a great mode of transportation—a little slow, but reliable.

Wildcrafting

Wildcrafting is the way man first harvested plants and is still practiced by small farmers all over the world. Crude tools were made out of stone and wood; and eventually, simple metal machinery was crafted that man could either pull or push to cultivate and harvest. Then the machines were adapted for horses to pull, and today "the old machines" are practically forgotten as high-tech equipment plants, cultivates, harvests, and even packages all that was once done by hand.

Machines still don't harvest on the mountainsides or down steep hillsides, and so with a basket and cutting tool in hand, the men and women go on foot to begin their small harvest.

Wildcrafting generally produces a small volume, which is not usually enough for commercial use. The same plants that have been growing in the same soil for perhaps thousands of years with absolutely no soil enhancement are not usually strong enough to be harvested every year.

It is no different than if you plant and harvest your garden vegetables every year and put nothing back into the soil. Soon the tomatoes get smaller and smaller, and the plants produce less and less. Some people choose to use synthetic fertilizer to replenish the garden soil, and some use cow manure and compost. For the first four or five years, there isn't a lot of difference. However, vegetables sprayed with synthetic fertilizers are less tasty, and the nutritional value will be different; but to the eye, they will look pretty much the same.

Many of our oils today are produced from wildcrafted plants such as ocotea, vitex, juniper, blue tansy, Canadian fleabane, tsuga, ishpingo, ledum, palo santo, myrtle, ruta, Idaho tansy, eucalyptus blue, copaiba, yarrow, etc. In reality, the conifer species of spruce, pine, Western red cedar, and all of our frankincense and myrrh species could be considered wildcrafted. The difference is that true wildcrafting is when the plants are not cultivated for production. When we prepare the land, replenish the soil with nutrients, weed, and cultivate, we are no longer wildcrafting.

Gary enjoyed visiting Morocco in search of blue tansy.

The cookers were small but perfect for blue tansy.

The firebox is antiquated, but it is carbon-neutral and burns the wood and brush gathered from the ground and works very well.

Members wildcrafting lavender in France.

Wildcrafted ruta is unloaded and weighed at the Ecuador farm.

Yarrow (small, white flowers) grows abundantly all over the Northern Lights Farm and could become a crop in the future.

Copaiba from Brazil is a very popular oil in Young Living.

When Gary first bought Helichrysum in 1990, there were only 90 liters produced worldwide, which were used primarily in the perfume industry as a perfume fixative; but as he continued to discover more uses for the oil and talked about it in seminars, the demand began to increase.

Crops like helichrysum from Croatia and blue tansy from Morocco have been wildcrafted for centuries, and the gatherers have been paid by the volume or weight of the plants. With the world demand increasing, the volume from wildcrafting is not enough.

The gatherers know that in order to get paid more money, they have to produce more plants; so they harvest as fast as they can. Even the women and children help. It is much faster to pull the plants out of the ground, roots and all, and make more money because of the weight than spend the day walking the hills and cutting with a scythe or shears.

This shortsightedness hurts the farmers and has caused a tremendous decrease in the wild plants and could permanently wipe out a crop. The people who are wildcrafting this way are raping the land with no thought for future generations.

So, where are people going to get their Helichrysum this year? Where are they going to get Blue Tansy in Morocco, since this country is experiencing similar difficulties? What will desperate buyers do who cannot get the oil they want? Will laboratories manufacture more nature-identical oils?

It makes much more sense to begin cultivating these declining plants in fields where they can receive proper care and nourishment to grow and multiply. Naturally, it costs more money and takes more time, but the long-term reward is a strong, sustainable crop that produces beautiful plants for distilling every year.

Because of this situation, Gary made plans to find a partner farm that would grow helichrysum, which he achieved in 2015. As he began to work with different farmers in Croatia, Gary stipulated that he would not buy oil that had been distilled from the helichrysum plants that were poached and/or pulled out by the roots. In 2014 he even went twice to Croatia during the harvest to make sure that only the tops of the plants were being harvested and that the whole plant was preserved and was not being pulled out of the ground.

Farmers in Ethiopia still cut and thresh grain the same way they have been doing for thousands of years.

THE ORIGIN OF PLANTS

Taken from Gary's *Power of Genuine* Presentation

Some essential oil companies tout that their oils come only from the country of origin where they are wildcrafted, which is why they do not have farms.

People who have no experience or knowledge might say, "That sounds reasonable." However, how many people have knowledge of the origins of plants in the world? Probably not many—and does the origin matter?

Can alfalfa grow in France? Can it grow in northern British Columbia? Can it grow at 6,500 feet in central Idaho, in Croatia at sea level, in Washington at 1,200 feet, or in Utah at 5,000 feet? Can it grow in Montana, Oregon, California, Ecuador, Texas, Wyoming, and Serbia? Of course, it can grow in all of these places.

Where is the origin of alfalfa? Certainly it didn't start in North America, so does this mean the alfalfa in Utah is of lesser quality because Utah or Idaho are not its origin? How is it that alfalfa from the Mona area of Utah has the preferred higher protein content for the dairies in California? Does that mean that the alfalfa in Montana is of lesser quality, even though it commands a price per ton equivalent to Utah, Idaho, and Washington, as well as the far northern reaches of British Columbia like Fort Nelson, 100 miles south of the Northwest Territories border?

Does this mean that alfalfa grown in other countries around the world has lower quality because it did not originate from where it is growing? The same might be asked about wheat that grows in almost every country in the world. When you eat commercially grown wheat products, do you know if the wheat came from its place of origin? What a ridiculous idea.

Very few people would even know that wheat originates from the Mesopotamia Region in Eastern Europe, and who would even care? Does that mean we shouldn't eat wheat because it doesn't come from Mesopotamia? If you eat wheat from somewhere else, will you have a nutritionally deficient body? This line of reasoning is absolutely absurd, considering that the origin of wheat is not the United States, as most Americans think, especially when they see millions of acres of wheat blowing in the wind as they drive the freeways in Middle America.

What creates the nutritional value in wheat? Is it the place of origin, even though the land is old and has become nutrient depleted over hundreds of years; or is it the soil condition, climate, where the crops are being grown, and how well the land has been taken care of with proper soil management and added nutrients?

Is the lavender from Idaho or Utah deficient because it does not come from France? How many people know that France is not the true origin of lavender but that its origin is actually ancient Persia, even though most of the world thinks it is from France? One might say, "That is just good marketing."

Why did lavender grow so well in France until the last 15 or 20 years? Why has there been such a tremendous decline in the production of French lavender—true lavender (*Lavandula angustifolia*)? Why did so many fields of lavender die, and why did farmers turn to other crops or sell their farms? What happened to the lavender capital of the world, to the farmers, to the soil in which the plants grew so heartily at one time?

Did the French farmers not realize that all the chemical fertilizers and pesticides used over so many years would contaminate the soil and eventually weaken the immune

Growing and harvesting the ancient way in Pakistan.

system of the plants? So what happened when a blight attacked the lavender, and then France had a severe drought that lasted for several years? Why did it not occur to the farmers that perhaps they needed to start irrigating? Why did the farmers not replenish and feed the soil with potassium and nitrogen or analyze the soil to see what the plants needed nutritionally or determine the effects of the chemicals? All these factors led to the dying lavender industry.

How is it that the lavender in Utah produces a higher percentage overall of linalyl acetate and a higher yield per acre? It is all about soil amendment that you cannot get in nature. Weak soil produces genetically weak plants that produce genetically poor oil quality.

Some companies claim their oils come from plants that are wildcrafted and slander people who farm and domesticate their plants and build the soil with organic and wholesome nutrients. Healthy soil produces genetically healthy plants that produce high-quality oil with well-balanced molecules for a strong immune system and reproduction.

When plants are cared for and nutritionally fed, they are able to do what God intended for them to do, to keep our planet balanced and to support humankind. This ability of the plants is greatly reduced when they are genetically altered and damaged with synthetic chemicals.

Any grower wanting to produce high quality oil must know how to analyze the soil, plow it, plant seeds or seedlings, and then cultivate the crop. How would someone who has never analyzed the soil, plowed and planted it, and then cultivated newly growing aromatic plants even know if they are growing in the right conditions, let alone never having distilled an aromatic crop before going to tell the world that they are investing in partner farms?

In what are they investing? Crop seed? Fertilizers and pesticides? Equipment for irrigation, planting, harvesting, or even distillation? How can they say they buy their oil only from crops grown and distilled in the place of origin, yet they do not even know the real country of origin? To really understand origin, we would have to follow the evolution of planting, harvesting, and wildcrafting from people and cultures of ancient times. Where would the world be if we depended on the wildcrafting of wheat, corn, beans, potatoes, etc.? The world would be starving.

Thirty to forty years ago, many plants were wildcrafted, even lavender. Gary learned to wildcraft lavender and thyme with Mr. Viaud and then distilled them in Mr. Viaud's distillery. Mr. Viaud said that wildcrafting was a thing of the past, because you can't harvest enough by hand to make any money, and the time would come when wildcrafting would stop. He was certain that the governments would stop it because they would see the natural resources being depleted. He couldn't stress that more when in 1992, he said, "Mr. Gary, the time will come that if you do not grow it yourself, you will not have pure oils."

ESSENTIAL OIL WORLD TRADE STATISTICS

"The global market for essential oils and oleoresins is poised to surge exponentially in the forthcoming years." According to research experts[1], "high growth is expected due to increasing medical applications with growing consumer interest regarding health benefits associated with essential oils and natural ingredients."[2] The global market size was 4.35 billion USD in 2018[3] and is expected to grow to as much as 13 billion USD by 2024.[4]

The world demand for essential oils is so much greater today than 30 years ago or even 5 years ago. Even though more oils are being produced now, there is still not enough to meet the demand for pure oils. Global demand is expected to approach 250 million tons by 2020[5] and 350 kilo tons by 2024.[6] North America comprises a significant share of the global essential oil and aromatherapy market,[7] but the U.S. is also one of the biggest importers of essential oils.[8,9]

1. *https://www.transparencymarketresearch.com/essential-oils-oleoresins-market.html*. Retrieved January 11, 2019.
2. *https://www.grandviewresearch.com/industry-analysis/essential-oils-market*. Retrieved January 14, 2019.
3. *https://www.statista.com/statistics/742159/us-essential-oils-market-value/*. Retrieved January 11, 2019.
4. *https://globenewswire.com/news-release/2018/10/24/1626070/0/en/Essential-Oils-Market-to-exceed-USD-13-billion-by-2024-Global-Market-Insights-Inc.html*. Retrieved January 11, 2019.
5. *https://www.statista.com/statistics/750725/global-essential-oils-market-demand/*. Retrieved January 11, 2019.
6. *https://www.gminsights.com/industry-analysis/essential-oil-market?utm_source=globenewswire.com&utm_medium=referral&utm_campaign=Paid_globenewswire*. Retrieved January 11, 2019.
7. *https://www.marketwatch.com/press-release/essential-oil-aromatherapy-2018-market-share-production-and-consumption-analysis-brands-statistics-and-overview-by-worldwide-top-manufacturers-2023-2018-11-16*. Retrieved January 14, 2019.
8. *https://www.statista.com/statistics/475103/us-import-volume-of-essential-oils-by-product-type/*. Retrieved January 14, 2019.
9. *https://comtrade.un.org/db/ce/ceSnapshot.aspx?qt=ss&cc=3301&px=H1&y=2015,%202016,%202017*. Retrieved January 14, 2019.

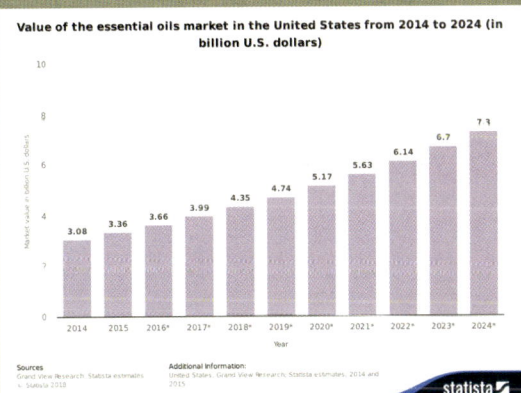

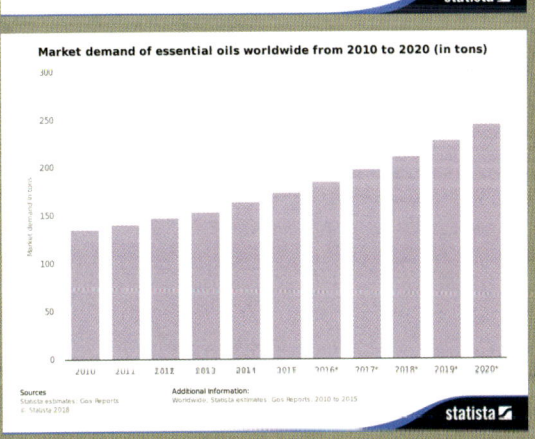

Carbon Dioxide (CO₂) Extraction

Carbon dioxide (CO_2) extractions are becoming more popular. The most common type of CO_2 extraction is supercritical CO_2 extraction. Under a specific range of temperatures and pressures, CO_2 exists as a supercritical fluid and will act like a gas in some cases and a liquid in others. In practice, the plant material is packed into a cooker and CO_2 gas is added. The pressure and temperature are then increased to change the CO_2 gas into a supercritical fluid that saturates the plant material and releases the essential oil.

When the pressure is released, the CO_2 reverts into a gas, leaving the oil behind. Supercritical CO_2 extraction is preferred over the use of chemical solvents and may remove heavier compounds not extracted through steam or hydrodistillation.

When Gary began distillation 30 years ago, CO_2 extraction was not available for the aromatherapy industry. It was basically used in laboratories for research and was not practical for large scale production. As the technology advances, large scale production using CO_2 extraction may be feasible.

Adulteration and Chemical Manipulation

More people are becoming educated about synthetics, so laboratories have become very sophisticated and can easily formulate what they call "nature-identical oils," but few people know what that means. Unfortunately, it sounds good but is just another name for synthetic products.

A common practice by brokers is to buy third- or fourth-grade oils and then cut them with synthetics and sweet chemical fragrances. Pure essential oils have distinct, individual aromas; and they are not all sweet. When an essential oil smells sweet like candy, you can suspect that it has been adulterated to make it smell more appealing. Pure oils do not smell like candy but have their own individual aromas.

Will a little synthetic hurt you? That depends on your immune and elimination systems, but why take that risk? Synthetics accumulate in the liver, reproductive organs, and fat cells; and some have a shelf life of more than 100 years.

The other way essential oils are adulterated for profit is by the addition of inexpensive oils that have similar constituents. For instance, cinnamon bark oil can be adulterated with cheaper cinnamon leaf oil. This can be detected by analysis because leaf oil contains a higher content of eugenol, but how many companies take time to check for purity?

Cheaper cornmint is used to dilute peppermint oil, but peppermint's menthofuran content should be from 0.4 to 14.6 percent, while in cornmint it is not detected or detected only in levels up to 0.01 percent. Viridiflorol is found in peppermint up to 0.9 percent, while it is not detected in cornmint at all. Those who spend the time and money to analyze oils will easily spot such adulteration.

Sadly, there are few essential oil companies that would make this kind of an investment to validate the oils they sell. Besides that, who would know how to have an oil tested? Where would it be sent and what would it cost? The average person would not generally entertain these questions.

Essential oils have become a big "money maker" because the unknowing public has no way of determining the quality or purity of the oils they buy. Most people go by the smell, and if it smells nice, "It must be good."

Today it is common to find a variety of essential oils listed as part of the ingredients on the labels of hundreds of consumer products like skin care and cosmetics, household cleaning products, and a vast array of food and animal products. How does the consumer know the quality of the oil listed on the label? Naturally, there isn't an easy way to know. But for the volume of oil that is supposedly used in the millions of products that are on the market according to their labels, it isn't possible that there are enough oils produced in the world to meet the growing demand.

Young Living has invested millions of dollars in very sophisticated scientific instruments needed to detect adulteration. There are many different tests conducted with various instruments by our chemists and technicians who have had years of experience testing essential oils.

In 1998 our laboratory began with one GC instrument and has grown into one of the worlds finest state-of-the-art laboratories for conducting analytical research to protect the purity of our oils and to expand our knowledge in this fast-growing industry.

Young Living invests in the farmers, buys land, plants crops, and builds distilleries with analytical laboratories on site, to secure our oil production and also to support local economies and create security for rural communities.

With this in mind, we have to be prepared for certain oils to go out of stock until the next harvest and distillation. It seems that we all want it when we want it, but the choice is to either wait until the next distillation to have a pure oil or buy a not-so-pure or synthetic oil.

Gary Young spent 30 years developing relationships with people all over the world. He often said, "My quest has always been to develop a strong foundation for the future supply of our members and their children for generations to come." For this reason, Young Living will always be the world leader in essential oils as new farms and partner farms are established to provide for the essential oil demand of our members. The strength of our dedication, sacrifice, and determination is the foundation of Young Living and our commitment to you.

Scientific Analysis

Using scientific instruments, analytical chemists are able to know an oil's compound structure and determine how it might be used for aromatic, physical, emotional, and spiritual benefits, as well as in the vast flavor and fragrance industries. They are able to test for a "balanced" chemical profile and also detect additives that are either natural or synthetic and/or the manipulation of the molecular profile of a pure oil.

When the chemical profile is different from the accepted library profile, the chemist knows that something "extra" has been added to the oil. A good chemist will often be able to tell what substance may have been added that will increase or decrease certain percentages of a compound.

Over the years, Young Living has added an essential oil library containing over one million index files for analytical comparisons. This library includes data purchased from CNRS in France that Dr. Hervé Casabianca has worked on for decades. The compounds that Gary identified in his research were also added.

We purchase libraries with our GC/MS instruments. For Ecuador alone, we bought a library of 500,000 profiles. When the GC/MS analysis is completed, we compare it to our database and also that of Dr. Casabianca. Then we check our retention indices library, which is a type of "address" that shows where a compound "elutes" or comes out on the GC analysis. It is a great backup to firmly document a compound.

The experienced analytical chemists at Young Living are amazing, and their combined experience on these instruments adds up to more than 200 years.

Synthetic components are also detectable with instruments such as IRMS, optical rotation, and HPLC. Young Living uses many test modalities to obtain analytical scientific data. Oils coming from our farms we know are pure; but with the GC/MS testing, we can see in the constituent profile the effects of the variables of the rain and sunshine, the correct time of harvest and curing, the time and temperature of distillation, as well as the nutritional content of the soil in which the plants and trees are growing. This information is extremely valuable in being able to determine the exact time and process of distillation to obtain the highest quality possible.

When an oil is "created" through the combination of different oils or individual compounds, the analytical profile will be very different from the accepted library index. If the oil is made with adulterated components, the profile will not match or be comparable to the library index. One oil can even be a combination of different species of the same genus.

For example, an oil can be sold as "frankincense" yet be a blend containing a combination of frankincense species: *Boswellia carterii, B. frereana, B. papyrifera, B. neglecta*, etc. Varying component molecules can be identified. Finding epi-lupeol and lupeol in a frankincense oil tells you that

---

Dear sir,
I'm a French exporter who exports products from Provence (south of France) to North America. select very typical products which quality is unquestionable. would like to know if you could be interested by Provencal products like lavender essential oil made in France?

(50% lavender & 50% lavandin) 100% pure.
15ml=$2
50ml=$4
100ml=$7
Bulk = $65/liter

hope to hear from you soon
Yours sincerely,

This gentleman probably gave no thought to the fact that he was selling a cut or mixed oil—definitely not a pure lavender. Cutting the lavender with lavandin is a well-known practice in the industry. Just business as usual.

frereana has been included in it. This compound is not found in other frankincense species. Individual compounds in such a blend can be identified, but they will not resemble any single oil.

If there is any question about any oil coming from a partner farm or vendor, then more instrument testing and analyses are used to be certain of the oil purity.

The Day of the Laboratory

From ancient times moving forward into the 19th century, a laboratory-made oil was not something anyone would contemplate. However, during World War II, the warring countries were not able to ship goods out of their countries; and so the United States lost its essential oil supply from Europe. This might be one of the reasons the chemical industry began to develop fragrances and flavorings in the laboratory. They discovered that these chemical creations were easy to make, cheaper, and more consistent in their "quality." People didn't seem to mind or they simply had no awareness as laboratory flavors moved into the food industry; and fragrances moved into cosmetics, soaps, and common everyday products.

Today, chemists use highly technical methods to synthesize oil molecules to increase the volume and change the aroma. The day of the laboratory has become highly sophisticated where anything can be modified and changed, and it is almost impossible to detect any kind of compound alteration.

Adulterated or modified oils are difficult to detect on a GC/MS because these instruments cannot determine if the molecule is natural or synthetic. A highly sophisticated IRMS analysis, or one done by someone with a trained nose such as Gary had, can usually determine the ratios and percentages of essential oil compounds and detect the presence of synthetics; but people like this are a very small minority.

Nature-identical oils are synthetics made entirely in the laboratory and are used mainly in cosmetics and food flavoring but are also found in the aromatherapy industry. It is truly fascinating how this industry's standards have lowered to accept synthetic chemical additives.

Adulteration can occur anywhere along the production process and is disguised in so many ways. Synthetic or adulterated oils can be mislabeled, diluted, and adulterated with various chemicals and cheaper oils to increase volume and change the aroma.

Common Adulterating Agents

Clary Sage	Synthetic linalyl acetate, linalool, lavender oil, bergamot mint oil
Geranium	Palmarosa, citronella, various synthetic fractions
Lavender	Lavandin from which the camphor is extracted, synthetic linalyl acetate and linalool
Frankincense (B. carterii)	Frankincense composites, various synthetic fractions
Melissa	Citronella, lemongrass
Neroli	Lemon, lime, orange, petitgrain
Peppermint	Cornmint up to as much as 85%
Rose	Palmarosa, citronella, and various fractions, synthetic and natural additives
Rosemary	Camphor, eucalyptus, sage
Sandalwood	Amyris, araucaria, cedarwood, castor, copaiba, glyceryl acetate, benzyl benzoate, other synthetic additives
Ylang Ylang	Other Cananga species, balsam, copaiba, various other fractions, and synthetics

Although the chemical industry has become very big and powerful, awareness is growing among people who don't want chemical adulteration. They want to be healthier and happier, living with greater wellness, and are looking for any and all products that are unprocessed or less-processed, wanting to live in a cleaner environment free of chemicals—and that is a tall order in today's world.

However, grocery stores are thriving as they offer organic foods and chemical-free products. Health food products are scattered on the shelves of well-known grocery stores, and even the average convenience stores are beginning to add better choices to their inventories with healthier snack foods and drinks. People are more aware of the dangers of chemicals to their bodies and the rampant abundance of toxins in our environment. More people are committed to living in vibrational-clean surroundings, which has to start within our own bodies.

Essential oils are a part of nature, and our bodies love what comes from nature. Our bodies know how to respond instinctively. The body is refreshed, revitalized, emotionally uplifted, spiritually strengthened, and given greater life awareness with the life-giving pure essence of the plant kingdom, whether it's touched, felt, or breathed. It is like water. We cook with it, we bathe in it, and we drink it without asking questions. It is a natural part of our lives.

Essential oils are God's gift to mankind, and we must respect them by keeping them pure to support our well-being freely as God intended.

Myrrh		
Botanical Name: *Commiphora myrrha*		
Country of Origin: Somalia		
	Accept	Reject
Components	C0527	72713
	6/18/14	7/20/14
	Area %	Area %
Beta-Elemene	3.7	3.0
Curzerene	22.3	24.6
Germacrene B	1.8	2.0
Furanoeudesma-1,3-diene	38.9	22.9
Lindestrene	11.5	11.8
2-Methoxy Furanogermacrene	6.0	Not Detected
Other Notable Components		
Diethyl Phthalate*	Not Detected	4.6

Vendor sample 72713 was rejected due to lack of 2-Methoxy Furanogermacrene and other unspecified components, as well as the presence of Diethyl Phthalate, a commonly known plasticizer. Contamination may have occurred due to interactions within certain plastics or plastic adhesives during the distillation or storage process.

Franken-Yeast Creates Expensive EO Molecules

Since "nature-identical" products are no longer accepted as consumer friendly, it was just a matter of time until a newer technology arrived. The newest and cheapest way to make flavors and fragrances is now Synthetic Biology.

High-value molecules (key components of essential oils) can be recreated by fermentation from sugar with Streptomyces enzymes or by creating synbio yeast (synthetic DNA is designed on a computer and inserted into the DNA of naturally occurring yeast) to produce a scent molecule like vanillin. Synthetic vanillin is added by unscrupulous vendors to thinned-down lavender and peppermint to make them smell and taste sweet like candy.

A September 2015 study stated: "With the tools of metabolic engineering, microorganisms can be modified to produce compounds such as esters, terpenoids, aldehydes, and methyl ketones."[1]

Researchers from Belgium reported that filamentous fungi are able to produce fruity or floral odors: "White rot fungi are known to metabolize ferulic acid into vanillic acid and vanillan... The fungal plant pathogen *Botryodiplodia theobromae* can also form methyl(+)-7-iso-jasmonic acid, which displays a sweet floral, jasmine-like odour."[2] The study also notes that rose and even galbanum scents can be created using yeast fermentation by *Saccharomyces cerevisiae* and *Kluyveromyces marxianus*.

Perhaps the worst news about these cutting-edge technologies is that, according to FDA rules and European regulations, since the flavor molecule comes from an edible yeast, it is considered "natural."

Seed to Seal is Young Living's commitment that our laboratories will reject fake vanilla-burping yeast additions that attempt bio-adulteration. Young Living provides essential oils that are the true essence of the plants and are 100 percent pure.

1. Carroll AL, et al. Microbial production of scent and flavor compounds. *Curr Opin Biotechnol.* 2015 Sep 28;37:8-15.
2. Vandamme EJ. Bioflavors and fragrances via fungi and their enzymes. *Int J All Facets Mycol.* 2003 13:415-421.

Terminology and Common Tests Used for Young Living Quality Assurance

The following terminology is very helpful in understanding the many methods of testing and the instruments used.

Optical Rotation is determined with a polarimeter, which characterizes or identifies the optical activity of a substance. The instrument measures the rotation of a polarized light source passing through the substance. Almost all oils contain optical active compounds that affect the rotation of light. However, if an equal mixture of chiral (mirror image or optical isomers) molecules are present within an oil (which usually does not happen in nature), the optical rotation reading will be zero.

A study on the discovery of the chiral differences in the two frankincense species carterii and sacra was published in 2012 in the *Journal of Chromatography A* by D. Gary Young and his co-authors. Sacra contains a majority of optical isomers that have a dextrorotary or (+) form, and carterii contains a majority of optical isomers that have a levorotary or (-) form. This was the first time that the two frankincense species have been shown to be different.

GC (Gas Chromatography Separation) is a technique whereby a complex mixture of molecules is separated into individual molecules.

GC/MS (Gas Chromatography/Mass Spectrometry) is where mass spectrometry is coupled to the GC instrument and allows identification of the molecules that are separated by the GC.

GC/IRMS (Gas Chromatography, Isotope Ratio, and Mass Spectrometry) When added to the GC/MS analysis, this additional step involves placing the material to be identified into a combustion chamber where under high heat (1500°C/2732°F), the molecules are pyrolyzed into the elements: carbon, hydrogen, oxygen, and nitrogen (if present). These are the basic building blocks of matter. Young Living purchased standards that will identify the ratios of isotopes and determine if those ratios are natural (created by plant metabolism) or synthetic (created in a lab). In other words, the IRMS allows us to identify whether a sample is natural or synthetic.

HPLC (High Pressure Liquid Chromatography) is used to separate, identify, and quantify the individual components in a material. Unlike the GC, the HPLC analyzes liquid mixtures that contain compounds that are difficult to volatilize or cannot be evaporated out of the mixture. The HPLC is ideal for separating large molecules like vitamins, hormones, and other biomolecules like synthetics.

The Refractive Index measures the penetration of a certain wavelength of light through a medium. The measurement varies from one material to another and is used to identify different substances.

pH is used to measure the activity of hydrogen ions in a solution. It is used to determine if a substance is acidic, neutral, or alkaline. The pH scale ranges from 0-14, with 7 being neutral.

A Brix Refractometer measures the sugar content of an aqueous solution. A high degree of Brix within a plant indicates that a high oil content is present and helps to determine the best time for distillation.

FTIR or NIR (Fourier Transform Infrared Spectroscopy/Near Infrared) is used to help identify oils, dietary supplements, and personal care products by measuring and graphing the absorption of light across a wide array of wavelengths. The resulting graphs are then compared to a known library for identification.

Specific Gravity is the ratio of the density of a substance to the density of water.

Viscosity describes the thickness of a liquid substance. A thick substance has a higher viscosity than a thin or runny liquid.

Microbiological Tests are used to identify and test for any pathogens or undesirable microorganisms that may be present in products. These tests ensure the safety and quality of those products. The microorganisms we test for are *Escherichia coli*, *Staphylococcus aureus*, *Pseudomonas aeruginosa*, *salmonella*, and coliform, along with yeast and mold.

Combustibility measures the flash point of an essential oil. The flash point is the lowest temperature at which there will be enough flammable vapor to ignite when an ignition source is applied. Once the company determines the flash points, it must list the flash points that are problematic in their Safety Data Sheets (SDS) for safe shipping.

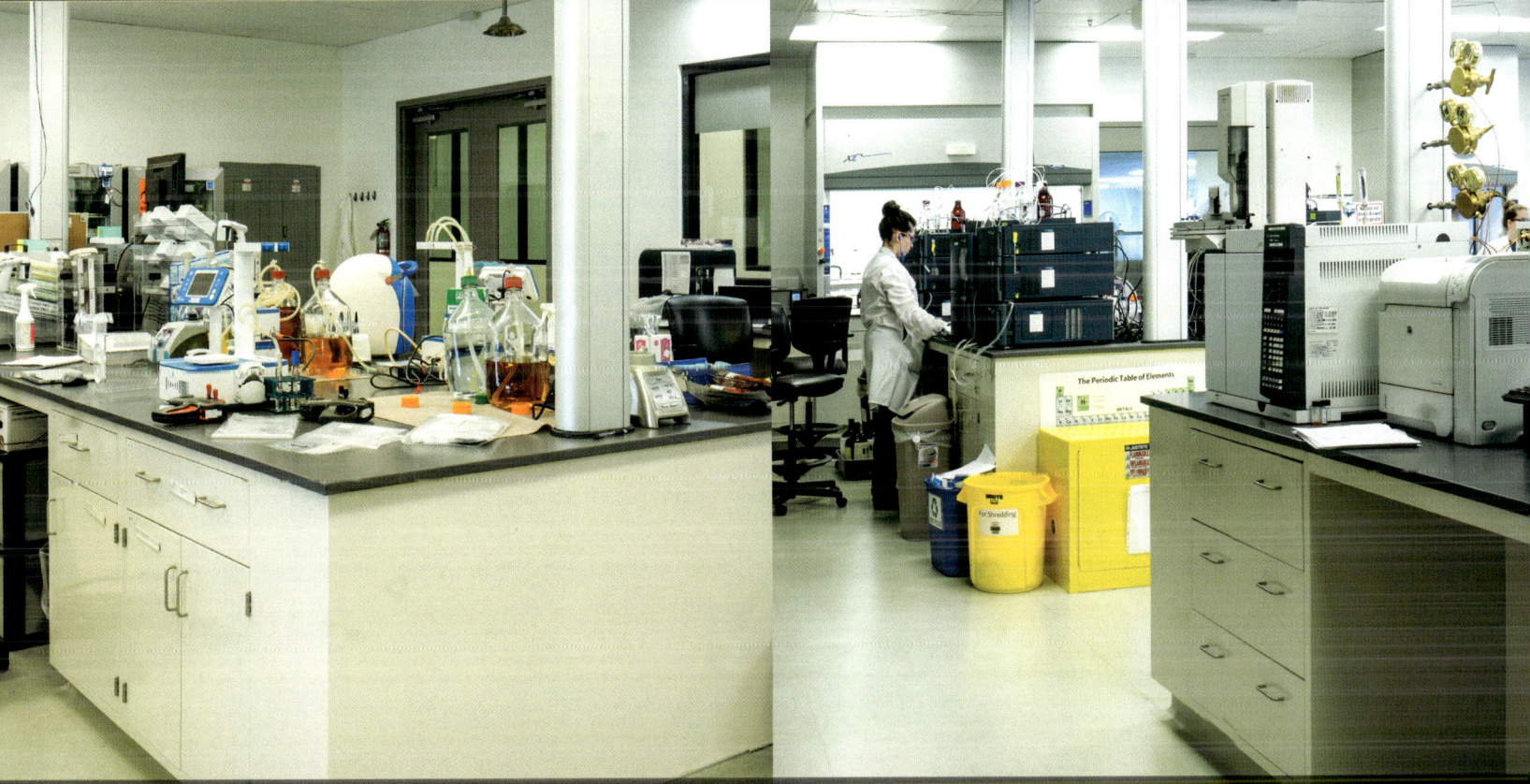

UHPLC (ultra-high-pressure liquid chromatography) tests vitamins and components of dietary supplements and foods.

This is the laboratory in the Spanish Fork warehouse, which is one of four research and quality control laboratories that make up the D. Gary Young Research Institute, which employs many experienced PhD chemists, scientists, and skilled technicians, who work with the most advanced scientific instruments and equipment, directing cutting-edge methods of testing to ensure the quality of our oils and to develop new products for market.

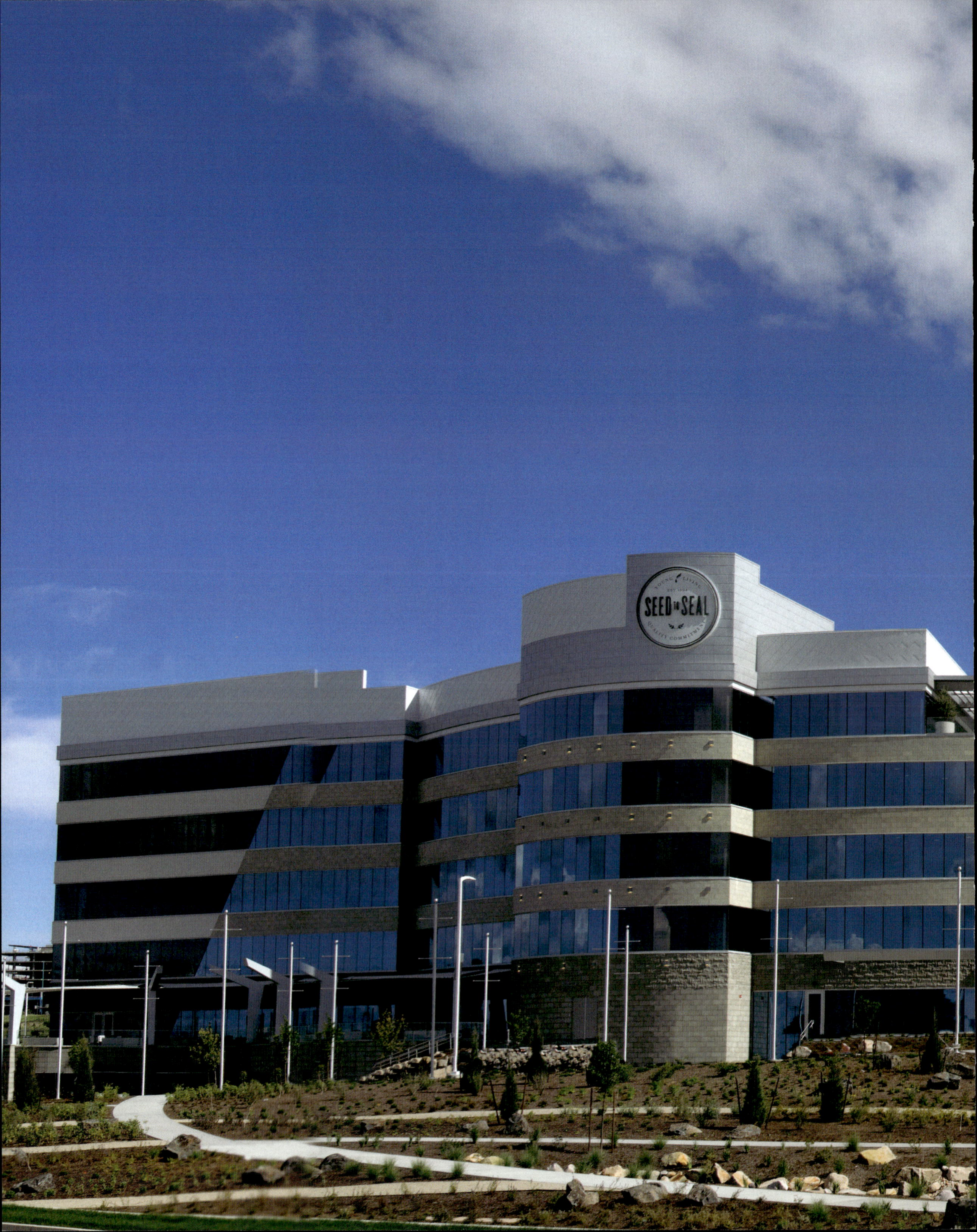
YOUNG LIVING
SEED TO SEAL
QUALITY COMMITMENT

YOUNG LIVING TODAY

The magnificent Young Living Global Headquarters fulfills the 25-year dream of Founder D. Gary Young when members and staff worldwide celebrated the ribbon cutting May 29, 2019, in Lehi, Utah. The small building in front is a research greenhouse that is part of the D. Gary Young Research Institute.

Young Living's global headquarters is in Lehi, Utah, with manufacturing in Spanish Fork, Utah, and Member Services in American Fork, Utah. In July 2015 annual sales reached $1 billion, with more than 1 million members in 138 countries and nine international offices.

In late 2019 Young Living reached $2 billion in annual sales with more than six million members worldwide. This is phenomenal growth for a company that started in 1994 as a tiny mom-and-pop business in a 5,000-square-foot building and averaged about $85,000 in sales per month.

Today Young Living has offices and experience centers in Australia, Brazil, Canada, China, Colombia, Croatia, Ecuador, Hong Kong, Indonesia, Japan, Malaysia, Mexico, the Philippines, Singapore, South Africa, Taiwan, the United Kingdom, and the United States, which collectively employ more than 4,000 people.

Young Living has 11 corporate-owned farms and distilleries in six countries and 17 partner farms worldwide that supply essential oils to meet Young Living's Seed to Seal standard. As we continue to grow, we will constantly expand our corporate and partner farms.

In 2003 Young Living's Global Headquarters moved from Payson, Utah, into a building in the Thanksgiving Point Business Park in Lehi, Utah. As the business grew, more space was needed, so a second building was leased in 2011, and by 2018 Young Living was leasing seven buildings in the Thanksgiving Point Business Park.

More than 25 years ago, Gary started drawing plans for the future Global Headquarters. In the Payson office (1997), Gary had a model, enclosed with glass, in the entrance way with a sign that read: Future Global Headquarters. There was often talk about it, and we always kept asking, "When?" Gary said, "When I'm ready. We have to build the farms first."

In 2008 Gary began looking for an architect, at which time various firms submitted their proposals. Gary chose Kevin Scholz of Scholz Architects. However, due to the 2008 recession, the project was put on hold, but Young Living was growing and had to lease more and more buildings. Many people urged Gary to start construction, but again he said the time was not yet right. The farms came first, and he knew that was where the money was needed the most.

In 2014 Gary finally gave the go-ahead for the building, and the search for an appropriate site began. Nestled between the rugged Wasatch Mountains and Utah's main traffic corridor in Lehi, Utah, 27 acres of farmland on the east side of I-15 were purchased in April 2016. Over the next year, architectural plans were finalized, contractors were hired, permits were secured, and construction preparation began.

On the morning of May 15, 2017, Gary climbed up on the excavator and proudly dug the first bucket of dirt, as everyone cheered enthusiastically. The groundbreaking ceremony brought tremendous excitement, as the reality of Gary's dream of 25 years began to take shape.

Two years later, on May 29, 2019, thousands gathered to watch the ribbon cut for the new 265,000-square-foot Young Living Global Headquarters.

This world-class building has a commanding presence among Utah's thriving business community, while bringing pure essential oils to the world and being stewards of the earth. The exterior finishing materials have an exquisite, natural-flowing design that is complemented by the beautiful landscape that surrounds it.

The foyer features a large member-recognition screen, a three-story waterfall with a stunning waterscape, and an atrium of aromatic plants and shrubs from around the world and those we grow on our farms that represent our source of essential oils. Two large walls are inset with beautiful live plants that also refresh and humidify the air inside.

The new headquarters has energy-saving green features such as solar panels on the roof and covered parking structure, liberal natural light in the building, selected variable refrigerant flow (VFR) HVAC system to optimize energy conservation, and tinted windows with shades throughout the facility to reduce demand for cooling.

The new, state-of-the-art water filtration system eliminates the need for bottled water, which will significantly reduce plastic waste. Water-efficient landscaping with a drip irrigation system minimizes the use of water by filtering and recycling the water supply.

Interior glass walls allow the sunlight into employee-friendly workstations, two huge skylights bring natural light into the core of the building, and low-energy LED light fixtures are used throughout the building.

Gary designed the overall plan for this beautiful atrium and waterfall to create the essence of nature—nature's living energy within our building.

Regionally sourced construction materials are used wherever possible to minimize energy-consuming transportation to the site. Recyclable materials used in furniture and finishes reduce volatile organic compounds (VOCs), which are gases emitted from certain solids or liquids that often have adverse health effects. Concentrations of many VOCs are up to 10 times higher indoors than outdoors and are emitted by thousands of products.

There are electric charging stations for 24 vehicles, prioritized parking for those who carpool or drive eco-friendly vehicles, and covered exterior bicycle lockers to promote cycling to work.

The building has both LEED Silver and Green Global NC certifications. LEED–Leadership in Energy and Environmental Design–is a third-party green-building certification program that focuses on specifications for building design, construction, and maintenance that are cost-effective and environmentally compliant. It designs highly efficient buildings that have a reduced impact on the environment, lowering operating and maintenance costs, increasing asset value, and decreasing risk. LEED certification is invaluable in today's market because it represents leadership in the business and marketing world.

Green Globes New Construction (NC) is a web application that helps architects, engineers, construction professionals, owners, and building operators to evaluate and improve the environmental friendliness and sustainability of new buildings, to evaluate opportunities for energy savings, reduced environmental impacts, and lower maintenance costs. Green Globes NC provides early feedback on projects before critical decisions are made that save time and money while benefiting from a cost-effective third-party assessment process.

About 240 percent more acreage (6.12 vs. 2.55 acres) than is required by Lehi City code is devoted to worker-friendly green space at the D. Gary Young Memorial Park and Demonstration Gardens.

A replica of the small cabin where Gary lived the first four years of his life sits next to the immensity of the new building—a dramatic contrast from his humble beginning—creating a moment of tremendous respect and admiration for all those who come to visit. Outside the cabin stands a life-size sculpture created by world-renowned sculptor Jonathon Bronson, which is breathtaking. Standing beneath this statue, one has a feeling of deep introspection about the opportunities that life offers and the purpose of life, as Gary's eyes seem to pierce one's very soul.

The Young Living museum inside the building displays memorabilia of historical events of our growth and Gary's unmatched vision, with colorful costumes, props from the frankincense documentary, early distillers, rare books, and unusual artifacts from Gary's explorations around the world.

A beautiful landscaped amphitheater seats approximately 1,000 people for assemblies or performances during warm-weather months, and a 1.5-acre park that honors our founder is a peaceful place where people can relax and visit.

Light rail and bus stations are planned adjacent to the property, increasing proximity to major transportation corridors.

Kevin Scholz, the Architect—Nature's Living Energy

"From our first meeting, Gary and I felt an immediate kinship as we started melding his original ideas with my exterior design concept and the story—Nature's living energy. Gary wanted special features that included gardens growing aromatic plants, the use of solar power and natural light, efficient heating and cooling, and building water purification. He even wanted the restaurant to feature locally sourced foodstuffs prepared in healthy and delicious ways. This design led to LEED Silver certification for energy efficiency and sustainability, and Green Global NC certification for new construction.

Working with Gary Young is one of the highlights of my career. His warmth, enthusiasm, vision, creativity, and philosophy touched every part of the project. We worked together to create a project that provides a welcoming place for visitors and members, a world-class business and working environment, and a physical expression of Young Living's commitment to its mission: "To honor our stewardship to champion nature's living energy, essential oils, by fostering a community of healing and discovery while inspiring individuals to wellness, purpose, and abundance."

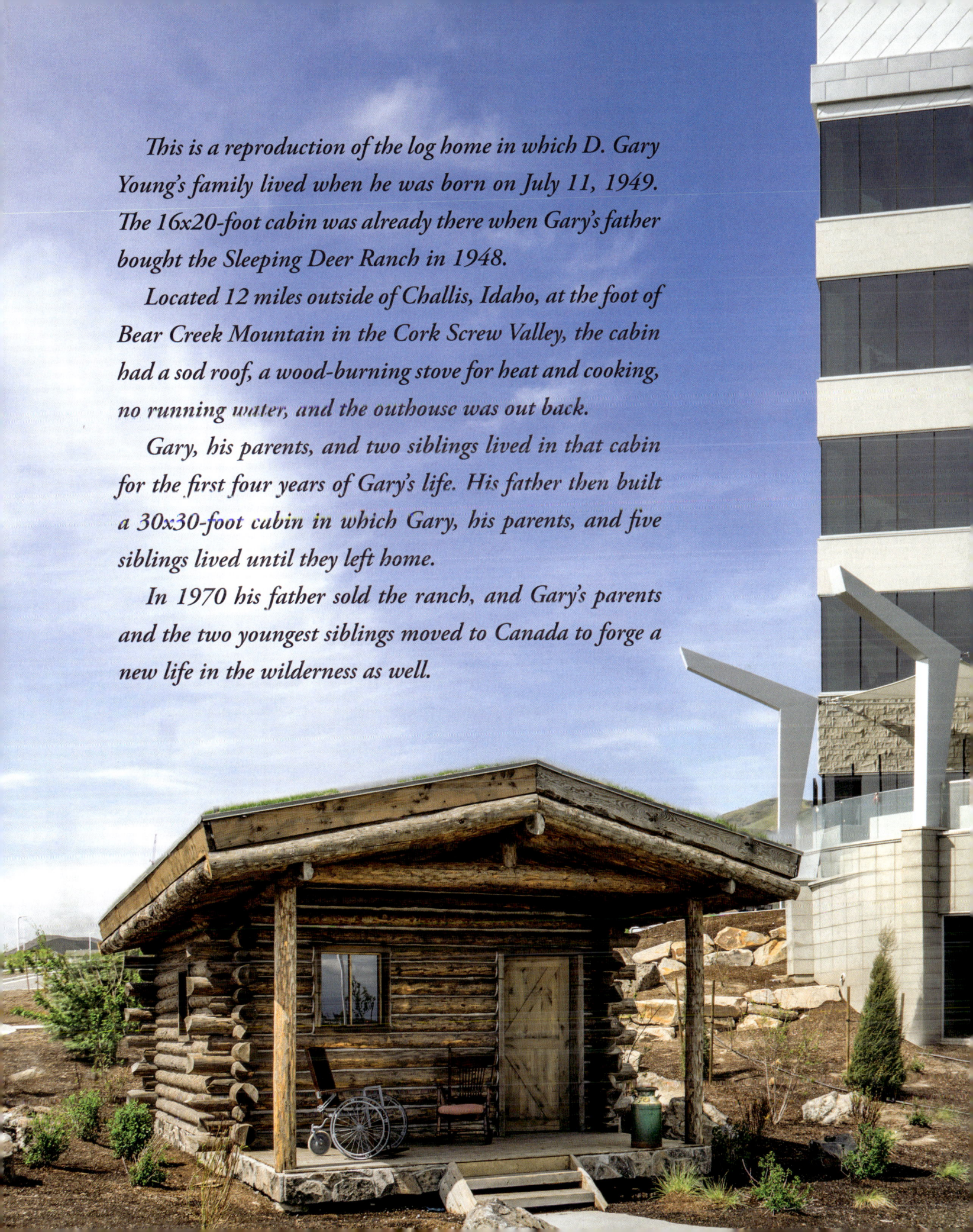

This is a reproduction of the log home in which D. Gary Young's family lived when he was born on July 11, 1949. The 16x20-foot cabin was already there when Gary's father bought the Sleeping Deer Ranch in 1948.

Located 12 miles outside of Challis, Idaho, at the foot of Bear Creek Mountain in the Cork Screw Valley, the cabin had a sod roof, a wood-burning stove for heat and cooking, no running water, and the outhouse was out back.

Gary, his parents, and two siblings lived in that cabin for the first four years of Gary's life. His father then built a 30x30-foot cabin in which Gary, his parents, and five siblings lived until they left home.

In 1970 his father sold the ranch, and Gary's parents and the two youngest siblings moved to Canada to forge a new life in the wilderness as well.

This magnificent five-story structure is one of a kind and a dream place to work.

Our beautiful Vitality Café provides delicious organic and nutritious meals every day.

Our state-of-the-art laboratory is featured on the first floor behind floor-to-ceiling glass for everyone visiting to observe.

Five Years, Five Key Goals, One Powerful Pledge.

In Gary's last few months, he spoke more about the future of Young Living and his vision for its growth. The 5x5 concept emerged from his conversations with Jared Turner, who spearheaded this enormous movement that is spreading across the globe with great enthusiasm among members and non-members alike. As Jared said, "We wanted to establish a set of goals that captured the magic and boldness that Gary always represented and envisioned for the future."

The thrill of celebrating our 25th anniversary with what began as one man's vision and has now become a worldwide mission was an event that surpassed our imagination and filled our hearts with joy beyond description. As Gary would say, "Remember: God, our Creator, sets no boundaries to our success. It is our responsibility to take our vision of wellness, purpose, and abundance to every home in the world." Gary's legacy lives on forever in the hearts of all of us.

FIVE x FIVE

PEOPLE POWERED
Our people make our pledge possible

EMPOWER
five times more people through The D. Gary Young, Young Living Foundation

ACHIEVE
zero waste in five years as stewards of the earth

REACH
five million additional households in five years

DEVELOP
at least five Corporate-owned or Partner Farms each year

OPEN
a minimum of five new markets each year

362   D. Gary Young | The World Leader in Essential Oils

This building, formerly the Young Living global offices, has now been converted to the headquarters for the United States market.

In 2018 we became more efficient in our processes through greater technology and staff expertise in manufacturing. We installed our newest production line, which fills 300 bottles per minute, bringing our capacity to nearly 142 million bottles per year and fulfilling 1.6 million orders sent to 126 countries.

WAREHOUSE AND MANUFACTURING

On August 15, 2007, Young Living moved into its new Spanish Fork warehouse. The 106,250-sqare-foot building seemed overwhelming at the time and would surely meet Young Living's needs for years—so everyone thought.

However, as with the previous warehouse, the racks spread out and went to the ceiling with the growth.

The building was engineered to ship 7,000 orders per day, but that soon became insufficient, so the engineers started redesigning and adding new equipment.

A new, innovative, state-of-the-art pick-to-light system was installed to speed up our capacity to pack between 18,000 to 24,000 orders that are shipped daily. In 2013 our first high speed Rota was purchased with a filling capacity of 300,000 bottles of oil a day. Production filled 10.7 million bottles in 2013, which made it our greatest growth year to date.

As we became overcrowded, boxes of inventory were stacked in the aisles, so outside warehousing space had to be leased. It became obvious that we needed to expand our facility, so plans were drawn and construction began for the new addition that was completed on July 14, 2016.

When the new expansion of 97,000 square feet was completed, the racks quickly filled, and manufacturing reached a capacity of 400,000 bottles per day, and filled approximately 52 million bottles that year. A new mezzanine for offices brought the total to 203,215 square feet, and staffing increased from 24 to 65 people.

In 2015 we installed another high-speed Rota line and added an additional 30 employees, which brought the total to 42.7 million bottles filled that year. One of the older Rota filling machines was sent to our Croatia warehouse that was in the beginning stages of production.

In June of 2016, the expansion of our distribution center opened, which included warehouse space, a rack-supported pick module, a seismically engineered pack mezzanine, and material-handling capabilities—all built while operating the facility and shipping out orders.

Our fulfillment operations were expanded from 1 pick line, 24 pack stations, and 8 manual shipping lanes to 5 pick lines, 96 pack stations, and 2 automated shipping lanes.

In 2017 growth continued stressing our capacity. In May a third shift was added with a total of 200 employees, and production reached 70.0 million units.

The need for more space and faster shipping to the East Coast of the U.S. was growing, so a second 175,000-square-foot warehouse went into operation in Memphis, Tennessee, on February 1, 2018.

The year 2018 was a solid year, as many people became experts in their roles, and we could focus more on people and process rather than on rapid expansion. We completed 71.8 million bottles, and by the end of the year, we installed our newest production line, manufactured by Bosch, which brought a level of intelligence and communication to our manufacturing that no other oil company in the world is using.

This new machine brings high-speed filling of 300 bottles per minute, an in-line weight-check system, automatic filling that adjusts the torque with recorded data, and a vision system with rejecting capability for any underfilled bottle, poorly placed caps, or broken tamper bands.

The labeler paired with this filling system incorporates vision capabilities that will reject a poorly placed label, a poorly coded label, or even a label with a bad SKU, automatically. Production capacity jumped to nearly 142 million bottles per year, giving us ample capability for future growth.

The warehouse facility is an awesome sight, and visitors are fascinated to see the different aspects of warehousing, laboratory testing, manufacturing, and shipping. The atmosphere is warm and friendly, and employees enthusiastically welcome our members, local authorities, and state agencies to see the efficient and organized way they all work together.

In February 2018 Young Living opened a partner distribution center in Memphis, Tennessee to increase our daily shipping capacity and reduce shipping costs and delivery time to our members in the eastern U.S. In December we shipped over 1.6 million orders to 126 countries from our U.S. distribution centers.

The warehouse totals 203,215 square feet. Thousands of visitors stand in awe at the immensity of the building and efficiency with which the staff works.

Barrels of oil are ready to go into production. The new machine fills up to 400,000 bottles of oil per day.

Our state-of-the-art, pick-to-light order-filling/packing system ships up to 24,000 orders daily, which is about 42.7 million bottles a year.

D. Gary Young | The World Leader in Essential Oils 367

In 2018 over 4.5 million personal connections were made globally through live chat, phone, and email, about 12,300 contacts per day.

MEMBER SERVICES CENTER

Member Services is a very busy hub of the Young Living business, where hundreds of service representatives are talking to thousands of members all over the world. In 2018 over 4.5 million personal connections were made globally through live chat, phone, and email, about 12,300 contacts per day. In the U.S. and Canada there are roughly 325,000 calls a month. Members first is the core objective of our business, where we strive to build lasting and personal relationships—to help them feel like family.

Our Member Services teams around the world support all global markets in 27 languages, with many more markets and languages on the horizon. Our largest service center is in Utah, with over 700 employees. An additional 300 employees in Member Services teams work in Latin America, Europe, and the Asia Pacific region. Our Utah representatives start at 5:00 a.m. and rotate hours until 10:00 p.m.

We have dedicated representatives from many different demographics and walks of life with very diverse backgrounds who are passionate about Young Living and our members. Together they create an amazing culture and build a stronger appreciation for the needs of our members, to determine the best ways to serve them.

"I get to meet new members every day, understand their struggles, and enjoy finding solutions; plus, the workplace is awesome." —Member Services representative in Malaysia

"If you ever have a concern, we are always here to listen, or if you have an awesome accomplishment, we are here to share in your joy. I love my job and even more I love the people I work with." —Member Services representative in Utah

Gary's first Young Living humanitarian trip in 2001 set him on a path that has grown into a worldwide mission. "When we are blessed financially, we have a great opportunity to share our abundance by helping those less fortunate in the world," and Gary practiced every word he spoke.

The D. Gary Young
Young ⊕ Living™
Foundation

Gary was born with a feeling of wanting to protect the "underdog." As a youth growing up, he was always the champion of the weak and those who couldn't defend themselves. Perhaps it was the poverty and the harshness of his life or maybe just his simple innate desire to help others that drove him to accomplish all that he did. Even though he had very little monetarily to give, he creatively found ways to help. When essential oils became a driving force in his life, he saw how they could benefit God's children; but with the growth of his new company, he saw even more how those in need could be helped—a new opportunity to change thousands of lives.

Mexico: Gary wanted to study the longevity of the Tarahumara Indians, which is why he chose to lead a small group to the high mountain plateau deep within Copper Canyon of Durango, Mexico, in June 2001. The members of the group carried heavy supplies up steep canyons, forging through fast-running water, and trekking up dangerously narrow trails that eventually brought them to the remote Tarahumara Indian village. They built two schools, and then at the base of the steep climb, a water-pumping system was installed to get water to this village that barely had enough water to prepare one meal a day for the children, with parents often going without food for two or three days.

The village men easily helped carry hundreds of sacks of supplies to the top.

The logs were heavy and the trail difficult.

It was a great reward when the school houses were finished.

There was so much joy and gratitude in the faces of those who were helped that it ignited Gary's drive to create more awareness with our members to join in the work with him.

Ecuador: When Gary started to build the farm in Ecuador and every day drove past a dilapidated excuse for a school, the feeling came over him to do something better for those children, and in 2009 the Young Living Academy opened its doors. Shortly thereafter, the Foundation was incorporated, which was the official start of a movement that would spread worldwide to provide a better education for children wherever possible—not just a bandage approach.

The Young Living Academy opened its doors in 2009 to 99 children, and today 350 students are enjoying the opportunity of having an education.

As Gary traveled the world, he saw need everywhere. He wanted to give back, to empower others to achieve their potential and defy limitations by providing wellness and education. He knew that by giving the children the opportunities to explore and develop their own skills and abilities as they grew into adulthood they would become strong examples for the next generation.

Gary said: "We envision a world where children are provided with the resources and opportunities necessary to become confident, self-reliant leaders who can take control of their own health, provide for their families, and positively change their communities."

In 2019 the Young Living Academy celebrated its 10-year anniversary and the announcement of the new Young Living Endowment Fund to support graduating students continuing on with higher education. The opportunities are immense as they venture into an exciting new future.

Uganda: Tragically, malaria is the leading cause of death for children under age 5, killing an estimated 42 children each day in Uganda. Since 2015 we have worked together with Healing Faith Uganda to put an end to malaria deaths in the rural villages of eastern Uganda and have helped increase its impact by 1,000 percent.

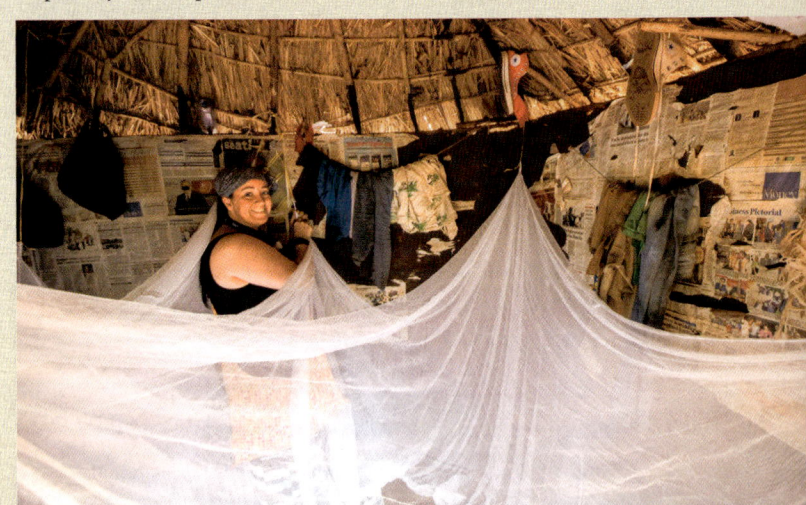

For less than $3 per net, thousands of lives are being protected.

Malaria is preventable and treatable, and our Foundation helped fund The D. Gary Young, Young Living Foundation Malaria Center, which is open five days a week and provides 80,000 individuals with feasible access to life-saving malaria prevention, education, testing, and treatment.

The Malaria Center provides urgent treatment and care.

Uganda: Our partner Sole Hope aids children infested with jiggers, a parasitic sand flea that burrows into hands and bare feet, causing infection, disease, and ostracism. As part of the removal process, children's feet are washed in tubs of soapy water that contain drops of Lavender and/or Purification essential oils, after which a medical professional removes each jigger. Once treated, the children receive a new pair of shoes and are educated on how to remain jigger-free.

Uganda and Ethiopia: The Foundation supports eight Lighthouse Centers in Uganda and Ethiopia that rescue children living on the streets who have only the clothes they are wearing and face starvation and violence daily. They are easily exploited by traffickers who thrive on their extreme poverty, which is why Hope for Justice creates women's groups in rural areas to empower women to save money and build businesses, thus bringing financial stability to their families, reducing vulnerability, and protecting themselves from traffickers.

Members wash children's feet before the jiggers are removed.

School is a dream for these young girls rescued from trafficking.

Cambodia: In 2016 we partnered with Hope for Justice, an organization determined to end human trafficking, a vicious crime that strips freedom from over 40 million victims worldwide. Hope for Justice rescues and rehabilitates these victims and works tirelessly through community outreach programs to prevent slavery before it claims lives. Survivors begin a new life when they come to Hope for Justice. The Young Living Foundation helps fund three programs in Cambodia, including the Phnom Penh Lighthouse, where victims receive treatment immediately after being rescued; the Poipet Pathways Project; and the Shine Career School, which empowers each girl to achieve their dreams.

Free of jiggers, the children proudly show off their new shoes.

Rescued girls in Cambodia learning Yoga.

Natural disasters: Sadly, the last few years have seen an overwhelming number of natural disasters, from wildfires and mudslides to hurricanes and earthquakes, which have impacted thousands of people everywhere, including many Young Living members. As Young Living has responded, service projects developed and have become an integral part of the Foundation, with thousands of members investing their time and money to contribute to the many needs. The Foundation quickly provided emergency supplies and relief teams that were ready to help in any way possible. The Foundation provided nearly $6 million in aid to those impacted by disasters in 2017 and delivered more than 4,000 care kits.

Nepal: In the spring of 2015, two earthquakes with magnitudes of 7.8 and 7.3 destroyed hundreds of villages in Nepal. While lecturing in Japan in 2016, Gary was asked if he would visit Nepal to see what could be done. He was overwhelmed when he saw the devastation that was caused by the earthquake, and wanted to help.

Members from all around the world joined Gary to help rebuild the village of Yarsa. Gary taught the villagers a new method of making bricks with a machine that mixes dirt with a small amount of cement, providing a more affordable means to build and offer work to locals who had lost their livelihoods in the disaster.

In May 2018 the Foundation had completely rebuilt all 100 homes in the village, as well as the primary school, which is called the Young Living Academy, Yarsa Primary School. Now, the focus has turned to rebuilding 16 schools and two educational women centers in other devastated communities.

"These people have had an impact on me as we help rebuild their village. They live in unimaginable circumstances, yet continue to thrive, be happy, and are welcoming. Helping these people is an amazing experience from which anyone would benefit," said Gary.

Ecuador: In April 2016 a 7.8-magnitude earthquake hit Ecuador 300 miles north of Guayaquil. The Foundation rallied quickly, and Young Living Ecuador farm workers and office staff, Academy graduates and staff, and community members traveled together for hours to reach the devastation. Survivors were curled up on mattresses or blankets next to decimated homes. Working through hard-to-imagine destruction, care kits were quickly distributed with clothing, blankets, and Young Living products to remote areas where people were still waiting for aid.

Gary, Jacob, and Hector work side by side with the villagers in Yarsa to rebuild.

The brick-manufacturing machine made rebuilding fast and efficient.

Ecuadorian earthquake victims are grateful for the relief supplies.

Greg Larsen, Foundation Executive Director, joins in the relief work in Houston.

Diana Patiño and Juan Arevalo pass out NingXia Red to earthquake rescue workers.

Florida members prepare relief packages to be flown to Puerto Rico.

Members unload a semi-trailer of product for hurricane victims.

Houston, Texas: Many members and Young Living employees joined relief efforts for Hurricane Harvey victims in 2017. Homes were destroyed within minutes as Harvey raged through Houston. It was total devastation, but everyone worked hard gutting, cleaning, and carrying relief supplies while giving hope and reassurance. One victim said: "They worked so hard and did such an amazing job gutting my home of damaged possessions and filling it with hope."

Mexico City: The 2017 Puebla Earthquake in Mexico City brought much suffering to thousands of people. Young Living Foundation staff was able to land at a small municipal airport that was still open and provide precious supplies to those in need. The Foundation made two trips in 2018 to help with rebuilding efforts to provide temporary homes for those still displaced from this disaster alongside a local organization called Techo. Young Living Mexico members and staff, along with Techo volunteers, were able to serve those in their local community, successfully building homes for 30 families.

Puerto Rico: After Hurricane Maria wreaked havoc in Puerto Rico in 2017, Foundation Executive Director Greg Larsen, and Director of Special Projects John Whetten flew nine round-trips from Florida to Puerto Rico carrying precious relief supplies, including 1,700 water filters, 12,000 pounds of food and baby products, and nearly 1,000 Young Living care packages. Because most of Puerto Rico didn't have power, on the way back to the United States, they flew out many evacuees in severe need of medical attention.

Florida and California: In 2018 the Foundation supplied several hundred care kits to hurricane victims in the Carolinas and the Florida Panhandle and to families affected by the raging wildfires throughout California. It has been so painful to hear the stories from those who lost all their worldly possessions. But out of that emerged a powerful, inspiring feeling of hope and connection that banded Young Living members together in one purpose—to help those in need.

Oh, Bearded Ones: At the 2016 Grand Convention, Jonny Turner, senior director of Media Productions for Young Living, and Stelios Xanthos, media production cinematographer, offered to let members cut off their mountain-man beards for the $100,000 Foundation challenge for the short time that they were on stage. Everyone was ecstatic and roared with laughter as they watched members shave off Stelios' and Jonny's beards.

Stelios loved the attention but Jonny didn't recognize himself.

Alaska: In early 2017 Gary entered the Tustumena 200 and the Willow 300 Alaskan dogsled races. He created different ways for members to donate to the Foundation through his challenge to finish. Members raised as much as $40,000 for Nepal, as Gary surpassed all the expectations of seasoned mushers.

Young Living members are always looking for ways to be involved and be creative in their support for the Foundation.

Ride for a Reason: In 2017 Scott and Brenda Schuler, Young Living leaders, spearheaded a new fundraising activity for our members. Scott's love of motorcycle riding has enticed others with that same passion to ride with him from Minnesota to the Young Living farm in Mona, Utah, arriving the day before the Young Living International Grand Convention.

Although riding was not one of Brenda's passions, she and Scott chose to ride together, and as Brenda said, "It was so fun and rewarding to be a part of something bigger than ourselves. What a wonderful way to partner with those we love."

The enthusiasm of Brenda and Scott was very contagious.

It was thrilling as they entered the farm. Scott auctioned the motorcycle he rode the first year and, along with two other donations, raised close to $150,000 for the Foundation.

Greeting the morning sun when cresting the top of the hill with his magnificent dogsled team was part of the reward of the race.

As Scott says, "The sweet spot in life is when you can leverage what you love for the benefit of others."

Many joined Gary to ride the last few miles to experience the thrill of finishing with everyone else when entering the farm, 2017.

In 2018 many members donated motorcycles, UTVs, custom scooters, and even a Jeep to help raise over $1 million for Hope for Justice in its fight against human trafficking. In 2019 the number of riders increased, and more items were auctioned at convention, resulting in more money raised for the Foundation.

In 2018 Jacob rode Gary's motorcycle into the farm with the other riders.

Josef rode as an enthusiastic passenger with Kevin Pace so that he could be a part of this amazing biking experience.

Gary's truck from Fort Nelson was the final spin of the auction. Thousands watched with anticipation to see who would claim this wonderful memory.

The impact of the Foundation is tremendous:
- Rebuilt 100 homes and a primary school in Yarsa, Nepal
- Service trips to Ecuador, Uganda, Mexico, Nepal, and Cambodia
- Hope for Justice partnership to end modern slavery
- Disaster relief care packages and supplies delivered to more than 4,000 individuals in 2017
- A 57 percent increase of donors to the Foundation
- Over $16 million raised from 2014 through 2018

When we are blessed financially, we have a great opportunity to share our abundance by helping those less fortunate in the world. It seems that the more we give, the more we are blessed. The donations continue to increase as does our ability to help with more projects and more requests.

Gary's heart was warmed to see our members catching on to his vision, knowing that they will continue to carry that torch for freedom. We all benefit by being part of that vision to serve humanity and better thousands of lives.

For more information, go to bit.ly/ylfoundation

The Young Living Foundation staff and members enjoyed their service project working together in Chongon, Ecuador.

The first international office opened in Japan in January 1999. In March 2011 the headquarters were moved to the 32nd floor of this beautiful building. The entrance is decorated with breathtaking dried lavender flowers that were flown in from the Young Living farm in France.

This beautiful office in Sydney, Australia, was opened in January 2016, having been moved from the Brisbane office first established in 1999.

INTERNATIONAL OFFICES

Members enjoy visiting our offices wherever they are in the world. It creates a feeling of belonging to something that is successful and spreading across the globe of which they are a part.

As we have grown, the needs of our members have made it important to have a business office and a place where they can take their friends and people who are interested to see what Young Living is about. All the experience centers are very beautiful and unique to their country yet carry the Young Living theme throughout the decor and message.

We invite everyone to come and visit and share their stories while drinking a glass of NingXia Red or munching on a Young Living snack. As we continue to open new countries, more people will hear our message and want to become a part of a vision that is bigger than all of us—a vision that we are fulfilling together as it reaches the far corners of the earth.

The Ecuador office first opened in 2006. In 2019 the new Experience Center opened in Mall del Sol, which is visited by 1.8 million people every month.

The fascinating France Experience Center opened in July 2012. It overlooks the Young Living farm in Provence through the windows of the amazing 12th-century castle, Château des Agoult.

Gary and I joined members in cutting the ribbon of the Mexico Experience Center in February 2017. It is located on Paseo de la Reforma, the most important avenue in a major historic area of Mexico City. Mexican leaders loved hearing Gary explain the Seed to Seal process.

European headquarters was established in England in April 2005. The new London office opened in February 2016.

The Singapore Experience Center and offices, October 2011.

D. Gary Young | The World Leader in Essential Oils 381

The office and Experience Center in Calgary, Canada, was first opened in 2013.

Malaysia headquarters, Kuala Lumpur, first opened in October 2014. The new Experience Center opened in 2017.

Corporate offices opened in Split, Croatia, in October 2015, with Member Services, a distribution center, distillery, and manufacturing.

Our unique Seed to Seal® commitment and its three pillars— Sourcing, Science, Standards— ensure that the cultivation, wild-crafting, distillation, quality testing, and legal compliance of essential oils and products produced by Young Living are done without compromise.

The Hong Kong office was established in October 2013 and then moved to this new Experience Center in 2017.

The Taiwan Experience Center opened in October 2016.

The Indonesia Experience Center opened in May 2017.

Canada's Toronto Experience and Training Center opened in June 2017.

Manila, Philippines, Experience Center opened in October 2018.

D. Gary Young | The World Leader in Essential Oils

Guangzhou, China, Experience Center opened in October 2018.

Perth, Australia, welcomes visitors to the beautiful new Experience Center that opened in November 2018.

The Bogotá, Colombia, Experience Center opened in February 2019.

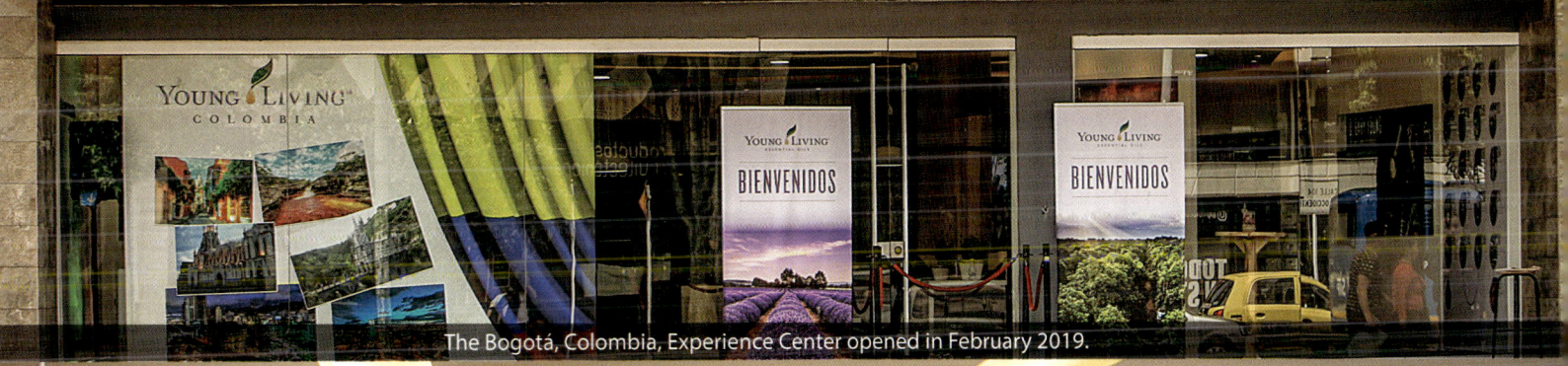

Members and visitors enjoy learning about Young Living in the beautiful Colombia Experience Center that opened in February 2019.

D. Gary Young | The World Leader in Essential Oils

Artistic rendering of Costa Rica Experience Center, opening November 2019.

Artistic rendering of São Paulo, Brazil, Experience Center, opening December 2019.

388   D. Gary Young | The World Leader in Essential Oils

Johannesburg, South Africa, opening October 2019.

Artistic rendering of South Korea Experience Center, opening in December 2019.

Creating Something to Believe In—Salt Lake City, Utah, 2002.

Achieve Your Highest Potential—Salt Lake City, Utah, 2003. Gary rode Goliath down the convention aisle and up on to the stage.

INTERNATIONAL GRAND CONVENTIONS

Convention is a time of excitement in learning about the latest discoveries, being first to hear about new products, meeting members in our organizations, and sharing in each other's success.

Young Living Essential Oils was registered in Utah in April of 1994, but that year Gary was building the distillery in St. Maries, Idaho. Besides that, Gary and I were married in September and off to Europe to a medical seminar.

The first convention was held in Spokane in 1995, with about 160 attending. Farm day in St. Maries was exciting, as Gary showed off his new distillery and talked about his visionary plans for farming and producing oils.

Convention was held every year, but growth was slow. In 2003 we were thrilled to see the number of attendees finally exceed 1,000, but it took us until 2014 for our attendance to pass the 10,000 mark. In 2017 Gary greeted 30,000 attendees cheering for him as he entered on his dogsled, pulled by the huskies that took him to the finish line of two races in the Alaskan wilderness earlier that year. The challenge and the accomplishment of these races filled Gary with excitement that was highly contagious. His last presentation at the close of convention was deeply inspiring and one of his finest.

The 2019 convention—25 Years Young—welcomed 50,000 members to Salt Lake City to the University of Utah Rice-Eccles Stadium. Being together to celebrate our 25th year anniversary, which began as one man's vision and has now spread worldwide, surpassed imagination and filled our hearts with joy beyond description.

As Gary often said, "Remember: God, our Creator, sets no boundaries to our success. It is our responsibility to take our vision of wellness, purpose, and abundance to every home in the world."

Live Your Dream—International Grand Convention in Salt Lake City, Utah, 2014.

The One Gift, 2010—Following the Frankincense Trail.

Jacob and Josef loved riding their camels.

The One Gift—Salt Lake City, 2010; Gary loved the authentic reenactment of history.

Transformation—Salt Lake City, Utah, 2012.

Journey of Discovery, Nashville, Tennessee, 2004.

Light the Fire—Dallas, Texas, 2015.

Live Your Passion—Salt Lake City, Utah, 2016. Gary loved the surprise of the unexpected—and the audience cheered with delight.

Fulfill Your Destiny—University of Utah Rice-Eccles Stadium, Salt Lake City, Utah, 2017.

Freedom—The Vivint Arena, Salt Lake City, Utah, 2018.

The Gifts of Convention

1995
Into the Future

1996
Yesterday's Wisdom,
Tomorrow's Destiny

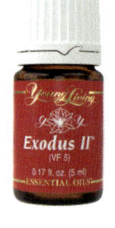

1997
Seek Knowledge
and Serve

1998
Magnify Your Purpose

1999
Live with Passion

2000
Building Our Legacy
of Freedom

2001
Life, Liberty, and
Longevity

2002
Creating Something
to Believe In

2003
Highest Potential
Chivalry

2004
Journey of Discovery

2005
Gold of the Gods

2006
Explore the Dream

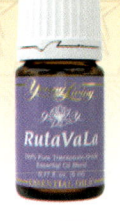

2007
Infuse Your Life

2008
Rise to Excellence

2009
One Mission, One Passion

2010
The One Gift

2011
Vitality

2012
Transformation

2013
Believe

2014
Build Your Dream

2015
Light the Fire

2016
Live Your Passion

2017
Fulfill Your Destiny
My Destiny

2018
Freedom

2019
25 Years Young

D. Gary Young | The World Leader in Essential Oils

Gary's heart was filled with tremendous satisfaction as he watched the first drops of Black Spruce oil bubble up in the separator during the first distillation at the Northern Lights Farm in Ft. Nelson, B.C., Canada, March 2014.

A MODERN-DAY PIONEER

Gary Young was a truth seeker, and he followed the path that led him there. He was not one to write about someone else's adventures. He had to know and see for himself. He wrote about his own experiences, research, and findings.

His determination took him to Shabwah, the ancient dwelling of Queen Sheba, hidden from the world in the "Forbidden Zone" of Yemen; to the unexplored tribal land of frereana frankincense in Somalia; to the tops of the Al-Hasik Mountains in Oman; deep into the jungles of the Amazon; to Sri Lanka to find the elusive blue lotus; and to many other previously unexplored places looking for the hidden secrets of God's oils.

As Gary said, his mistakes were numerous, but they all taught him more about life and what works and doesn't work. Sometimes, through trial and error, he was led down a wrong path, from which he gained greater understanding and tolerance. He lived on the edge of life with pain and suffering that taught him endurance and persistence.

He ventured into unknown danger seeking truth, giving him courage and gratitude for God's blessings in his life. His adventures were an open book, and he eagerly shared his discoveries with those who would listen and benefit from his knowledge and experience. We are grateful that his life's story has been preserved in the photos of this book.

He grew up farming and living off of what Mother Nature offered, which gave him a tremendous advantage in his life's path. He invested 36 years in the research and discovery of essential oils and their benefits and 31 years learning how to blend oils for enhanced benefits and infuse them into food supplementation.

In addition, he spent over 27 years farming aromatic plants, learning distillation and analytical evaluation, and traveling to the far corners of the earth in his study of essential oils. He designed and built eight large distillation facilities around the world. No other company has the history of research and development of essential oils in the areas of production, usage, research, and education as D. Gary Young and his company, Young Living Essential Oils.

Members of Young Living, the World Leader in Essential Oils, spread the knowledge of God's precious oils to every corner of the globe, giving hope to the needy and an opportunity for those looking for a way to help our world physically, spiritually, and financially.

For more than 25 years, thousands of Young Living members have come to one or more of the farms to help with a harvest and reforestation to expand their understanding and their appreciation as they learn what it takes to produce an essential oil. The camaraderie, sharing, working together, and helping each other in this kind of work in these conditions cannot be experienced anywhere else in the world. It is truly a life-changing experience.

Young Living sets an example in the network marketing industry in the integrity of its products and a compensation plan that makes it possible for those interested to realize their dreams. It creates an honest environment where its members are invited to be a part of the Seed to Seal process, so they can speak with a knowing of the value of their products and from where they come.

D. Gary Young was truly a pioneer in essential oil research, an inventor of equipment, a developer of the process, a scientist and formulator in the laboratory, an educator on the cutting edge of discovery, and a leader in usage and application, who taught millions of people in many countries.

He was a writer with deep human insight and understanding, a man with an inner knowing of God's great gift of essential oils to mankind.

Today, with the education and experience of almost 30 years in growing crops for essential oil production and designing, building, and operating distilleries around the world, D. Gary Young certainly earned the distinction of being the World Leader in Essential Oils.

The Many Facets of D. Gary Young

The life of D. Gary Young has many facets. He was a man who was comfortable wherever he was and whatever he was doing, from riding his horse in the mountains, to formulating in the laboratory, to teaching thousands of people from stage.

His life is an inspiring story of what most people would say is impossible—to overcome monumental obstacles and succeed. We hope this book about his life's journey has warmed your heart, motivated you, and excited you to go for it and live your dream.

Teaching at the St. Maries Farm in Idaho.

Offering relief in the Tarahumara Indian village in Mexico

Warm Springs—the Idaho wilderness: Gary's favorite place.

With "Nitro" in the engine, what would you expect?—2013.

Salmon fishing with his boys was the best

Teaching from the old French portable distiller during convention.

Gary was most at home in the saddle.

Live Your Dream, 20th Anniversary, Convention, 2014.

Convention 2007

No one ever knew it was Gary; he always fit in with the culture.

Bartering was in Gary's blood.

1st place division over 50 in 2002

Following the Frankincense Trail.

Vita Flex was always taught first before Gary went on to Raindrop.

At age seven, Jacob was a natural. "Just don't tell Mom."

Convention Farm Day, a moment of precious information.

The faster and more dangerous, the better.

GARY'S QUOTES

- It's never eaten as hot as it's cooked.

- If you're not living on the edge, you're taking up too much space. Live life like you're on an escalator, always going up and always moving.

- It's an awfully thin pancake that has only one side.

- Being difficult is not a problem, and the impossible just takes a little longer.

- I believe that essential oils are the closest physical and tangible substance on earth to God.

- Vitality is waking up in the morning and hitting the ground running.

- I'm always short of time, so I planted some.

- The two greatest powers on this planet are the power of prayer and the frequency of oils. When you combine the two, you're in God's frequency.

- I'm happy with the accomplishments of the day, but could I have done more?" I don't believe God sent me here to rest on my laurels thinking I've already accomplished enough, so I'm going to push until I die.

- Focus on where you want to go and don't let anyone take you off your path. Let the Spirit guide you as you follow your dreams and reach your highest potential.

- A fellow asked me, "Gary, what happens if something happens to you, what's going to happen to Young Living?" I said, "Don't worry about it, Mary can handle it all. Piece of cake. The company will just go on. The office staff can run it. It will just go on without me, and it will be fantastic, and that's what I want." Then the man asked, "Well, what about formulas?" and I said, "No problem. Mary will dream and they'll come to her. I'll give them to her in her dreams. Don't worry about it. It's all covered."

- All the information in the universe is out there, and all you have to do is ask for it.

- I believe that if something doesn't work, then try another way until it does. That is how I have been with learning about the oils. I did not have someone to teach me the Raindrop Technique. It was shown to me in a dream, and I tried it different ways until I found the way that it was the most effective.

- Life is a grand journey and can be whatever we choose it to be. We often spend our energy locked into lack, limitation, and unproductive choices. Because we are insecure, we feel that we have to undergo the abuse, hardship, and trials put upon us by our own choices.

- We have the God-given right to shape and control our own future, and perhaps our own destiny, by the very thoughts we project. We often feel that we will never have enough, life is harsh and terrible, and that we must go through all these trials and the experiences because of what our parents or someone else did. However, God gave me the insight to see that we go through these trials only because we choose to. When we choose to have happiness, peace, and abundance, those attributes will flow to us more quickly and freely than misery, suffering, unhappiness, and lack.

- Whenever there's a need, the Lord puts an experience in front of me, and then I create something for that need. That's why I formulated many of the Young Living products that we have today.

- I have found throughout my years that the greatest secret of life is loving life.

- Take the responsibility to be the master of yourself and realize that if you want the answer, it lies within your reach. Those were the very words that were given to me years ago at 2 in the morning. But I had to have an open mind and heart and be willing to explore every aspect of life. I was not to go with blinders on down a tunnel, and it has truly paid off.

Publications by D. Gary Young, 1996-2015

Co-Authored Research

Detecting Essential Oil Adulteration. Boren KE, Young DG, Woolley CL, Smith BL, Carlson RE. J Environmental Analytical Chemistry. 2015 2:2.

Differential effects of selective frankincense (Ru Xiang) essential oil versus non-selective sandalwood (Tan Xiang) essential oil on cultured bladder cancer cells: a microarray and bioinformatics study. Dozmorov MG, Yang Q, Wu W, Wren J, Suhail MM, Woolley CL, Young DG, Fung KM, Lin HK. Chinese Medicine. 2014 Jul 2,9:18.

Management of basal cell carcinoma of the skin using frankincense (Boswellia sacra) essential oil: a case report. Fung KM, Suhail MM, McClendon B, Woolley CL, Young DG, Lin HK. OA [Open Access] Alternative Medicine. June 01, 2013 1(2):14.

Extraction of biologically active compounds by hydrodistillation of Boswellia species gum resins for anti-cancer therapy. Lin HK, Suhail MM, Fung KM, Woolley CL, Young DG. OA (Open Access) Alternative Medicine, 2013 Feb 02;1(1):4.

Chemical differentiation of Boswellia sacra and Boswellia carterii essential oil by gas chromatography and chiral gas chromatography-mass spectrometry. Woolley CL, Suhail MM, Smith BL, Boren KE, Taylor LC, Schreuder MF, Chai JK, Casabianca H, Haq S, Lin HK, Al-Shari AA, Al-Hatmi S, Young DG. Journal of Chromatography A. Oct 2012.

Frankincense essential oil prepared from hydrodistillation of Boswellia sacra gum resins induces human pancreatic cancer cell death in cultures and in a xenograft murine model. Ni X, Suhail MM, Yang Q, Cao A, Fung K-M, Postier RG, Woolley CL, Young DG, Zhang J, Lin HK. BMC Complementary and Alternative Medicine. Dec 2012.

Boswellia sacra essential oil induces tumor cell-specific apoptosis and suppresses tumor aggressiveness in cultured human breast cancer cells. Suhail MM, Wu W, Cao A, Mondalek FG, Fung K-M, Shih P-T, Fang Y-T, Woolley CL, Young DG, Lin HK. BMC Complementary and Alternative Medicine. 2011.

Inhibition of methicillin-resistant Staphylococcus aureus (MRSA) by essential oils. Chao S, Young DG, Oberg C, Nakaoka K. Flavor and Fragrance Journal. Vol. 23 2008.

Essential Oil of Bursera graveolens (Kunth) Triana et Planch from Ecuador. Young DG, Chao S, Casabianca H, Bertrand M-C, Minga D. Journal of Essential Oil Research. Nov/Dec 2007.

Inhibition of LPS Induced Nitric Oxide Production in Murine RAW Macrophage-like Cells by Essential Oils of Plants, Chao S, Young DG, Nakaoka K, Oberg C. Journal of the Utah Academy of Sciences, Arts, and Letters. Vol. 82, 2005.

Assessment of Antimicrobial Activity of Fourteen Essential Oils When Using Dilution and Diffusion Methods. Donaldson JR, Warner SL, Cates RG, Young DG. Pharmaceutical Biology. Vol. 43, No. 8. 2005.

Pre-Clinical Study: Antioxidant Levels and Immunomodulatory Effects of Wolfberry Juice and other Juice Mixtures in Mice. Chao S, Schreuder M, Young DG, Nakaoka K, Moyes L, Oberg C. Journal of the American Nutraceutical Association. Winter 2004.

Composition of the Oils of Three Chrysothamnus nauseousus Varieties. Chao S, Young DG, Casabianca H, Bertrand M-C. Journal of Essential Oil Research. Nov/Dec 2003.

Antimicrobial Effects of Essential Oils on Streptococcus pneumoniae. Horne D, Holm M, Oberg C, Chao S, Young DG. Journal of Essential Oil Research. Sep/Oct 2001.

Screening for Inhibitory Activity of Essential Oils on Selected Bacteria, Fungi and Viruses. Chao SC, Young DG, Oberg CJ. Journal of Essential Oil Research. Sep/Oct 2000.

Effect of a Diffused Essential Oil Blend on Bacterial Bioaerosols, Chao SC, Young DG, Oberg CJ. Journal of Essential Oil Research. Sep/Oct 1998.

Papers Presented at Conferences

Inhibitory Activity of Essential Oils Toward Cellular Proliferation in a Lung Cancer Carcinoma Cell Line. International Food Chemistry Conference. SICC-5, Singapore, 2007.

Comparative Study of the Essential Oils of Three Betula Species: B. alleghaniensis, B. lenta, B. pendula. Gualin, China, Conference, 2004.

Autolysis Induction by Essential Oils in Streptococcus pneumoniae. Annual Meeting of the Utah Academy of Sciences, Arts, and Letters. Salt Lake City, UT, April 1998.

Cultivating and Distilling Therapeutic Quality Essential Oils in the United States. Proceedings from the First International Symposium, Grasse, France. March 21-22, 1998.

Organic Farming and Germination: UNIDO World Congress on Essential Oils, Anadolu University in Eskisehir, Turkey, 1997.

Books Published

Ancient Einkorn: Today's Staff of Life – 2014
Shutran's Ancient Apothecary – 2011
The One Gift – 2010
Raindrop Technique – 2008
Discovery of the Ultimate Superfood – 2005
Essential Oil Integrative Medical Guide – 2003
A New Route to Robust Health – 2000
Pregnenolone – 2000
Longevity Secrets – 1999
The Truth Behind Growth Hormone – 1999
An Introduction to Young Living Essential Oils – 1999
Aromatherapy: The Essential Beginning – 1995

Essential Oils Desk Reference—First published in 1991, this book chronicles Gary's life work, which started in 1981 when he was recovering from his accident and studying the human body and nutrition. This set him on his path to discovering the miracle of essential oils and his recognition as the world leader. The 8th edition was published in November 2018.

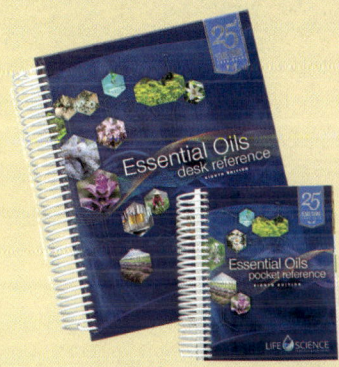

www.discoverlsp.com

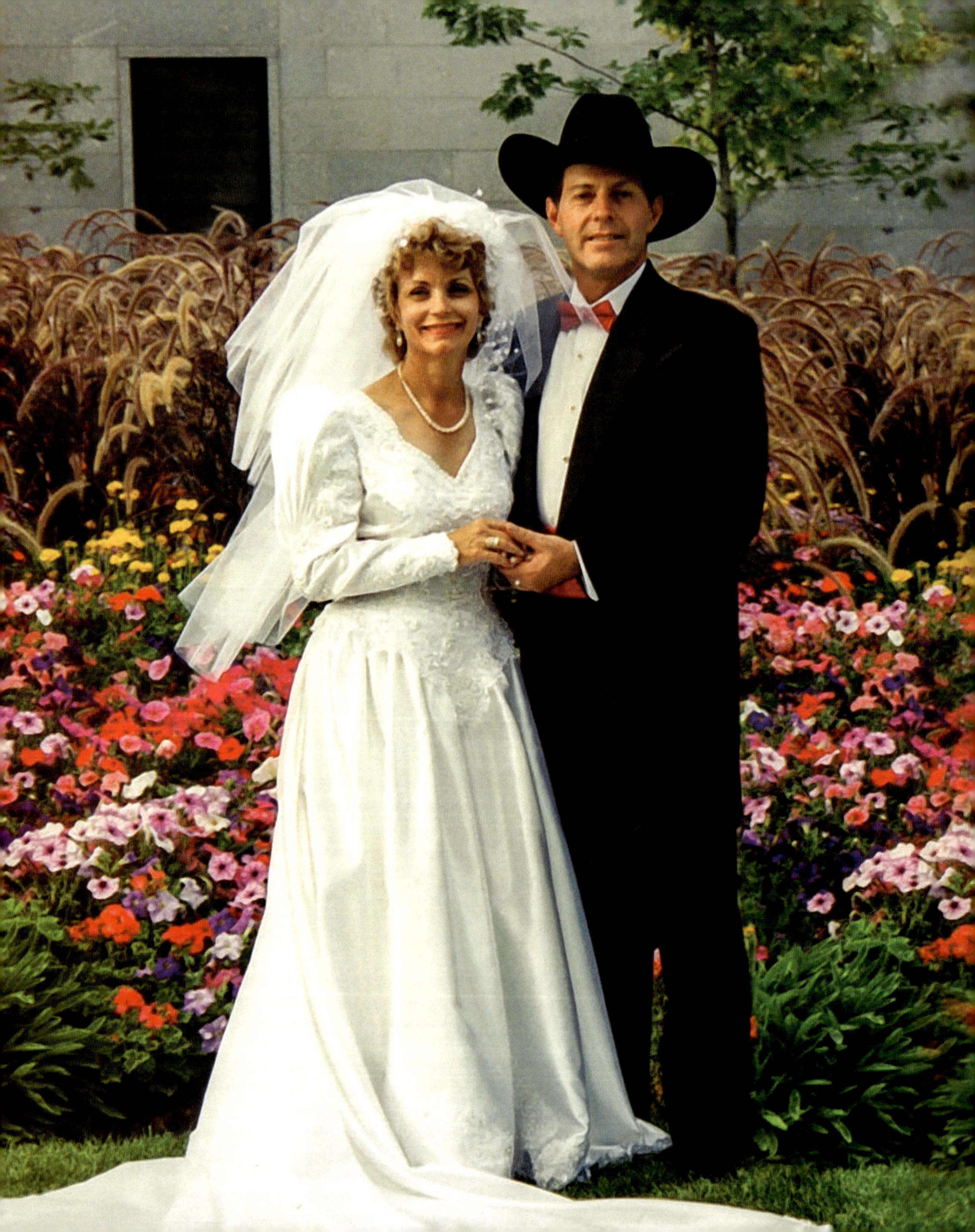

A LOVE STORY

Young Living is a remarkable success story, built as a labor of love from the ground up by husband-and-wife team D. Gary and Mary Young. Young Living is a global phenomenon—largely a result of their tireless work ethic, uniquely complementary chemistry, and passion for sharing pure essential oils. Here is a glimpse into their love story, which Mary shared with us:

Gary and I met in October of 1992 at an expo at the Salt Palace in Salt Lake City, Utah.

A young man working in the Young Living booth invited me to a meeting the next day, which I couldn't attend, but I suggested he call me the next time they were in town. Surprisingly, I was called a month later. I was fascinated with what I heard and signed up with someone I didn't know, since I just wanted to use the products. However, I also wanted to know who this Gary Young was and if he was for real.

A month later Gary came to give a meeting. I was amazed that anyone could talk so fast, talk about places, dates, history, and quote scripture without any notes. We spoke briefly by way of introduction, and then I left.

A month after that, I received a call from his office asking if I could pick Gary up at the airport and drive him to where he could buy a few things that he needed on his way to Egypt. I reluctantly agreed, not knowing if I wanted to get that involved. We went to the bank and the camera shop and talked a lot about the plans for his company. He was a wealth of information, which I enjoyed. Before taking him back to the airport, he took me to lunch and offered me a marketing job, to which I said, "No. I'm financially independent, and I don't want any job, but I will help you."

His business in Spokane was plagued with problems and a lot of debt, and he wanted to move to a new location and start over. After a lot of conversation and sharing of ideas, we decided to become partners and start a new company. He moved to Utah, and Young Living Essential Oils was birthed on Thanksgiving Day 1993.

We started in an old, dilapidated building with 5,000 usable square feet. Gary put up walls and built his laboratory and the offices. He did all the texturing and painting, while my mother, LaRue, and I did the cleaning and organizing. Gary blended the oils and traveled all over the county giving meetings and seminars, while I took care of the office.

Our lives became entwined in growing our new business. Everything revolved around Young Living, and dating was lunch with everyone else at a local Mexican restaurant. It was a tough time with no borrowed money or investors, but it was also exciting with Gary's compelling vision.

We had many fond memories with some funny stories of those early days, such as when he was building the first distillery in St. Maries that he built with PVC tubing. Everything worked just as he planned. The steam was sizzling through the pipes into the cooker, and we were making oil. It was very exhilarating, and we could hardly wait to get started the next day.

However, the next morning Gary made a not-so-happy discovery. The hot PVC pipes had become soft and stuck together as they cooled down during the night, so Gary had to replace all the tubing with steel pipes. Those times were frustrating, but the thrill of seeing the oil bubble up is all part of what brought us to where we are today.

It must have been the aroma of the lavender or the alluring beauty of the sun sitting on top of the pine trees at dusk, but when he asked me to go to Europe with him for a medical seminar he was attending in September, I told him I wouldn't go unless we were married. That was in July, so there was no time to think about it; we just had to move quickly. We were married on September 2, 1994, and on September 3 at 7 a.m., we boarded the plane for Europe.

Gary came from the mountains, and I came from the opera stage; and yet we thought alike, our standards were the same, we wanted to help people, and God was always our foundation. We believed that health and vitality were to be found within the wonders of Mother Nature and not in the chemicals of the laboratory. We had the same goals: to help others discover true wellness, so they could share and help carry Gary's vision to the world.

We loved planning, working, and doing meetings together, and we loved sharing the challenge and success of Young Living. Gary was the visionary, and I was the realist, but it was a great dynamic that worked very well. Our boys, Jacob, born in 2000, and Josef, born in 2004, have been an integral part of our Young Living journey. We always took them with us wherever we went. They spoke on stage, greeted our members, joined in all the activities, and were always creating fun and laughter with everyone.

We are about truth, honesty, and integrity, deeply grounded in our love of and belief in God. We are about family—our own family and our Young Living family. Our boys love God, the oils, doing what's right, eating healthy, and being an example so that they can help further this great company that their father founded, that Young Living has become.

Who's kidding who?

Honeymoon in France.

Laughing with Japanese friends on the bullet train to Tokyo.

Oh, no, another flight?

"Hang on, Mary," Cairo, 1999.

Baby Jacob coming our way.

Gary taught at the Izmir University, Turkey, 1996.　　　Josef has no fear.　　　Go faster, Dad.

Can't start too young!　　　Brotherly love?

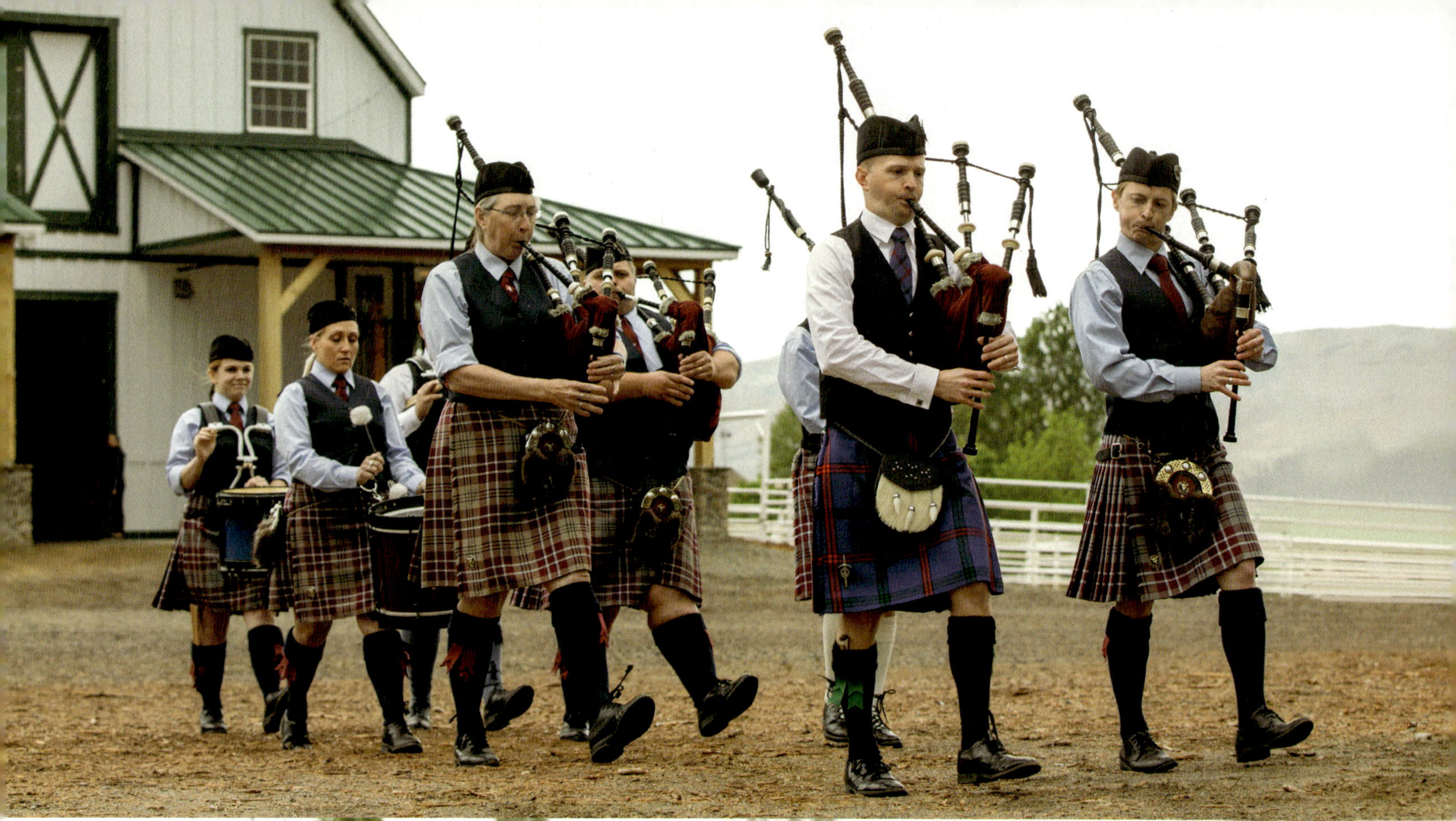

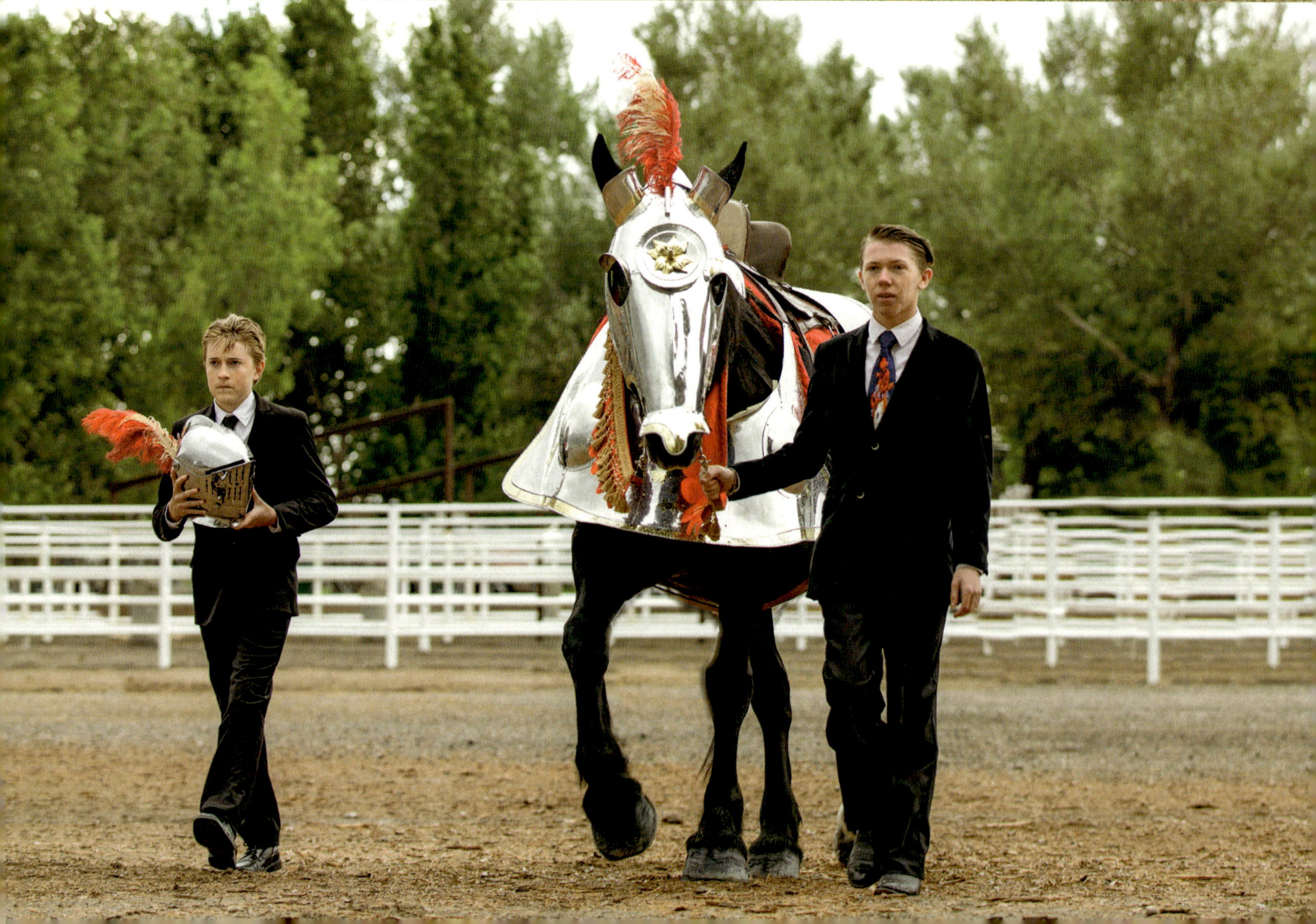

CELEBRATION OF LIFE
D. Gary Young—July 11, 1949-May 12, 2018

D. Gary Young, the undisputed leader of the essential oil movement in North America and the founder of Young Living Essential Oils, passed away on May 12, 2018, in Salt Lake City, Utah, due to complications following a series of strokes.

In December 2009, Gary was deep in the jungle boating up the Amazon tributaries and sleeping in native huts in small villages along this mammoth river. One morning he awoke with a huge welt on his side that was already oozing. By January of 2010, he was coughing a lot with a fever and feeling quite weak. He ended up in the Infectious Disease Ward at the University of Utah Hospital for about 10 days. After many tests and several possible diagnoses, the official diagnosis came back as an "unknown virus."

The fever was gone but he did not seem to get better. He continued to cough and was always short of breath. But typical of Gary, he just forged ahead with what he had to do and gave little thought to his condition. As time went on, he seemed to have more heart problems, which led to more tests.

Dr. Olivier Wenker, a friend and long-time physician in Houston, invited Gary to come down to where Dr. Wenker knew many doctors and could help us get through the maze. We met with a well-known cardiologist to whom we told the story about the welt, which we had determined to be a bite. He looked at Gary and said, "That sounds like Chagas." What's Chagas? We had never heard the word before, but after looking it up on the internet, Gary had or had had every symptom.

Because of his severe arrhythmia, Gary agreed to have oblation surgery, which did seem to help. While probing in Gary's heart, the doctor discovered a hole and a large scar where several nerves converge. That seemed to answer many questions but didn't help the situation, and no one really knew what could be done.

Gary had a PICC line put in so that he could have some IVs, but his body rejected the line, and he developed blood clots. He'd had blood clots before with several accidents and resolved them his way, but it wasn't until this incident that we realized how prone he was to forming clots.

Besides this situation, Gary still dealt with the internal damage from the accident of 1974 and several more accidents later in life. After breaking his back four times and now dealing with this treacherous disease, the pain became debilitating and unbearable most of the time.

Over the past 10 years—maybe even longer than that—Gary had some small strokes, which lasted between 5 and 30 minutes, but nothing longer. Unfortunately, we didn't recognize what was happening early on, when perhaps we could have been doing more to strengthen his brain tissue and blood vessels.

His first "real" stroke came in January 2018, which paralyzed his left side. He made remarkable progress and was lifting and working his left arm and hand. He went out to the gym every day and was really determined to walk again. Perhaps he pushed himself too hard and overworked his body. In any case, he broke his leg and needed surgery. The surgeon was very pleased with the results and said everything went better than he had expected. He told us Gary could stand on his leg and start exercising the next day.

However, the surgeon also said that Gary had bled a lot, which was a precursor to clotting. That night, Gary again had trouble breathing and was put on an oxygen machine to help him. As I watched and visually continued to communicate with him, I could see him struggling. He couldn't talk and was in great pain. He didn't want to leave us, but he was trapped, which was contrary to Gary's whole being. I felt his suffering—we all felt his suffering.

The next day, Saturday morning, he was taken for a CAT scan, which revealed that he'd had another big bilateral stroke. He had so much brain damage that his body started to shut down. He went into lung failure, kidney failure, and septic shock. The doctor said Gary could recover perhaps from an individual problem, but putting them all together, recovery would be unlikely or very difficult. We had reached the point of no return.

With deep sadness, I had the breathing tube taken out and the machine turned off so that he could be free. Now it would be his choice; his spirit and body would decide.

At the end, Gary was surrounded by those he loved and those who loved him dearly, who worked with him, and who had traveled the world with him. Surrounding his bed, we held hands and prayed. The spirit was strong, and we could feel such relief from him. I know he could hear us, and he knew that he was surrounded in love; but he had enough and was ready to go—to be free of his broken and tortured body.

I put my arms around him, Jacob and Josef each held one hand, and the rest held on to him to be a part of his decision. He was anointed with Sacred Frankincense, Palo Santo, and Journey On, which filled the room with a feeling of peace and resolution. His breathing became slower and slower until it stopped. He was gone, but he passed away peacefully and without pain.

Gary was a driven man—a man on a mission with a vision that had no boundaries. He was always concerned about everyone else and the well-being of his company. He would never rest and went from trauma to trauma never taking time to heal because so many members and others were depending on him, and he refused to let them down.

God was Gary's foundation, and his word was his bond. To let anyone down was to disappoint God—and Gary wasn't about to do that. He called the Bible his owner/operator's manual. He trusted and believed in others until they proved him wrong. He always saw the best in others until their actions said something different.

Gary's personality was bigger than life itself. Wherever he was, his spirit filled the room, the convention hall, and even his farms. He always gave 200 percent, never allowed the word "can't" to be spoken, and always looked for the solution, the best way to accomplish a goal.

He accomplished more in his life than 100 men combined. He founded the essential oils movement against tremendous opposition and slander, but he never wavered in his desire to serve God's children. He touched millions of lives for good. His work was brilliant beyond his time, which is still being proven by modern science.

Surely history will see him as an iconic pioneer and educator for essential oils and their benefits to all people. Gary had a knowing, a destiny, that has given so much to our world.

To explain Gary's accomplishments seems never ending. He spent 35 years studying the benefits and perfecting the extraction of essential oils while building a multibillion-dollar global business designed to share what he deemed "the gift" of essential oils with millions of people.

Described as a "modern pioneer," Gary was part inventor and part historian. He was determined to discover the ancient practices and benefits of herbs, plants, and trees that had been lost to the modern world. His research took him to the remote corners of the earth and often back in time to learn about the power that Mother Nature offers.

Young Living is well-positioned to follow the path he envisioned 25 years ago when we started our company. The farms are thriving and in this second edition, we have added 2 more corporate farms and 11 partner farms.

The farms were Gary's great love, and I'm sure he will be smiling as he looks down and sees the amazing people who are directing their growth. Our Seed to Seal promise to those who use our oils is the foundation of our farms, the vision of D. Gary Young, and of all those who are part of this great mission.

Mary Young

A Tribute to Gary

On May 18, 2018, a beautiful tribute to Gary and the celebration of his life began at the Young Living Lavender Farm in Mona, Utah. Many people sat in the bleachers, and with live streaming, thousands more viewed the celebration from around the world.

Dale Billeter, Gary's brother-in-law, who with his family was always there to help on the farms, with the Young Living business, and especially with family needs.

Dale offered the family prayer with deep-felt love and admiration, and family and friends were given the opportunity to bid their final farewell to our beloved leader.

The pallbearers carried the beautiful mahogany casket to the wagon, where Gary's magnificent Percheron horses were waiting. The bagpipers led the procession with a stirring sound that penetrated the patter of the falling raindrops. The heavens seemed to be weeping with all of us as we stood waiting for the wagon to arrive. Toward the end of the celebration, the sun broke through the clouds, spreading its light and warmth as if to say, "What a glorious time we have spent together."

Ben Riley conducted and led the tribute with a tone of dignity and love.

We want to welcome you all here to the memorial services for Don Gary Young.

Gary has been a part of my life for about 30 years. In the early 1990s, he approached my family to see if he could grow lavender, clary sage, and other botanicals on the Riley family farm near here in Genola, Utah. A few years later, in 1998, Gary helped put me through college when I was working in the warehouse. During the last couple of years, it has been my distinct honor to work side by side with Gary at his company, Young Living Essential Oils. I am very honored and proud to be here as we commemorate the life of this great man.

Alene Frandsen, Gary's sister-in-law, worked closely with Gary on various projects, especially editing his books, making sure that his writing was clear, precise, and polished.

Her prayer was heartfelt in expressing our loss and asking for God to comfort us. She expressed a resoluteness to go forward sharing Gary's vision of essential oils and the well-being of mankind and to see his legacy spread throughout the world.

Matthew French, Young Living's Chief Legal Officer, has been close to Gary as a friend and one who was always concerned about Gary's well-being and the protection of our company. As he read the obituary, there was greater insight and understanding into Gary, this amazing man.

D. Gary Young, the undisputed leader of the essential oils movement and the founder of Young Living Essential Oils, passed away on May 12, 2018, in Salt Lake City, Utah, due to complications following a series of strokes. Gary spent 35 years studying the benefits and perfecting the extraction of essential oils while building a multibillion-dollar global business designed to share what he deemed "the gift" of essential oils with millions of people.

Described as a "modern pioneer," Gary was part inventor and part historian. His pursuit of new wellness discoveries was rooted in ancient practices, and he attempted to unlock and share the benefits bestowed by herbs, plants, and trees. His research would take him to the remote corners of the earth and often back in time to better understand nature's powers that modern society may overlook.

In 1993 Gary founded his company in Riverton, Utah, and in 1994 Young Living Essential Oils was incorporated. In 1995 Gary bought 160 acres in Mona, Utah, and started a new farm.

In 2005 his path took a unique turn when he was invited to develop a natural medicine program and farming project for the University of Azuay in Cuenca, Ecuador. However, the climate in Cuenca has only a three-month growing season, so Gary went to Guayaquil, a very busy city on the coast, where he found the climate and unidentified plants to be an irresistible opportunity.

In 2006 he purchased 2,300 acres of "unfarmable" land on the edge of the jungle, which has become the largest farm and distillery outside the U.S. He was excited to begin exploring the country with the intention to discover new plants that could be distilled and shared around the world.

While fascinated with the teachings of ancient cultures, Gary was also a modern thinker. In 2014 the Young Living Highland Flats Distillery became the first automated, large-capacity, computerized steam distilling facility ever built in the world for essential oils.

The company has many international offices, 10 corporate-owned farms, 18 certified partner farms, over 4,000 employees, and well over 6 million members, a company that will continue to grow and share Gary's vision around the world.

Gary's research led him to the far corners of the earth and to unprecedented findings that improve health and wellness today. But perhaps the most important role essential oils played in his life was bringing him together with his wife Mary of 25 years. Together, they have two sons: Jacob and Josef.

Today Mary continues to serve as CEO of Young Living, the company they founded together. Mary's experiences as a networking distributor prior to Young Living and her business experience give her an unusual balance of understanding in this amazing essential oil company they built together. They were the perfect match, with Gary the visionary and Mary the realist.

Mary will continue to carry Gary's vision forward with a unique understanding of her visionary husband and with an extraordinary executive staff who will carry Gary's torch forever. We love you, Gary.

Jared Turner was knighted by Gary as president of Young Living just a few short months before Gary's passing. Like Gary, Jared loves Mother Nature and the things of God, which bonded the two men in a way that only they knew. Jared walks in Gary's footsteps and is committed to carrying forward Gary's great legacy.

It has been a hard week, and it's reminded me of a night I spent with Gary in Coeur d'Alene, Idaho, scrambling from western-wear store to western-wear store, trying to find the perfect western clothing for the meeting that he had to give that night.

In Gary's inspiring obituary, you can see why we affectionately called him "the most interesting man in the world." Overcoming tremendous adversity and poverty, disabling injury, and ridicule fostered in him an unstoppable desire to help others in need and to serve God. He once said, "Whatever path I walked, God was my partner. After my terrible accident at age 24, I promised God that if He gave me back my legs, I would spend the rest of my life serving His children."

Gary was a healthy mix of Indiana Jones and John Wayne with a touch of Chuck Norris. He was a cowboy, inventor, botanist, farmer, explorer, jouster, author, businessman, philanthropist, adventurer, and healer. He was a husband and father and was my friend and mentor—and he was that to many of you.

He was a master craftsman who learned the art of distillation in France from the families who had distilled lavender for generations. He then brought the craft to North America, where he modernized it and made it better.

Everything about Gary was bigger than life: his smile, his curiosity, his laugh, his love, and, most importantly, his dream. All of us sitting here today at this beautiful farm are here in fulfillment of that dream, from the millions of Young Living members to the 4,000 employees and many others. We are all manifestations of his original vision. Around the world, the name Gary Young is cherished. Why is it cherished? Because he connected people to their purpose, to their own personal "why," allowing them to live an empowered, entrepreneurial life.

He advocated for natural healing as he taught about essential oils and their healing properties. He connected people to the earth through farming experiences, letting people plant and harvest botanicals, to drive tractors and other farm equipment, and to participate in the distillation process.

The memories I have of Gary have come flooding back this week. I will miss the 5 a.m. phone calls to go snowmobiling, the midnight emails celebrating a recent draft horse show win, and crisscrossing the globe on helicopters, planes, boats, dogsleds, horses, motorcycles, and sand rails.

There was always a lesson in these adventures that we participated in with Gary. I learned a valuable lesson in how important it is to experience a farm firsthand when I crisscrossed land in Serbia with Gary, searching for suitable ground to grow helichrysum. When Gary found a farm that he thought was potentially suitable, we walked around the freshly tilled soil. He reached down and picked up two dirt clods; he smelled the dirt clods and said, "The only way to know if this dirt is good enough is if it is sweet. Taste it." He popped a dirt clod in his mouth and I popped one in my mouth. I tasted it and swallowed it and did not realize that Gary had spit his out. I will always have a piece of farming and Serbia with me.

He had a great sense of humor. On that same trip the next day, we toured a blue yarrow distillery. As many of you know, blue yarrow, like blue tansy, has a chemical constituent called chamazulene, which has a beautiful blue hue. Gary said, "Jared, blue yarrow is amazing for the skin."

So, I thought, "With all these premature wrinkles Gary has given me, maybe I could use this oil." So I covered my face with blue yarrow, and everybody started laughing. I went to the mirror in the bathroom and discovered why: My face was dyed that same beautiful, blue hue—I looked like a Smurf. I tried to wash it off with soap and water, but it did not come out. "Gary, I tried to wash it off, and it would not come out."

With a smile on his face, Gary said, "I know!" So, I spent the rest of that day a much-chagrined shade of blue, and Gary just kept laughing.

Gary had a childlike joy and curiosity that you all knew well, that smile and look. One time with our Diamond leaders in Oman, a beautiful country in southern Saudi Arabia, we were touring the ancient frankincense trails and our distillery there. We were all dressed up fairly nicely for dinner on the beach of the Arabian Sea, and Gary came over and said, "Let's run into the ocean, into the waves."

Looking at those big waves, I said, "Okay." So, we ran into the ocean in our jeans, cowboy boots, and buttoned-up shirts yelling with excitement, when a huge wave came over and took Gary under the water. I pulled him up because I'm a little bit taller, and as he came out of the water, the fear had passed, and it was that look of childlike joy that we have all seen.

The question I get most from people now is, "What can we do to keep Gary's legacy alive?" I would wager that Gary would tell you to heal, to be healers. He would say there are enough marketers, salespeople, and business people in the world. What the world needs more of today are healers, people who give to others without expecting anything in return. This company, this movement, was founded to help those in need of healing. He would ask for each of you to care for each other and to extend that community wider and wider until the world is taken up in Gary's vision of community and tribe. Watch for the signs.

How are we going to secure this legacy? As leaders of this company, we will continue to build farms, we will continue connecting people to nature, we will continue putting people over profit, and we will never compromise on quality.

It was a sacred honor for me to be in the room with Gary during his last moments. I committed to him as I said goodbye that I would never, ever deviate from the path that he has set us on. I would ensure his values and love are magnified even more.

And Mary, I promise you here today that we will never deviate, and Gary will live within us as we expand on that work.

I would like to end with a quote from Steve Jobs, the founder of Apple, that I believe perfectly summarizes our friend and mentor, Gary:

"Here's to the crazy ones. The misfits. The rebels. The troublemakers. The round pegs in the square holes. The ones who see things differently. They're not fond of rules. . . . You can quote them, disagree with them, glorify or vilify them, [but] the only thing you can't do is ignore them. Because they change things. They push the human race forward. While some may see them as the crazy ones, we see genius. Because the ones who are crazy enough to think that they can change the world, are the ones who do."

May the powerful spirit of Gary abide in all of us, from today, moving forward. Thank you.

Jacob Young sang with great poise and confidence. He knew how much Dad loved to listen to him sing with his beautiful, deep bass voice, which was soul stirring to everyone listening. To Dream the Impossible Dream was so fitting, as the words certainly describe Gary's fighting spirit.

We were grateful to have Larry Gee (Jacob's vocal coach) at the piano, and Craig Nybo, a good friend and well-known musician, added so much with the beauty of his guitar.

"I would like to dedicate this song to my father that I believe perfectly summarizes his life."

"The Impossible Dream (The Quest)"
from Man of La Mancha—Mitch Leigh and Joe Darion

To dream the impossible dream,
To fight the unbearable foe,
To bear with unbearable sorrow,
To run where the brave dare not go,

To right the unrightable wrong,
To love pure and chaste from afar,
To try when your arms are too weary
To reach the unreachable star!

This is my quest:
To follow that star,
No matter how hopeless,
No matter how far,
To fight for the right
Without question or pause,
To be willing to march into hell
For a heavenly cause!

And I know, if I'll only be true
To this glorious quest
That my heart will lie peaceful and calm
When I'm laid to my rest.

And the world will be better for this.
That one man, scorned and covered with scars,
Still strove with his last ounce of courage
To reach the unreachable star!

Kelly Case was the one Gary called for whatever he needed. She was calm and peaceful and helped him find solutions to many problems of a man traveling all over the world. She was a close friend and confidant and worked closely with Mary to help Gary achieve his goals. She was always there for him, and he loved her like a daughter.

My earliest memory of Gary happened over 17 years ago. I had been an employee of Young Living for just a few months when I was invited to go snowmobiling and sledding in the mountains. We were a small operation then, and I am fairly certain that all employees—from marketing to R&D, the call center to the warehouse—were invited on this snowy adventure.

I was standing at the base of an awesome sledding hill because, of course, Gary found the biggest hill in the mountains that he could. I had my inner tube in one hand, and I was debating how to get to the top of that hill when Gary pulled alongside me and playfully offered me a ride to the top of the hill on his snowmobile. Keep in mind, I was a brand-new employee and did not know any better. I had not yet learned that you never get on the back of a snowmobile with Gary Young.

I naively climbed on the back of that machine and, with my one arm holding tight to the inner tube and the other holding tight to Gary's sled, he took off at full speed. I was fairly certain I was going to meet my end on the back of the snowmobile that day. Thankfully, I didn't fall off and made it to the top after a very fast and very scary ride.

You will probably hear this many times today, but Gary lived by the motto, "If you are not living on the edge, you are taking up too much space."

If you have ever wondered what it is like to work closely with Gary, I think those of us who have been blessed with that opportunity would agree that working with him was a bit like that snowmobile ride—you were always moving fast, and it was often a little scary; but in the end, the rewards were worth the ride.

Kelly was always ready to help Gary.

Thirteen years ago, I made the difficult decision to quit my job at Young Living so that I could be a full-time stay-at-home mom to my two young children. After being home for almost eight months, my phone rang one day, out of the blue. I looked at the display, and "Gary Young" was flashing up at me. I immediately thought, "I am NOT answering that call. He is going to ask me to come back to work, and I won't do it. I refuse." But that thought only lasted a second, because who was I kidding? You never ignore a call when it comes from Gary Young. Sure enough, I am standing here today because of that phone call.

I would answer thousands of calls from Gary over the next 12 years. People always teased me because I carry two cell phones. I have my personal phone and I have my "Gary phone." I like to think of my "Gary phone" as his lifeline. I would answer his call, day or night, weekday or weekend. In fact, I prided myself on being available to Gary 24/7 for years while Gary traveled, particularly when he traveled studying the Frankincense Trail. He often put himself in harm's way, living that life right on the edge. He was in Somalia, Yemen, Saudi Arabia, and Oman, among many other places. I worried, Mary worried, we all worried; but Gary had a mission and he never failed to answer the call of that mission.

So I would sleep with my "Gary phone" under my pillow when he was traveling. I figured if it was under my pillow, it would be muffled enough that it would not wake up my sleeping husband, but I would be able to hear it and take his call. He did call, many times.

Some have often wondered, "Why are you willing to do what you do? Why would you sleep with your phone under your pillow and be available 24/7?" To me, the answer was always so simple: How could I not? Because Gary was traveling all over the world, he gave me the greatest gift and encouraged me to stay at home and be a mom first.

I also believed, with all of my heart, in Gary and what he was doing and in the mission of Young Living; the least I could do was answer a phone call.

Wednesday, this last week, I got home after a long day. I was feeling completely spent, emotionally and physically. I had not yet had a quiet moment to even begin thinking about what I was going to say to you all today. As I went to bed, I said to Gary, "How am I supposed to stand up in front of all those people and say 'goodbye'? How do I share the love I have in my heart for you without completely falling apart?"

I went to sleep with a heavy heart and feeling stressed about how to find the words for this moment. At 5:20 a.m. Thursday morning, I sat straight up out of bed. I reached for my phone and started typing frantically as the words and memories flooded my mind. I believed Gary had called, and I answered.

Gary, I promise you that I will continue to listen, and when you call, I will answer, always.

John Whetten traveled the world with Gary, experiencing many unique and challenging adventures. He was always there for Gary, helping him stay on track and documenting so much that we would otherwise not have.

First of all, I have a sense that Gary is here with us today. I would like to just point out, Gary, in case you have not noticed, I am wearing a suit. You see, Gary and I had this unwritten agreement that if I was going to work for him, in a largely undefined role, then I would never have to wear a suit and tie. I know at times this bothered him a little bit, but he let me get away with it, and for that, I am grateful.

First impressions are everything. The first time I ever saw Gary was about 10 years ago. I had just been hired, and the 2008 convention was a few days away. Gary and a small group of people were standing in the parking lot, unpacking a new CO_2 cannon. It was fashioned in the shape of a NingXia Red bottle that was designed to shoot T-shirts into the crowd at convention. He loaded the cannon with a T-shirt and said, "Let's turn it up all the way and see what happens." The T-shirt shot out with so much force that it broke a window of a car in the next parking lot over. Gary said, "Wow. It's a good thing we tested this thing before using it onstage." He then turned to someone standing next to him and said, "Have legal write a letter to the owner of the car and let him know that we will pay for the window." I knew then that Gary was someone fun to get to know better.

Mary asked me to share a story today to illustrate what it was like to work and travel with Gary. As I thought of which story to share, I thought of the tens and possibly hundreds of other people in attendance today who have also traveled with or worked closely with Gary and who love him dearly, and all of us have stories. So I want to tell a story that all of you could relate to, a story with a common theme that would be universal to all of us. So here it goes.

A few years ago, I was feeling burned out, as maybe some of you have also felt before. Of course, I felt lucky to be a part of Gary's adventures, but the nonstop travel was exhausting. It is not that I did not want to travel with Gary, but five years of more than 200 days a year on the road was starting to take its toll, so I came up with a plan to find someone with whom I could divide the travel work in half. All I had to do was get Gary to agree to the plan.

I was nervous about bringing this up to him; after all, I did not exactly want to admit that a man twice my age was running me into the ground, so I decided to couch my proposal not as being burned out but, instead, as a desire to have more work/life balance, more time for a social life, maybe even find a girlfriend. So on a car ride between Petra, Jordan, and the Israeli border, I shared my plan with Gary and started to lay out my justifications.

He saw right through me because he said, "John, don't worry about it. You're not the first person I have burned out." The good news was that he gave me the go-ahead to post a duplicate of my position and begin the search for someone with the right qualifications.

A few days later, when I got back to the office, I sat down, read through a few recent postings to try to figure out what a job description was supposed to look like, and came up with this:

Job Summary: Traveling assistant to the founder

Primary Duties and Responsibilities: Travel with the founder and handle any technical issue that might come up with any electronic equipment, which includes, but is not limited to, smart phones, computers, cameras, projectors, or other AV equipment. Help build and edit keynote presentations for meetings and trainings where the founder is presenting. Shoot photos and videos to document the founder's travels, discoveries, and general working conditions and prepare these photos and videos for internal distribution. At times, assist in purchasing farm equipment or something related to the operation of farms and distilleries. Drive large trucks and operate earth-moving equipment and farm implements and assist in harvesting and distillation.

Qualifications: Must be a certified Mac Genius. Must have a background in graphic design and video editing and knowledge of Photoshop, Illustrator, Keynote, and Final Cut Pro or Premiere. Must have at least a basic competency in any 3-D drafting or 3-D design software. Must be a competent photographer and videographer and demonstrate a thorough understanding of photographic techniques and terminology. Must be a native English speaker or possess native fluency in English and be a competent writer and editor. Foreign languages, particularly Spanish (and I do not speak Spanish), while not required, would be extremely beneficial.

Must have a valid driver's license with an excellent driving record. Must be able to drive a manual transmission. Must be familiar with auto mechanic tools and construction practices. Must be able to work long hours outside in extreme temperatures and be able to carry heavy loads long distances over uneven terrain. Must not be afraid of heights, claustrophobic, or have any reservations about flying in small aircraft. Must be able to travel at a moment's notice and be away in foreign countries for long periods of time, often working extended overtime for several weeks continuously without days off. Must possess a U.S. passport. Prior foreign travel required. Must be able to handle a very stressful working environment, often dealing with extremely short and unreasonable deadlines.

Education: This employee must be able to learn new skills almost immediately under extreme stress. College education not required.

I emailed this job description to HR multiple times, requesting that it be posted, but it never was and I'm not quite sure why.

I know there are a few people here today who feel that by swapping out just a few words, this could perfectly describe what they did for Gary. There are many, many more of you whose job description reads quite differently but contains an equally long, fun, and entertaining list of seemingly random and unrelated things that Gary has tasked you with over the years. In many cases, these things have required immense growth and learning.

As I look back at the job description, I now realize that the person we were looking for would not necessarily come with a specific skill set; rather, we were looking for a person with a very specific attitude. Gary built a great company because he found people with can-do attitudes and then gave those people immense opportunities to learn and grow, often tasking them with accomplishing things for which they had few qualifications.

As people grew, Young Living grew, and it was this growth that made Young Living a living company. Opportunities for growth and learning—these are the common threads of the narrative that unite all of us. This is our story.

Gary was full of one-liners. Kelly has already shared one, and I hope many more people share one today. I have spent a lot of time this week trying to think of a one-liner I could share that would sum up Gary's ethos of the way he looked at the world, but I have come up empty-handed. But then I was thinking about the things we do not say or will not say that define us more than the things we do say.

If you were to ask me what Gary Young never said, it would have to be, "That is not my job." He was a man who labored endlessly in every aspect of the pursuit of his vision and dream to bring health and wellness to the world, a goal that he clearly achieved.

All of you who have been lucky enough to work side by side with Gary and been willing to adopt his attitude will clearly know and understand how your lives have been blessed by your association with him.

I think the greatest compliment Gary ever paid me was when he said, "John, you're a good man to ride the river with." I also know that I am not the only person who he expressed this to, so for all the men and women here today who labored beside Gary, I would like to say, "Gary, thank you for the adventures. Thank you for the opportunities to grow and to learn, and thank you for the memories. But most of all, Gary, thank you for your friendship and allowing us to 'ride the river' with you."

Tamera Packer was Gary's closest family member who worked side by side with him doing research in the jungle and helping him build the NovaVita Rejuvenation Center and Spa in Ecuador. She was constantly by his side during the last few months of his life, using her knowledge and skills to help reduce his pain and comfort him.

I am honored to share a few thoughts about my dear cousin, mentor, and particularly, my dear friend. I think each of us here could call Gary our dear friend. He made everybody feel so important and like you were his only and best friend.

The song comes to my mind, "You Are the Wind Beneath My Wings." Surely many of us think that Gary was truly our hero—for he was, indeed, that.

Gary Young carried the knowing within his heart that his purpose was to help and prevent people from suffering. This knowing started for Gary at a very early age, as he watched his mother suffer with arthritis and would rub her hands to relieve some of her pain. He said from that moment, he knew that his mission was to help people, and that is exactly what he did throughout his life.

When we were traveling through Ecuador looking for palo santo, Gary decided to go to Vilcabamba, which was just a few hours away. He had been there previously studying their longevity and wanted to see if they, indeed, were still experiencing that same longevity. There was a 99-year-old woman sitting on the street with crippled hands. He went over to her, took an oil out of his pocket, and rubbed her hands, just like he had done for his mother.

I worked with Gary for over six years at the Nova Vita Wellness Center in Ecuador, where I had the privilege of learning many things from Gary: Raindrop Technique, neuro-auricular therapy, live and dry blood microscopy, and various other therapies. I learned a lot about the physical and emotional aspects of the human body, as well as the application of essential oils. I learned about compassion through Gary's example while I worked with him and how he constantly focused on people and the solutions they were seeking.

One time, we were in a small village with the Cinterandes Mobil Surgical truck, with which Gary traveled many times to assist with surgeries. It was amazing how he could do anything the first time, and it looked like he had done it a thousand times; that's what he did in the surgery truck. The doctors were extremely interested in Gary's research and his pain formula that was blended with essential oils for pre- and post-surgery. The back of the trailer had been turned into a surgery room, which worked very well out in the jungle. We would give half of the patients just the V-6 Vegetable Oil Complex, and the other half of the patients received Gary's special pain formula. Then we would analyze the blood to see the difference.

One little girl, about six years old, was given V-6 rather than the pain formula, and we could hear her sobbing in the other room after the surgery. Gary became frustrated and said, "I don't care about the research; we have to help this little girl," so he went to her with his formula.

Gary loved both the old and young. In Ecuador, we had people from the villages come to the Wellness Center. I remember particularly one little old man from Chongon who had no money. He came once a week and paid Gary with a sack of mangoes, his payment for treatment. I witnessed many things like that, which were so heartwarming, and for certain, no one was ever turned away because of their inability to pay.

Gary built the Young Living Academy for the children attending a deplorable school on the corner of a dirt road on the way to the farm. It was a horrible little place with no windows—just one big room and an outhouse that was a hole in the ground. That first Christmas, long before our school was built, Gary decided he wanted to do something special for the children. He put a Santa Claus suit on, and we wrapped presents, and he gave all the children a present, which was the best Christmas they had probably ever had—but I think Gary had the most fun.

Traveling through Ecuador with Gary was really an adventure. We all know the phrase, "Stop and smell the flowers." With Gary, it was stop and smell anything, everything, any plant. It was great fun. We would be driving and all of a sudden, he would stop the car, jump out, and start smelling the plants and flowers along the road. He was looking for aromatic plants, which was how he discovered dorado azul as well as eucalyptus blue, palo santo, ocotea, mastrante, and many of our wonderful oils from Ecuador.

Gary always knew how to push us beyond what we thought were our limits. I remember the first time in Ecuador when he asked me to teach Raindrop to the members who had come for a Raindrop training. I was not prepared. I did not know what I was doing. He looked at me and said, "Okay. It's your turn" and put his hand in the small of my back, so I would not be frightened while I taught. I like to think that Gary would be supporting us that way now, with his hand in the small of our backs, giving us his energy and his love.

I watched Gary's face time after time as he showed us how one person could make a difference through vision, belief, faith, and manifestation. One time I was with Gary, Mary, and the boys and his dear friend Eldon Knittle when we went to his favorite place in the entire world, Warm Springs—a very remote wilderness area in the mountains of Challis, Idaho, where Gary grew up. This was a difficult three-hour horse ride—particularly for Mary and me, who did not love the horse ride—but Gary made no allowance for fear, so down the steep mountain trail we went, hoping the horses knew their way.

We made it to camp, finished putting up the tents, and were eating dinner around the campfire when we noticed a brightness in the sky. Mary and I were not sure what we were seeing, but when Gary looked up, he immediately knew we were facing a blazing fire that was coming right toward us. At that very second, Gary asked us all to kneel down, and he said a prayer that we would be safe and protected, and I knew that he had faith that we would be protected.

He and Eldon had to find the horses that were somewhere hiding up the mountain, so they headed into the mountain darkness while Mary and I packed up the camp. Josef had fallen asleep on one of the tarps, and Jacob sat on a chair continually praying, almost chanting. The thought of riding out in the dark was frightening. Gary said we would have to move fast, and we might have to leave all the camping gear. As the night went on, the fire was all around us but had stopped moving toward us, and the shooting flames diminished to what seemed like amber coals and then completely stopped. We waited until dawn, packed the horses, and started up the mountain in awe of what was happening. I know it was through Gary's faith and his deep belief in God that the fire stopped.

Two hours later, when we arrived on top at the horse trailers, the mountain was ablaze again. It was a three-hour drive down the mountain, but looking back, the fire was raging and spewing black clouds of smoke and burning thousands of acres. When Gary talked to the forest ranger at the bottom, he said the Warm Springs fire was the only one that stopped and then went in a different direction, and if that had not happened, we would have been consumed by the fire, if not the smoke first.

Gary's teachings were not just about prosperity, but also about how to be free from negative beliefs and anchored emotions. He often shared his own lifetime struggles as he taught us how to use essential oils and assist us with bringing ourselves from these negative beliefs so that we could be leaders to help change the world. He taught passionately from his soul.

It seems that we had to let go of his physical presence much too early; however, he has left us with a great legacy that he taught so passionately. Let your heart lead the way. If you are struggling, let the oils help you, guide you. Gary taught us how to manifest prosperity from which so many of you have benefited.

Visiting the waterfall Pailon del Diablo near Baños, Ecuador.

In the last few months, I spent a lot of time with Gary and had many conversations with him. If he were here, he would say that we can do much good in the world with our prosperity; however, more importantly, he would have us look to the state of our physical and spiritual well-being. Prosperity will not bring contentment until our hearts are right with God. That is what I think Gary would want us to know.

Gary's legacy will empower us to be balanced leaders who continue to ease the suffering of ourselves first and then of the world. As we do this, his legacy will live on for generations and generations as he has given his life to us to carry on. Now it's time for us to say "goodbye" to our dear friend and mentor but with his memory forever in our hearts. We love you, Gary.

Mark Harris was Gary's pilot who worked side by side with Gary. Mark stayed with Gary many nights in the hospital as a trusted and loyal friend.

I had the pleasure of working with Gary, side by side, for the last four and a half years. My journey with Gary Young started out a little strangely. Five years ago, I was contacted by an aircraft broker to do a pre-purchase inspection on an airplane.

I was asked if I could fly the plane to Idaho and pick up the buyer, whose name was Gary Young. The next thing I knew, I was standing at the airport in Sandpoint, Idaho, but the broker could not get ahold of Gary. We could not reach Gary, since he was busy out in the woods, harvesting trees.

When I finally met Gary, he had this overwhelming smell of a Christmas tree. Little did I know how much this man was going to change my life. Gary kept asking me if I wanted a full-time position, but I refused because I lived in Florida with my family.

That was until June 4, 2014, when we landed in Fort Nelson, and I realized that there just might be something to this essential oil thing. From that point on, I remained by Gary's side, starting with the construction of the Northern Lights Distillery in Fort Nelson through so many amazing experiences.

Fort Nelson is fascinating with the aurora borealis at night, the rapidly changing seasons, and the extreme winters. I remember the mayor coming out to our construction site to talk with Gary. He was wondering when we were going to halt construction because, as the mayor explained, "Winter is upon us."

Gary replied to the mayor, "We will stop when we are producing Black Spruce essential oil." I know the mayor did not believe Gary, but anybody who knew Gary's determination and work ethic knew that this man did not let anything stand in his way, not even Mother Nature.

We pushed on, stopping only on days when the temperature literally got to 20 degrees below 0. He set expectations high, almost unobtainable, and he would endure and push each of us to limits that we did not even know were within us to make a dream a reality. I remember he told me with a wink, "Mark, the difficult is not a problem; the impossible just takes a little longer." One of my favorite memories was when Gary had rented a track excavator and said, "Have you ever run an excavator?"

My reply: "Does that include today?"

I remember him laughing, and he finally said, "Yes, it does." He gave me about 30 seconds of instruction and sent me off to dig. He had confidence in me, which gave me confidence in myself. Gary made people feel like they could do anything.

I recall a melissa harvest in St. Maries. I set my alarm for 4:30 a.m. because I was going to be the first in the field, but to my surprise, Gary was already checking the melissa to see if it was ready for harvest. Gary wakes the sun up and puts it to bed, but only when he is finished for the day.

Gary was so innovative that many times he would engineer custom equipment due to the uniqueness of our harvests. One time during the melissa harvest, the swather had failed, so we welded a folding chair behind the rotating head of the cutting blades. I used my belt while holding onto the chair to prevent me from falling into the blades of the swather; however, there is no photo evidence.

Just recently at the last Men's Camp, the "face your fear" challenge was a hike in the dark through the Uinta Forest. Skylar and I were going to meet the group in the forest at a place called Soapstone Pass, but when we arrived, the whole group seem to have disappeared. Suddenly, we spotted what appeared to be at least a 60-foot campfire. We looked at each other and said, "That has to be Gary."

Gary always did everything 110 percent, no matter what the task, no matter what the cost. He was bigger than life. The best tribute I can give to my friend is that God looked down on His newly created world and thought:

I need someone I can trust to take care of the lands and the fields and someone strong enough to till the soil, plant the seeds, and tend the crops. I need someone who will work 18-hour days, tend the horses, mend the fences, and do the chores. I need someone who will work the fields all day, fix the equipment until dark, then stay up half the night feeding a newborn elk calf.

I need someone who is strong-hearted with family values in sharing, caring, and disciplining, who has patience and perseverance to go the extra mile. I need someone who is willing and kind enough to extend a helping hand to a neighbor. I need someone who is thankful for the rain and the sun, who loves the harvest, who graces you with blue, smiling eyes and feels so proud when his children say they want to spend their lives doing what their dad does. So, God created a farmer in the image of Gary Young.

Gary, wherever you are, you will be met with love. I regret that you did not have two lifetimes to teach me half of what you know. Goodbye, my mentor, my friend. I will truly miss you.

Sabina DeVita, a close friend for several years, spent many hours helping Gary with various projects and concerns.

This is such a great honor and a privilege for me to share a few memories of my journeys with Gary. As I look back, I think, "Wow. Destiny." I look at myself here, I look at Mary, Gary, the family—destiny, a magician of time.

I joined Young Living in 1997. I was sent one brochure and one handwritten letter that caused me to want to meet this man, Gary Young. I felt he has been touched by the hands of God in a very unique and different way.

I asked Gary if he would be a guest speaker at our Total Health Expo in Toronto, which he did in March of 1998. I loved his presentation and knew he had a message for the world.

Gary loved to challenge other people, so in 2001 he asked me to help him with an emotional-clearing training he had scheduled, since I work in the field of emotions and psychology. I told him I hadn't ever done anything like that before, and he responded, "That's okay. You'll be fine."

The fire walk in Cancun, Mexico, was a very "hot" experience. Some people did not quite make it to the other side of the burning coals, but Gary made sure that everyone had the opportunity. He wanted all of us to be able to walk across those hot coals because he believed in us.

Gary had amazing intelligence that superseded many a college education. He had a GQ, which I call the God Quotient or the Genius Quotient. God was his foundation and the genius within drove him beyond all imaginable.

Gary talked to and communicated with the plants, trees, and animals and told us his amazing groundhog story. In the fields of the St. Maries farm, the groundhogs burrowing in the ground made it almost impossible to grow the lavender and melissa; there were just too many holes.

Gary said, "Early in the morning, I went out to pray and talk to the groundhogs. I spoke to their spirits and explained that I needed them to leave because they were interfering with my planting and harvesting."

The next day, a neighbor came to the farm and asked Gary if he had any idea why his property was overrun with groundhogs and wondered where they came from and what he could do about it. Laughingly, Gary said, "Just tell the little critters to leave."

Gary lived a life without any boundaries. He pushed the limits and has now become boundless with the Infinite. Gary was an effervescent spring of creation and was always putting another idea into motion. Our dear friend and brother is free. It is interesting that this year's convention theme is Freedom.

The poet Kahlil Gibran said this about death: "In the depth of your hopes and desires lies your silent knowledge of the beyond and like seeds, dreaming beneath the snow, your heart dreams of spring. Trust the dreams, for in them is hidden the gate to eternity."

My dear Gary, thank you for all you have given humanity that will live on forever. Your legacy is infinite, and we are the ambassadors who will continue to carry that light to mankind. The world loves you, Gary. I love you. May God bless us all.

Sabina loved filming the frankincense documentary with Gary.

Joe Walker is a long-time, trusted friend, who was always there to help Gary, who had a difficult time transitioning into the digital world. Without the slightest sense of frustration, Joe was there to help.

The weather has been a little bit crazy today, but I think Gary is enjoying it. He loved being outside in the elements of Mother Nature, anytime, anyplace. Today, I think the rain and wind would actually set him free.

I am the vice president of IT operations and have been with Young Living for 13 years. My heart is filled with a lot of emotions and stories and not enough time to tell them all. We are here to celebrate Gary's life and mourn his passing. He was a man who lived life to the extreme and fulfilled his lifelong dream of bringing back the ancient art of essential oils to the world.

Wherever he went, people wanted to be there. He simply had an infectious nature about him. Gary and Mary always wanted to interact with their employees and members on a personal level. That family feeling thrives today and is one of our strengths as a business. It is why we have such loyal employees and members to this day.

Joe was always living on the edge with Gary.

I will never forget the first time I met Gary. I was called to his office to help him with a computer issue. As I walked into his office, he looked up and I said "Hi, I'm Joe, here to work on your computer issue." He stood up and reached out with those strong hands, and grabbed mine and said, "Gary Young, cowboy, not a computer guy." We both laughed, and I said, "Well, I'm your guy," and ever since, we built a strong bond not only in the workplace, but in living on the edge together.

Gary had many close relationships with those of us in the office over the last 12 years and with many of you—Gary loved us. He loved all of us and wanted us to interact with him, no matter where he was or what he was doing. Throughout the years, we have continued to strengthen our business and personal friendship, which is why I have always called him "The Cowboy." All the farms and distilleries around the world are because he had that "cowboy" in his heart.

One thing that sets both Gary and Mary apart from anyone I have ever known is the personal sacrifices they have made for you and me. How many business owners do you know who would move their family to another country to build out a farming infrastructure living in what was once a jungle but is now transformed into the Ecuador farm?

Gary's thirst for knowledge was an adventure of discovery. One time I was walking with Gary through the raw jungle that was part of the Ecuador farm. I asked him if I should have gotten a yellow fever shot. He laughed and said, "You'll be fine."

Have you ever been bitten by 1,000 mosquitoes at once? I have. Later that night, I was a mess, but Gary wasn't. I wondered, "Why is that?" Then I remembered, he told me to put on some essential oils, but I didn't do it. He told me bugs in general don't like the smell. I learned my lesson and from then on listened to Gary when he gave me advice.

Whether Gary was jousting, engaged in a gunfight in Wolfberry Creek (the old western town here at the farm), preparing the fields for seed planting, or making a deal with just a handshake, those talents served him well. I always thought he was born a few centuries too late.

One time, Gary called and said, "Let's go snowmobiling somewhere different this weekend." We started from Strawberry Reservoir and finished at the Bear River Lodge in Wyoming, about 13 hours and 118 miles. When we finally pulled in and were all wiped out, Gary said, "Anyone up for a night ride?"

"No way." Most of us ate something fast, and a few of us fell asleep in our clothes.

From where did his energy for life come? He pushed it to the limit and always said, "When most people are starting to slow down, that is when you need to push even harder."

Gary could outwork anyone. First up in the morning and last to bed, always working, teaching, studying, and always engaging his mind. Many of us interacted with him either in the office, at the farms, working at the distillery, preparing new land, or just doing something fun. He loved inviting people on his adventures, whether it was hunting, fishing, snowmobiling, riding horses, dogsledding, or just hiking in the mountains and talking about the land in all its splendor.

He was successful in life because he demanded excellence of himself and set the example for everyone. It was one of his biggest strengths. People are drawn to that type of individual, and he definitely had the skills to teach people to believe in themselves.

I feel true sadness for Mary and the boys. We have spent many hours throughout the years together all over the planet. This has been a heartbreaking experience for the Young Living family—for all of us. I have lost a good friend, our mentor, and one of the last cowboys I knew.

Most importantly, Gary believed in me, you, our planet, and the natural wonders it can provide us. I will truly miss him and all the amazing adventures we shared together. We have been left with his vision. We have the people and the best products earth can provide. Let's keep his dream alive.

Jean-Noël Landel was Gary's partner and very close friend in France who brought Gary into the world of the French lavender farmers, which developed into a lifelong friendship of trust and corroboration. More than any other person, Jean-Noël facilitated the opportunity for Gary to learn "the art of distillation," which laid the foundation for Gary's expertise in the production of essential oils.

My accent is French, and it has been almost three years since I have spoken English in public, so my talk will be much shorter. I have known Gary for 28 years and was distilling lavender in the south of France when he first came to visit me. I have been doing this for 30 years, until one month ago when I retired.

I first met Gary in October of 1990 when I attended a natural product show in Los Angeles, hoping to sell the essential oils that I was producing for health purposes and not for the perfume industry, which was the tradition of our production in France. I had some samples in my pocket and went around the whole show for about three hours. By the end of the morning, I saw only one little booth that said Essential Oils on it, and that was all it said. It was the only place where essential oils were displayed. I met a cowboy, dressed like a cowboy from his head to his foot. I handed him one of my samples; he opened the bottle and smelled it. I have never seen somebody smiling so much by just smelling a bottle of lavender oil. He said, "Do you really distill this in France?"

I said, "Yes."

He said, "I will be at your place in about three or four months." I went back home thinking, "I really spent a lot of money traveling all the way to California just to meet a cowboy, who says he will be coming to my home because he likes lavender."

Jean-Noël and Gary were close friends and partners for 28 years.

How surprised my wife and I were when he showed up exactly four months later, and that was the beginning of a long, long passionate relationship. On Gary's first visit to France, he was so excited to learn about our distillation techniques that every morning he would be the first one on site to start working, taking pictures, and checking everything out.

Some of the farmers were afraid he was only there to steal their oil. When I shared this with Gary, he told me to tell them that the only concern they should have was to be able to produce enough quality lavender oil for him in the future. Remember: At that time, there was no aromatherapy lavender oil at all, because all our production was going to the perfume industry.

My farmers kind of laughed at him, but that is exactly what happened. From then on, I knew I could always trust Gary, and he always kept his word. He proved this to me on many other occasions. One time, he was in a very bad position financially, and in order to pay me for the oils I had supplied him, he sold part of his land that he had just purchased. This is something that is very hard for a farmer to do—believe me. So he really was one of the most honorable people I have ever known.

The early days with Gary were very exciting. He had great energy and an enormous thirst for learning all he could from the Frenchmen who had been growing and producing lavender for almost 100 years, but he also loved sharing his ideas and discoveries on the cultivation of aromatic plants and the distillation to produce essential oils. This led to many long evenings of discussions and sharing ideas.

One thing about Gary is that he never kept his innovations for himself. He always wanted everyone to benefit from them. The day Gary inaugurated a distillery here in Mona, which implemented his new ideas of distillation, my partner, Marcel Espieu, said that Gary was considered the master of distillation and his mentor and declared that the pupil had exceeded the master. That is absolutely what happened within two years after Gary started learning about distillation.

Gary's knowledge and innovation in the world of distillation enabled him to be accepted into the circle of the French distillers, which led to him to become the first American to own a lavender farm in France, which we purchased in 2002.

A true friendship developed between Gary and the French growers and distillers, and Gary's dedication to having the best quality of lavender oil became the salvation of true lavender in Provence. One of the growers, who is here today, declared that Gary saved his life. He was depressed and tired of producing industrial lavandin oil and was thinking of selling his farm and quitting. Gary proposed to him that he grow a true lavender of excellent quality that Gary would buy from him, and this completely changed his life and his state of mind.

I remember the last few times Gary came to visit in France that because of this true bond he had established with the growers in France, he often said when arriving, "It's good to be home."

We all know that Gary was a very spiritual man, and this has always been a very important factor in my life as well. Gary and I often had discussions on spirituality in general and on the aspect of essential oils in particular.

When we first met, essential oils were used only in aromatic application for the medical, physical healing side, but Gary taught me about the effect that essential oils could have on our emotional well-being, on our psychological well-being, and on our spiritual well-being. This was a true revelation for me and the beginning of an amazing revolution in the world of essential oils in France.

Gary often spoke about his Father in Heaven and the fact that he was on a mission here on earth to help people alleviate their suffering. I noticed when I arrived here two days ago that one of the releases Young Living sent about Gary was that he was called the father of the modern-day essential oils movement, and this is really true.

He had ideas about essential oils and many other things that were far ahead of anyone else 20 years ago. The capacity he had for seeing things and just doing things far ahead of other people was not always understood nor appreciated by others, which caused him great suffering in the beginning.

Today, I am convinced that Gary is back in unity with his Father in Heaven, full of peace and joy. He is at peace, but you know Gary—he is certainly not at rest. I feel that he is still sending help for us all from up above. Gary considered everyone his family for whom he always had time, compassion, and love.

He is physically far away and that is painful for us, but I can still feel him with me and have a strong feeling that he is saying that it is important to continue his life's work as a family by caring for one another. Thank you.

Lauren Walker had many first-time experiences with Gary. Coming from the corporate world, she found it amazing to step into a world of love and friendship in a business environment.

Hello, Everyone. I am responsible for supply chain and warehouse operations.

In October of 2016, I received an email from Kelly Case—three months into my tenure with Young Living—informing me that Gary wanted to take me hunting—me, Lauren, the girl from Brooklyn, who saw a deer for the first time in her late 20s when she hit it on the highway, was going hunting? I was overcome with complete fear. I had no idea what I was getting myself into, but I did know I was going to spend this time with Gary.

So we went on this trip, and it was not me alone, it was actually a pretty large group of executives who had all gone together. We expected this to be maybe a one- or two-day trip. We would harvest our deer and head home. That was the case with the other executives who had gone, and they had their deer and were already back home in their warm beds, and I was still on the mountain.

Lauren followed Gary's every word and got her bull.

I was there for three days, and we kept seeing deer, and Gary kept saying, "No, that's not the one."

Silently, I kept asking myself, "What are we doing here?" But I just kept up with him, wondering what was going to happen.

Gary constantly kept looking back, checking on me and saying, "Just follow my lead," but I was so nervous. He put his arm on my shoulder before we got up there and said, "Don't worry. Follow everything I do, and I will teach you everything you need to know. You will be just fine."

Two days went by, but no deer. It was freezing and I still had no idea what I was doing out there. On the third day, high up on the mountain, Gary said, "Okay. Now is the time. Follow my lead. Do exactly what I say and you're going to be just fine."

In a whisper Gary said, "Get down on your stomach and crawl about 50 yards over to that bush."

I'm like, "What is going on?" I am probably the only person who has ever gone hunting with pantyhose under my camouflage. Gary didn't tell me what to wear, so I was guessing and just did what I knew.

I crawled army style over to the bush with this heavy rifle in my arms, and I heard softly, "Okay, quiet."

"Just wait until the deer turns toward you and then go for it," and I did. First shot—250 yards—flat on. It was great. However, the deer ran off and we ended up chasing it down the mountain for the entire day.

While all of this was going on for three days, I got to spend quality time with Gary. We did not just talk about hunting; we talked about everything sourcing-related. We talked about every farm and every partner farm; we talked about oils that were challenging to get and what our plan should be to go after them. We talked about regions to stay away from with regard to certain oils and regions that flourished.

We planned our first oil summit, where he mapped out a plan for the next 10 years for Young Living for all of the oils we would need and where we were going to get them. We talked about everything and at the end of that third day, when I finally had my deer, I was walking down the side of the mountain with sheer pride and joy and the biggest smile on my face. I did not just have that deer; I had knowledge that I could never have gathered in a conference room. I could never have gathered it reading a book or just out in the field. I learned it from the best, and I will never forget that.

Gary told me to follow him, follow his lead, and he would teach me everything. Gary, I want you to know that I feel I am now ready to lead. I am ready to take what you taught me on that mountain and what I have lived for the last year and a half since then and move this company forward in the direction that you want, embracing your vision to reach your purpose and your goal. I truly honor this moment, and I will for the rest of my life. I am so proud to serve all of you, and I am proud to serve Gary and execute his wishes. Thank you.

Ben Howden became a close friend while helping Gary build the Northern Lights Farm. As the contractor, he helped Gary in numerous ways with government permits and the many needs of such a huge project.

I ponder the life of my friend Gary Young, and I realize when I look back, I see so much more about him now than when I was with him. The first time I was introduced to Gary, I was excited because I had seen my wife's life transform, and she was so happy because she had found an answer to her health problems.

Over the next few years, I saw and heard many amazing stories about Gary, and then, when we came here to the Mona farm, I was overwhelmed as I saw the greenhouses full of new plants and the fields of lavender. We were here during the 5K run through the lavender fields that takes place every year during Lavender Harvest, so Gary and I ran together.

That winter I took my team from Canada to work during the harvest at the Highland Flats, Idaho, farm—the tree farm, as everyone calls it. Gary depended on the members to help him on the farms, and there was great anticipation and excitement by those who had never been to a harvest. This is where I really got to know Gary. He led by example and said, "When you work hard, you earn your stripes."

In 2007 we went to Ecuador, and I saw the amazing farm he had built with fields and fields of plants to produce oils for the world. It was so inspiring.

I realized that when Gary had a direction from his Father above where to find new plants for oils, he always accomplished his plan. In 2008 in St. Maries, Idaho, on the first week of harvest, we worked 20-hour days, getting the distillery ready for Gary when he arrived with the chips from the Highland Flats farm. He drove the semi-truck with two trailers 125 miles through snow and ice and horrible winter conditions.

When he arrived at 5 in the morning, we would quickly unload the chips, so they wouldn't freeze into a solid mass in the trailers. Then, without any sleep or food, Gary would head back to the tree farm, so the trailers would be there when the crew was ready to start chipping after breakfast. He often had to thaw out frozen brakes on the chip trailers and chain up to climb the hills into the farm over icy, slippery roads—all of that and every day—so that there were always chips ready for us.

Every year we went to the Idaho harvest and took other distributors with us. We were thrilled to spend time with Gary and looked forward to the after-supper stories he would tell and the journeys he took us on.

After a week with Gary, we left with a new vision, committed to our goals, and changing whatever was necessary. Gary always brought Mary and the boys to conventions, and everyone shared his boys. They were part of Gary and he shared them with all of us.

In 2014 on the Diamond trip to France, Gary came to me with a question: "Will you help me build a farm in Fort Nelson to produce Black Spruce? We are out of Valor because Black Spruce is a major component, and we cannot get enough. You are Canadian and have a contractor's license in BC, and I would be grateful if you would help."

My first thought was, "It's cold up there and during the winter the temperatures could drop to as low as minus 40 with so much heavy snow and icy roads." I asked him, "When do you want to build this farm?" He said, "We will start this fall and work through the winter."

As I digested what he said, some of the people who were with me expressed concern: "Ben, you will never keep up with Gary, and when you don't, that will be the end of your good feelings together, and you will end up having hard feelings." My thoughts were stirring, wondering what I should do.

On the last day of the trip, Gary came nose to nose with me and said, "Ben, are you going to help me or not?"

Without any more thought, I said, "Yes, Gary; I will."

Carol and I arrived home Saturday night, and the very next day, I got a call from Gary: "So, when are you coming to Fort Nelson?"

I said, "Gary, I just got home last night from France."

He said, "Yeah, so did I. Can you come up tomorrow, because I am here in Fort Nelson?"

I called our oldest son Cory, who was mining in the Philippines, and told him I needed him to come home and help me build a farm for Young Living in Fort Nelson.

He said, "If it's for Young Living, I'll come and help you." So, together with family, great friends, members, and employees, we embarked on one of the toughest jobs I have ever done.

Gary had great principles and always lived by those principles. He was there every day, working for four and a half months from 7 a.m. to 8 p.m. seven days a week, and during the summer days, we worked until 11 p.m. because of the long daylight hours. Mary and the boys came up, and Gary even had the boys operating the heavy equipment. Many members came from faraway places and donated their time and efforts in helping whenever they could. There was a bigger purpose: to share Young Living oils with every home in the world.

One morning after breakfast, Gary said, "I've talked to seven different country leaders this morning before breakfast." His drive was endless—and then the winter came. It was bitter cold, and Gary's ears and fingers were freezing, so I said to him, "Why don't we just shut down until March when the weather gets better, and then we can finish this project?"

Gary looked at me with frozen tears curled down his cheeks and said, "Ben, you can go home, but I'm not going anywhere. You don't have 50 emails a day with members begging for Valor, but I do."

That was a defining moment for me. I was committed. Everyone was committed, including my son Cory, who eventually became the farm manager. Because of Gary, who was an amazing leader who possessed dedication and perseverance, we now have Northern Lights Black Spruce oil, which is a component in 27 Young Living blends.

We all have so many friends and relationships all over the world because of Gary, and now it is our privilege and responsibility to carry the torch and continue to build relationships and share oils with every home in the world.

In December of 2017, we visited the corporate office for our Royal Crown Diamond event and afterwards had the privilege of having lunch with Gary—our last visit. It was also his last message to us, which was, "This business is built on relationships. There is a lot of social media now, and it is all good, but Young Living is the world leader in essential oils because of our relationships."

So how do we keep the spirit of Gary alive in Young Living now? We work consistently and we build relationships. We stay committed and we lead by example and tell our story.

Thank you, Gary, for all you have taught us and shown us—and yes, Gary, we will carry the torch for you.

Mary Young, Gary's wife of 25 years, who probably has the greatest challenge, spoke with courage and a knowing of Gary's genius and what he gave to the world. Gary loved Mary's singing, and this song was one of his favorites. He always asked her to sing it whenever there was an opportunity.

Gary loved this farm and his spirit will always be here, and those who come to visit in the future will surely feel his presence. I am blessed to see how Gary is being honored this day. There is so much that I would like to say, but to find the right words is my challenge.

It was said to me, "This program will be too long."

I replied, "But there are so many people who have come from so far. I want to make sure that they go home feeling it was worth their time to be here." I think we have had a magnificent view of who Gary was in a different way from each individual who has spoken.

Before Jacob was born, when we first bought this farm, Gary and I worked all day long down here. We had a bed in the Visitor Center, so we stayed here many nights because Gary started so early in the fields. He was driven to get seed in the ground, and there was always more in one day to do than he could accomplish.

He so wanted to have the distillery in operation for our first convention, but all he had was one cooker that he brought to the distillery site with the only backhoe we had. He was so disappointed, but that caused him to just work faster.

At night we would sit out on the patio and just talk about our feelings and what was in the future. Gary gazed out over the fields that were yet to be planted and said, "It is so beautiful here. It is so peaceful. It is so quiet," and he started expounding on all the things that he was going to build here at the farm, and we all know that Gary's vision wasn't small.

My realistic self responded, "But, Gary, we're so far away from everything. Who's going to come down here?"

With his all-knowing smile, he said, "You watch, Mary; you just watch them come."

Every year the numbers have grown as we have watched thousands come for Lavender Days with the harvest and the 5K run, conventions, the jousting, the Easter egg hunt, Christmas, Silver Club, and Gary's great dream—the draft horse show and rodeo.

It did not matter what the event was—the people were coming, and his heart was so full. He was so happy, seeing his vision come to fruition. The farm meant everything to him, and to have the people he loved, his members, his friends, come and be a part of that which he loved so much was the most rewarding thing I think I ever heard him express.

Now the sun is shining as we come to the close of this celebration. We feel the sun's warmth as our hearts seek comfort. I thought about the many people we learned about in our history classes. There was only one Galileo, there was only one Einstein, there was only one Michelangelo, there was only one Mozart, and there was only one Gary Young.

No one will ever take his place. No one will ever walk in his shoes—and I wear only a size 5½, so I am a long way away from walking in his shoes. But, together, we will keep his vision moving forward. We all loved him in our own individual way. We had our own experiences with him that were different and unique, and, yet, together, the path is the same.

I would like to read to you a very interesting text message I received from a medical doctor at Iowa State University with whom Gary was doing a special research project.

"Mary, I just saw on the news that Gary died. I am so sorry. Gary was a great man and had such vision. He taught me not to be afraid, to take chances, and not to be afraid to fail. You and your family will be in my prayers. I keep thinking about Gary and how advanced and how ahead of his time he was, how great his ideas were, and all the things that he wanted to do that the rest of us are still thinking about. He was inspired and truly a genius. I miss him. As I said, his ideas were crazy enough to change the world, and they did."

This is a medical doctor who did not know Gary very well and with whom we connected immediately but with whom we were not able to spend much time. He did not know what Gary was all about, but he saw the genius in Gary and that he was inspired to not be afraid to follow his dreams.

The thought came to my mind that "Gary's family was the world." Everywhere he went, he always looked for the good in other people, and I said to this friend, "It is amazing to think about all of the things that happened to Gary—the people who tried to take advantage of him, the people who betrayed him, the people who stole from him."

This friend replied, "He was so amazing. No matter what happened, he never stopped trusting people. He never stopped seeing the good in people. He never stopped wanting to make it better. He never stopped looking for a solution."

I had not thought of it that way, and it caused me to reflect on watching Gary in action, and it is true. He always looked forward; he never looked back. He never complained about what happened in the past, except only for a moment to consider that which he could learn and how he would do things better.

He was a forward-thinking man, and we all know his vision was bigger than anything I and perhaps even you could imagine.

I have had it said to me, and I have heard through the grapevine, that many out there are saying, "Well, Gary had the oils. Why couldn't he heal himself? Why didn't he use the oils? What did he do? Why is Gary gone?"

The thought came to me—and this has helped me a little bit, and maybe it will help you a little as well. When Gary had that terrible accident when he was 24 years old, he had 19 broken bones, 3 open skull fractures, his brachial plexus was broken in 3 places, and his spine was herniated in 3 places. He had severe cerebral hemorrhaging and blood clotting. Who could live through that? Why did Gary live through that?

They left him in the hallway of the emergency room because they knew he was going to die, but he did not die. What was it inside of him that kept him alive? We do not have that answer, but surely it is part of that fighting spirit that was within him.

I believe that by the grace of God, after that terrible accident at age 24, Gary was given another 40 years to fulfill his destiny—and give to the world his knowledge—his God-given knowing, which has blessed the lives of millions of people.

After we were married, I rubbed his legs down with oils every single night; he had so much pain. I would wake up in the middle of the night, hearing him groaning, and I would say, "Gary, what's the matter?"

He would say, "My legs, my legs," and it would be 2 in the morning, 3 in the morning, and I would go and get the oils and would massage and rub his legs, and he would say, "That helps. It helps a lot."

Sometimes, I was so tired, I would put my head down on the bed while I was massaging his legs. Many of the formulas that we have he made for himself: Thyromin, MultiGreens, ComforTone, and PanAway were some of his early formulas. He was always looking for things that would give him some relief and a little bit more strength.

I probably was the only one who really knew how much he suffered. The first and only big event we had for the community of Tabiona was a big Christmas party, a barn dance on the top floor of his new horse barn. It had to be a barn dance with all the children and parents alike. He loved everything that had to do with the farm, the cowboys, and the spirit of the Old West.

Many people said, "Oh, Mary, it was so fun to see you dancing with Gary."

Yet while we were dancing, appearing to have so much fun, Gary said to me, "Mary, I can't move anymore. Mary, I have to stop. It hurts too much. I can't move my legs. Help me to the side and have one of the boys take my place." Nobody knew because he had a big grin on his face.

The accident when he was 24 years old confined him to a wheelchair for 27 months. What kind of pain did he suffer while trying to get out of that wheelchair? I do not think that any of us can even fathom what he went through because we have not gone through it. During the 13 years that it took him to walk freely again, and throughout the duration of his life, he never let anyone see his pain.

I cannot describe how difficult these last two years were for Gary and all that he went through. We let very few come to visit because we did not want anyone to see him suffering because he had so much love for you, and I know how much you all loved him. He was physically and mentally so powerful, and to see that power dissipate was unbearable for those of us near him to watch. He did not want anyone to see that. We wanted you to remember him as you knew him, the powerful person that he was.

He talked many times of dying. He was not afraid to die. He wanted to be with God. God was his friend and many times Gary went to the mountains to talk with God. That was God's living room, and when Gary needed answers to questions, he would go there and talk to God and come back with the answers. That was his special time.

He loved the mountains so much. He loved the earth so much. He loved what God created so much. He was happy when his hands were digging in the dirt. He was happy when he was on his hands and knees, planting with everyone else.

The office wasn't his favorite place; he hated the cement city. But we had a lot of fun when he came to the office. We had great meetings. We did a lot of planning, but when I would say, "Do you want to go to the meeting?" he would ask, "Do we have to?"

And I would say, "Yes, I think we should go." So we went and had fun being with so many who we absolutely loved, with whom Gary shared new ideas and made great plans.

We always knew when Jared was in the office because everyone was laughing in the halls. There was so much laughter, and it was just fun to be there.

I have a very, very deep sadness within me. I have a void in my heart that will be there for as long as I live, until the day I die, but I will think about the 40 years that God granted us to have Gary live among us.

What he has given the world is beyond my ability to express. All of you are here because of something Gary did for you. Somehow, he touched your life, and the thousands who are out there, all over the world, listening to this service, are listening because Gary touched their lives. He truly was a man of the world. He truly loved the world as his family, and he was a man of God.

He loved God. For him, the Bible was his owner/operator's manual, and in many meetings, Gary would stand up on stage and chuckle and say, "Well, who has their owner/operator's manual?"

Everybody wondered, "What is he talking about?"

And then he would hold up that special book and say, "Who has a Bible?"

He always wanted to live by the Word of God. He always wanted to do what was right. He was not capable of manipulating, or lying, or tricking people. He just was not capable of it. He would never spout off, he never used bad language, not ever; that was not part of who he was because that would offend God.

There were so many times that we could not understand why things happened the way they happened, but he would still go forward. He would still plan. Sometimes we tried to get him to slow down, but he must have had a sense about his days being numbered because he would not stop, no matter how tired he was, no matter how he hurt, no matter how sick he was. He had one more thing he had to do, and he had to do it as fast as he could.

I asked so many times, "Gary, why can't you stay home? Why can't you rest? Why can't you heal?"

He always said, "No, Mary, I can't wait. I've got to get it done. I've got to get to Tabiona. I've got to get here. I've got to do this. I've got to do that."

Kelly and I have had a thousand conversations about it. "Why won't he stop?" Because he had so much he had to do. You heard about what his needs were, as John Whetten so poetically described. What amazing insight John gave us into what Gary was all about.

Gary gave us something that we can take to the world. There are people in need, people who are waiting for us to come with a message of something better, something that will help them.

Gary chose Freedom as our convention theme. What was that all about? What is life all about? What is helping other people all about? It is about freedom, being free to live the way you want to live, be it health, be it finances, whatever it is. Everyone wants to be free and if you know of something that will help someone else, that might enlighten their minds and give them the freedom they are looking for, you will be held accountable if you do not give them that message.

We are here to serve each other. We are here to serve God's children. We are His children and we serve, help, and love each other, which was the example Gary set.

Gary loved music; he loved country western, but he also loved the music of God. When we were in Egypt with about 100 members, and some of you were there, we were in one of the pyramids, and he went to the guards and said, "Would it be all right if my wife sang in the pyramid?"

I thought, "Oh, Gary, come on," but, you know, when he wanted something, he went after it, and he wanted me to sing. He always requested "My Redeemer Lives."

He always wanted me to sing about God, and it was interesting in the hospital; he was almost comatose, and we were all hanging onto a breath of hope, yet knowing he was getting ready to leave. We started talking about what we were going to do when the day came to celebrate his life, and I said, "Well, I'm going to sing 'My Redeemer Lives,'" and Gary opened his eyes and moved his head and looked at me and almost nodded. We all gasped and then he closed his eyes and went back into the deep recesses of his mind.

I could not let him leave without doing this for him. I do not sing this for me. I sing this for him because this is what he wanted.

My Redeemer Lives—*B. Cecil Gates*
I know my Redeemer lives, my Redeemer lives.
What hope, oh, what joy this gives, hope and joy this gives.
All glory to His blessed name, to His blessed name.
He is my Savior still the same, Savior still the same.
He lives to wipe away my tears;
To bless and comfort me through the years.
He is my everlasting head.
My Lord, my Lord, who once was dead.
My Savior is my heav'nly friend, wise and heav'nly friend.
He lives and loves me to the end, lives and loves me to the end.
I know my Redeemer lives, my Redeemer lives.
What hope, oh, what joy this gives, hope and joy this gives,
To know He lives, my Savior lives.
I know He lives, my Savior lives.

Thank you all for being here, for sharing with us. We love you dearly, and we so appreciate the love that you have shared with us, for the thousands and thousands of prayers that we have felt, for the messages of love and concern and support. They will always live strong within our home and within all of our hearts.

Josef Young is our 14-year-old son, who will rely heavily on his big brother to teach him the things that Dad would think are important, and Mom will be his rock as he grows into manhood without his father. Josef's beautiful talk showed him to be a young man far beyond his age.

Good afternoon, Young Living members, friends, and family. Thank you all for coming in honor of my father. It means the world to me.

My father was a great and caring man. I've had some amazing experiences with him that would take more time to tell than we have today, but I would like to share a few of them with you.

Dad was a great storyteller which was a lot of fun around the campfire in the mountains of Warm Springs, Idaho, that made us laugh 'til our faces were red, and we were almost crying.

He always wanted us to be with him in whatever he did and wherever he went. His latest adventure was dogsled racing in the Alaskan wilderness. My mom, Jacob, and I would wake up at 4 in the morning, so we could meet him at the finish of the race, and when he saw us, he cried because he was so happy to see us there. It was not always possible to be with him, but we did the best with juggling school and all of our activities.

I eat, breathe, and sleep soccer, and Dad was at every game possible, and when he couldn't be, he would ask Mom to record it, and then he wanted to hear every detail when I came home.

My dad was always planning something fun for us, especially for our birthdays. He'd ask me how I wanted to celebrate, and then he'd go to work. He made every single birthday a memory I will never forget.

Our family lived in Ecuador for several years, and since we've moved back, I am always excited to return for a visit. We usually visit once or twice a year, so I can be with my lifelong friends, Nayeli and Liseth, who I call my sisters. Dad loved the children as I do, and we love to be with our Ecuadorean friends.

My dad's creativity at Christmastime was off the charts. He wanted Christmas to be unforgettable. One year he bought a whole bunch of Christmas trees and set them up in the conference room. He set up tents, and we slept under the trees. My dad was a great cook, and on Christmas morning, he would make a huge breakfast of waffles, pancakes, eggs with Yacon Syrup, smoothies, and more. It was such a feast.

He was always looking for ways to make us laugh, so he created a scavenger hunt to find our last gifts. He started a new tradition called "cut the tree" in Tabiona. We would go into "God's living room," as dad would say, and cut down a tree, and the bigger the better, even if we had to cut it smaller to get it through the door.

My dad will always be my hero and is the greatest teacher and man I have ever known. My respect goes deep for him. When I was feeling sad, he would comfort me. When I was hurt, he would put oils on me and then pray to God for me. I will miss that strength and love that I felt with him. I will cherish these wonderful memories throughout the rest of my life.

Thank you for your love and support for me and my family. As long as we remember all that my dad has done and follow his example, his dream and vision will live in all of us. Please bow your heads with me in a moment of prayer.

Dear Heavenly Father, our gracious and loyal Father, Thank You for bringing all these wonderful people here today to celebrate the life of my father. We are thankful we could share our lives with my father, Gary Young. We are grateful for all that he has done for the world, for his great gifts and talents.

We ask You to watch over us through this difficult situation, so we can get through it. We ask You to give us strength and courage to go forth and carry Dad's mission to the world. May we follow Dad's example of showing love and kindness to each other. Be with us this day.

In the name of Jesus Christ, Amen.

Ben Riley: I would like the Young Living executives to join me on stage to kick off an International Day of Life to honor Gary. We would encourage each of you to go back to your homes and plant something that will be a reminder of this day and our commitment to carry forth the legacy of this great leader, who we all loved, who has enriched our lives in a most amazing way. Cultivate life, just like Gary has done for so many.

We now have reached over 100,000 live streaming connections worldwide, and people around the world continue to join us via simulcast, and many more will join us later as their day begins. We hope that, symbolically, each of us can embrace life, can be cultivators of life, creators of life, and make the world a better place, just as Gary did for us. It's a pretty inspiring marker to see the impact Gary has had on so many lives.

Many of us have ridden the river with Gary and are blessed because of it. As we go our various ways, let us remember this time together celebrating Gary's life. We have more river to ride, and may we ride it with excitement, the thrill of the adventure, and a sense of knowing that all is well and that we are all better people because we knew Gary Young.

We stood in solemn silence as the horses pulled the wagon away, carrying Gary out of sight to the other side of the farm. Jacob and Josef climbed into the wagon to accompany their father as he left the farm for the last time.

Young Living
ESSENTIAL OILS

D. Gary Young
1949-2018
Father of the modern-day Essential Oil Movement

My beloved Gary,

    May your spirit soar with the wind as it whistles through the trees, enveloping this beautiful ranch and preserving it as a sacred place for all those who come to visit. Fill our souls with a knowing that the future will bring us together again, but until then, I remain your Sweetheart, and those of us who love you will remember your vision and carry that love within our hearts.

                                      —Mary

SKYRIDER WILDERNESS RANCH
Gary's Final Resting Place, May 20, 2018

It was a cold, rainy two-hour ride for the motorcycle cortège that escorted Gary to the ranch. A quiet peacefulness greeted them as they came through the gate where the horse-drawn wagon was waiting. As the wagon traveled the dirt road carrying Gary to his final resting place, a feeling of reverence filled the air. The wind was blowing, and the rain drizzled down on those who were there to be with Gary for a final goodbye.

Jacob welcomed everyone and expressed the family's appreciation for their love and support.

Kevin Pace, who had spent many long hours with Gary in those last few weeks, offered thoughts of comfort and hope of one day being reunited with Gary and believed that thousands of people would come here to pay their respects.

Mary expressed Gary's feelings about his love for this beautiful ranch. "This is exactly where he wanted to be buried, overlooking the fields, the elk, the buffalo, and all the beauty that he had created." It was Gary's desire that people would come to his ranch to enjoy a time of peace away from the confusion and noise of the cement city. Gary was the happiest of anywhere he could be, here on his beloved Tabby Mountain.

Jared Turner offered a prayer of protection for this beautiful spot surrounded by the trees on the mountain in God's living room, as Gary called it. "He wanted to be with God on His mountain, and that is exactly where Gary is, his wish in life and death."

A musket tribute was made by Jacob and a few of Gary's friends: Joe Walker, Dave Wood, Scott Schuler, Max Hopkins, Skyler Olsen, Cory Howden, Chip Kouwe, and Mark Harris.

Several people lingered for a moment of silent communication to throw flowers and small mementos on the grave; a time of deep reflection of Gary's transition and the love we all shared.

Three weeks after Gary's passing, the Young Living International Convention took place in the Vivint Arena in Salt Lake City. Over 30,000 members were in attendance, desiring to learn more but also wanting to pay their respects while wondering about the future without Gary. Many great tributes were given, and the atmosphere was one of reassurance, excitement, and an even greater commitment to go forward and carry Gary's legacy throughout the world—the legacy of his vision and mission to see Young Living essential oils in every home in the world.

JOURNEY ON

Jacob sang **Journey On** at the Young Living Convention 2018, a beautiful song written for Gary by Janeen Brady a few years ago. It is a gentle, lilting western song that tells Gary's story and how he would have us go forward.

Journey On

We'll journey on. We've only begun, journey on.
There are souls to be healed, millions yet to be revealed, we'll journey on.
There are loved ones in pain, bring them back to health again.

The secrets we know from knowledge long ago we'll nurture.
The healing you'll share will help the world prepare for the future.
There are friends yet to meet, so our love becomes complete, journey on.

We're here together and love surrounds us, for our hearts are all in tune.
We're here together and hope has found us, and our faith is in full bloom.
But there are others we know are waiting, who have cried and suffered much.

We will gently reach out 'til we find them, and the world awaits our touch.
We'll journey on, there's work to be done, though you're only one, journey on.

Gary was truly a great visionary, and that gift has blessed the lives of millions of people throughout the world in so many ways. We can never forget our own experiences as we visit the farms, walk through the fields of plants ready for harvest, or watch the oil drops bubble up in the separator, filling the air with beautiful, enticing aromas.

In every bottle of oil, the essence reminds us of the dedication of one man's life—Gary Young—that invites us to carry that purity to those in need. May God bless you all as you walk your life's path and carry Gary's mission, our mission, to the world.

These are some of Gary's favorite oils from his bathroom counter that he used daily.

D. Gary Young | The World Leader in Essential Oils 439